AMERICAN EDUCATION

Its Men

Ideas

and

Institutions

Advisory Editor

Lawrence A. Cremin
Frederick A. P. Barnard Professor of Education
Teachers College, Columbia University

Theories of Americanization

A Critical Study

Isaac B. Berkson

ARNO PRESS & THE NEW YORK TIMES
New York ∗ *1969*

Reprint edition 1969 by Arno Press, Inc.

*

Library of Congress Catalog Card No. 77-87743

*

Reprinted from a copy in
The New York State Library

*

Manufactured in the United States of America

Editorial Note

AMERICAN EDUCATION: *Its Men, Institutions and Ideas*
presents selected works of thought and scholarship that have
long been out of print or otherwise unavailable. Inevitably, such
works will include particular ideas and doctrines that have been
outmoded or superseded by more recent research. Nevertheless,
all retain their place in the literature, having influenced educational thought and practice in their own time and having provided
the basis for subsequent scholarship.

Lawrence A. Cremin
Teachers College

Theories of Americanization

A Critical Study

Theories of Americanization

A Critical Study

With Special Reference to the Jewish Group

ISAAC B. BERKSON, Ph.D.

*Supervisor of Schools and Extension Activities of the Bureau of
Jewish Education; formerly Executive Director
of the Central Jewish Institute*

Teachers College, Columbia University
Contributions to Education, No. 109

Published by
Teachers College, Columbia University
NEW YORK CITY
1920

To the Memory

of

My Teacher

ISRAEL FRIEDLAENDER

Interpreter between Past and Present,
East and West, Israel and America

ACKNOWLEDGMENTS

This book has been accepted in partial fulfillment of the requirements for the degree of Doctor of Philosophy under the Faculty of Philosophy, Columbia University. Such acceptance, it is understood, indicates a judgment only in reference to quality of work; it does not imply that the views expressed are sanctioned by the University authorities or by the members of the committee which passed upon the dissertation. For the point of view presented, the writer must bear the sole responsibility.

I wish to acknowledge my indebtedness and to express my sincere thanks to my teachers in Columbia University; to Professor John Dewey, whose inspiration and encouragement led me to undertake the writing; to Dr. Isaac L. Kandel, Associate in Education, for many valuable suggestions; and especially to Dr. William H. Kilpatrick, Professor of the Philosophy of Education, who has given me at every point painstaking, constructive, and clarifying criticism. Of my associates, I wish to thank Dr. A. M. Dushkin, now secretary of the Vaad Hahinuch in Palestine, and Dr. Julius Drachsler, Assistant Professor of Sociology at Smith College, for what I learned from our many discussions as well as for their criticism of various parts of the study. I am grateful to Mr. Sol Bluhm for giving me unstintingly of his time in the revision of the manuscript and in the reading of proof. There are many other friends to whom thanks are due for helpful services.

My deepest debt of gratitude is due the Bureau of Jewish Education, brought into being by the will and genius of its director, Dr. Samson Benderly. Ten years of close association with him and this work have given me an unexampled opportunity to gain an insight into Jewish affairs, a sense of discipline in organization, a technique in practical work. Most of all, through the Bureau of Jewish Education I have had the rare and profound experience of conversation and comradeship with a group of men and women, teachers and co-workers, devoted through many trials, with single-mindedness and purity of purpose, to the practical realization of a spiritual ideal.

Isaac B. Berkson

October, 1920

CONTENTS

PART I

PART II

INTRODUCTORY

The problem of proper adjustment of the foreign ethnic groups in our midst to the life of America—popularly termed "Americanization"—was a subject of great interest even before the War. Now, in the aftermath, a heightened national consciousness has made of this question one of those burning issues which it is difficult, nay impossible, to discuss without stirring deep prejudices. Patriotism intensified by the experience of war immediately conjures up the spectre of foreign intrigue whenever the subject of the unassimilated immigrant is broached. In addition, the problem has become associated in men's minds with the whole discussion of internal political and industrial reorganization which seems to many to threaten the stability of present forms of government. Closely linked with the fear of foreign enemies and with the apprehension of "Bolshevistic" revolution, it is small wonder that much of what is said nowadays concerning "Americanization" savors of hysteria.

It may be urged that in such critical times as these only drastic measures are expedient. Our own recent experiences in the war, however, have sufficiently demonstrated that even in those moments when the need for action seems most urgent a decision which reckons with the fundamental principles involved serves not only justice and the right, but also in the end the practical. The war was won only because men had come to believe that they were fighting for a basic principle—for democracy.[1] A careful analysis with reference to fundamental principles becomes all the more necessary because our problem is a pressing one. What are the implications of democracy for the relations of foreign ethnic groups to the state? This question requires clear thinking, because we should seek to be true to the fundamental concept of American thought; the correct answer will avert failure in the practical task confronting us.

This book attempts a critical study of our question with special reference to the problem of the Jewish group. *What place has the*

---

[1]Likewise, if in the end the hope for a lasting peace shall prove to have been empty, it will be because the fundamental principles, the proclamation of which had won the war, were forgotten in the final settlement.

1

Jewish group in our democracy?   May it retain its identity or must it fuse entirely with the total group?   Second, if it may retain its identity, under what limitations and through what agencies may it do so?   These are the questions which must concern us in any consideration of the problem of the relationship of ethnic groups to the state.   While, therefore, our specific interest is the Jewish group, the whole discussion is in the main applicable—with the proper qualifications—to other ethnic groups.   Especially will this be true because the discussion here deals mainly with the general principles which should govern the relationship, not with the description of the actual processes of assimilation taking place in this particular group.   The fact that the Jews are not only an ethnic group, but also a cultural and religious community, enhances the appropriateness of using it in our discussion to elucidate the general problem.   For this very reason the Jews, as the following pages will make clear, present a crucial case where the significant elements are thrown into distinct relief.

Perhaps it is not superfluous to state plainly that the conclusions offered in reference to the Jewish group are in the main precedent to the argument presented here.   No pretense is made that they are the result of theoretical analysis alone.   This discussion is a rationalization of a point of view derived from the writer's personal history and experiences and confirmed by subsequent study and speculation.   It represents an attempt to clarify, to make explicit, and to introduce the balance of reason into a conviction which has been many years in the forming, rather than an effort to contrive a conclusion out of the objective study of abstract premises.

The whole argument rests upon the assumption that the United States aims to be a democracy.   The discussion may be conceived as an explication of the significances inherent in that term for the relations of ethnic groups to the state in the conditions prevailing in the United States.   Since the word 'democracy' has come to be used as a general term of approval and each man tends to see in it his own ideal, it will be necessary first to give some notion of what the writer implies in the assumption.   The first chapter, then, will deal with an analysis of the basic concept, democracy.   After this

orientation the following chapters will consider the various types of
ethnic relationship possible, reviewing them with the fundamental
notion in mind and developing finally that plan which seems to
harmonize best with the basic concept. The concluding chapters
will deal with the implications of the proposed method of adjustment
for the educational situation. There is added a chapter on the Central Jewish Institute, an institution which will serve as a basis of
discussion for the type of educational agency conceived as adequate
and proper in a democracy for the solution of our problem. The
description of this institution will furnish a concrete illustration of
the implication of the theory projected and will serve as a check upon
the meaning of the more abstract discussion.

The discussion, then, while setting out to consider the question
before us from the point of view of principles involved rather than
from the point of view of expediency or the seeming immediate need,
nevertheless at no point leaves out of consideration the actual situation and offers an opportunity for comparison of the moral conclusion
with the practical feasibility.

PART I

THE DOCTRINES OF DEMOCRACY

I refer to a Democracy that is yet unborn.
—WALT WHITMAN.

CHAPTER I

THE DOCTRINES OF DEMOCRACY

I

THE SCOPE OF DEMOCRACY

Democracy has become much like an established religion; everyone avows it and untold sacrifices are brought in its name, yet few seem to have any clear idea of its profound meaning. Such is the complaint that is frequently met nowadays in the numerous articles which attempt to present to us a more adequate conception of the fundamental principle assumed to underlie our civilization. In one form or another we find reiterated, "We have repeatedly professed this creed on many solemn and public occasions. Do we *really mean* it? And if so, *what* do we mean by it?"[1]

To most minds the term still brings primarily political connotations, and such a limitation of usage is supported by much more than mere philological derivation. The tendency to identify democracy with a method of political organization has its justification in the prime importance that government has for life.[2] Where one may dwell, how one is to earn a living, what a person can know and believe—all of these practical questions are affected by the systems which the state permits and supports. Political organization rather than prayer, we might even say, determines our salvation in any real sense of the word. Undoubtedly it is the recognition of the controlling importance of politics that has led in modern times to the ascendancy of the State above the Church.

The history of the United States as an experiment in democracy adds much force to this emphasis on the political aspect of our life. Undoubtedly the democratic ideal has indirectly been a factor in the shaping of many phases of our social life, in the development of

---

[1] Ralph Barton Perry, "What Do We Mean by Democracy?" *International Journal of Ethics*, July, 1918.

[2] Cf. Ogg and Beard, *National Government and the World War*, preface.

education, in the adjustment of racial and class differences, and even to some extent in the reorganization of industry. The main and direct applications, however, have so far been governmental, and this tendency in the course of our history has stamped itself upon the meaning that the word 'democracy' carries to the average American.

The emphasis upon the political connotation is well brought out if we compare the Declaration of Independence with the subsequent great documents of American history. From the Constitution on, so a leading American thinker[1] points out, the epoch making documents of American life reveal a constantly widening application of the concept of democracy. The preamble is inspired with the desire *of securing the blessings of liberty for ourselves and our posterity.* In the Monroe Doctrine the boundaries of our homeland have been surpassed and the European countries are warned *that these hemispheres must remain inviolate.* The Civil War extended the idea of freedom racially, proclaiming that *the nation cannot remain half slave and half free.* Our entrance into the European War was justified by an international aim *that the world be made safe for Democracy.* As Alexander says, *"The World:* Here, indeed is expansion; our globe has shrunk too small for democratic and autocratic states to subsist together, nor can Ocean herself constrain them in separation. Democracy has issued her final defiance to all the citadels of absolutism, proclaiming no longer her right to independences, nor merely her right to her own free field, but now her purposed supremacy in all fields and over all polities. Here is arrogance of pretension outmatching Monroe's, whose broad-limned compromise breaks futile, like the old compromises of North and South. Democracy claims for itself no less thing than the world."

The full significance of the new epoch, however, resides not alone in the expansion of the concept to an international application. If we examine the Declaration of Independence we find there the idea of democracy already expressed in universal terms: "All men are born free and equal and endowed by their Creator with certain unalienable rights." Indeed, the thought transcends even international implication and rises to cosmic and religious terminology.

---

[1] Hartley B. Alexander, essay "Americanism" in *Liberty and Democracy,* p. 131.

The aspiration for humanity's welfare is not new; it was the subject of the burning message of the Prophets of ancient Israel and the inspiration of the cosmopolitans of the eighteenth century. All great religions have expressed the longing for a universal good. The present epoch is particularly important not because for the first time we meet an aspiration in international terms, but because a tremendous effort is being made to create the *political institution* which will make possible a *realization* of the age-long dream. American history is to be seen not as a struggle for the development of the idea of freedom but as an experiment with the political institutions that shall guarantee freedom. The entire significance of the recent struggle is lost if the emphasis is placed anywhere else than on the international governmental institution which must be created in order to convert the desire into a reality. The important distinction between a longing and a political guarantee is clearly felt and finds expression in the explanatory phrase following President Wilson's famous pronouncement: "The World must be made safe for democracy: *its peace must be planted upon tested foundations of political liberty.*"

Democracy must be embodied in political institutions; that is the conviction that has animated American history. Many recent writers,[1] however, while agreeing heartily with the importance of the political phase tend to feel that it is a grave error to identify democracy with principles of government exclusively. It is pointed out that political democracy cannot be an end in itself; it is a means of gaining human freedom. There are instances where the end can be reached more directly through reform in the industrial or educational field than through the agency of the ballot and political methods. Furthermore, conditions of education, of economic organization, of social prejudice, so affect politics that even political democracy becomes unattainable, if political democracy alone engages our attention. To limit the definition to political reform without realizing the in-

---

[1] Hobhouse, *Liberalism*, see especially Chaps. II, VIII, IX; Herbert Croly, *Progressive Democracy;* Walter Weyl, *The New Democracy;* Alfred Zimmern, *The War and Democracy*, Chap. I; Dewey, *Democracy and Education;* Jane Addams, *Democracy and Social Ethics;* Giddings, *Democracy and Empire;* MacVannel, *Outlines of Philosophy of Education*, Chap. IX.

fluence of other phases of life is often to block the development of democracy.

Not alone theories, events, too, urge upon us new implications beyond the political. With the Russian attempt at control of industry by the workers already in the process of experimentation and with an industrial unrest of unprecedented extent and turbulence threatening the present capitalistic order it seems necessary certainly to consider immediately the extension of our concept to the field of industry. Beyond this, still in the realm of the vague unconscious begins to loom the problem of the reorganization of our educational system, implying radical changes in fundamental conceptions, philosophy, aims, methods and agencies far surpassing mere pedagogical improvements. Still there are some who maintain that we cannot speak of Industrial or Social Democracy, or of Democracy in the abstract, because we do not yet have actual examples of what these signify, and it is therefore impossible to know them. Such 'practical' minds refuse to recognize anything as existing unless a precedent can be found in application. It must be remembered, however, that the accomplishments of democracy in the political field did not wait for precedents. Must not the application to other phases of life be made with the same bold hazard (in thought and act) that carried through the experiment in the political field? We have certainly gone far beyond the primary meaning of the word 'democracy' and conceive its political implications as manifestations of an underlying and far-reaching principle full of significance for industry, education and the many other phases of social life.[1]

Indeed, democracy is so touched with deep emotion that even this broad definition in terms of a general principle applicable to all social institutions seems inadequate to express the fulness of its meaning. We feel somehow that our ideal cannot be attained by reorganization of institutions alone,—our most hidden and intimate conversations and our casual actions and relationships must be pervaded by a democratic spirit. It is the creation of a type of personality that the democratic ideal envisages. Democracy is not

---

[1] Charles A. Elwood, "Democracy and Social Conditions in the United States," *International Journal of Ethics*, July, 1918.

only something political and institutional; its real essence is spiritual. Definitions in terms of a rule, of a principle, or even of a philosophy are too pale, too platonic, too formal, too balanced, too finite in meaning and in application, too static. The forces of democracy seem to rest in the unfathomed depths of human and world nature; there is something elemental in the term. It reaches upward, too, towards unattained heights of the spirit; it is essentially an urge— a dynamic force in life.[1]

Democracy is a religious aspiration as well as a form of social organization. Only by realizing what is implied in its final goal can we judge whether any particular embodiment leads in the right direction. However efficient our organization may seem to the mind that loves perfected form and judges by accepted standards, any activity must prove meaningless unless it serves the ultimate ideal. "To what purpose is the multitude of your sacrifices unto Me? Who hath required this at your hand, to trample My courts? Incense is an abomination unto Me; new moon and Sabbath, the calling of assemblies. . . . Cease to do evil: learn to do well." Thus cries the prophet divining that there is no service of God in the performance without the spirit, in the activity unrelated to the abiding aim. What is the essence of the striving we call democratic and what are the conditions *sine qua non* of its fulfillment? The answers to this catechism will yield us what may be called the Doctrines of Democracy, the inviolable assumptions which must guide us in any subsequent discussion.

Often the attempt is made to define Democracy in terms of older ideals, such as equality, liberty or justice, etc., leaving the impression that the new term is little more than a new name for old aspirations. Such a procedure misses the point entirely. Undoubtedly old ideas and aspirations as well as older religions have contributed to the idea of Democracy. But the essential point to emphasize is that Democracy is a *new* synthesis, a *new* outlook and evaluation. To translate it into the older terminology robs the new concept of its unique character, of its specific connotations and associations, of its own

---

[1] Walt Whitman, *Democratic Vistas;* Edward Carpenter, *Towards Democracy;* Oscar L. Triggs, *Browning and Whitman, A Study in Democracy;* A. G. Flack, *Democracy.*

emotional driving power. A more direct examination into its meaning without recourse to the aid of the mediating agency of the familiar spirits, liberty and equality, is less likely to divest the new idea of its specific implications. Moreover, the error will be avoided of identifying democracy with a meaning derived not from itself but from one of its extensions, as is often done, for instance, when we confuse it with egalitarianism (from equality) or with *laissez faire* and individualism (from liberty). What we need to hold clearly in mind is the particular emphasis, the essential significance of the new ideal.

II

THE BASIS OF DEMOCRACY

The analysis presented below follows a hint offered by Professor Dewey in his suggestion that "Democracy, the crucial expression of modern life, is not so much an addition to the scientific and industrial tendencies, as it is the perception of their social or spiritual meaning."[1] *What the modern development has told us of the way of life—our new experiences, knowledges, and ideas unified into a principle—that is democracy.*

Development in methods of human communication and of diffusion of knowledge, the discovery of the potentialities of steam and electricity, the opening up of America, mechanical inventions, expansion of industry, progress in popular control of government, accumulation of bodies of scientific fact, all these have contributed to make what we call modern times. But more than all of these many inventions is the formulation of the Doctrine of Evolution. Through it a change of mental attitude has come about; all our thinking has been shot through with an idea of movement, development, growth. Our sciences of man, and the expression of our ideals of man, our psychology, sociology, anthropology, philosophy, ethics are undergoing a transformation under the influence of this powerful ferment. It is this idea ultimately which divides the mediaeval from the modern, the platonic from the pragmatic, and dissolves the dualism of the Christian scheme of morality into the unity of the physical and the

---

[1]"Intelligence and Morals" in *The Influence of Darwin on Philosophy*, p. 59.

spiritual demanded by the democratic ideal. What democracy is can be understood only when we recall what is fundamental in the modern situation, when we consider the influence exerted by the theory of evolution on modern thought.

Whatever may justly be said concerning the insufficiency of the Doctrine of Evolution as an ultimate explanation of the genesis and development of the world we cannot pretend, as the obscurantists do, that since the Biblical and the scientific accounts are both inadequate, it is immaterial which one of these we accept. The modern theory, it must be conceded, has wrought a fundamental change in our mental attitude. Previously accepted attempts at explanation had ended with the assumption of a preexisting conscious creator, who had created and who ruled the world in accordance with some divine plan. One idea was dominant in the minds of laymen and priests, of the masses and the scholars: namely, that a definite plan preexisted creation, that some divine purpose was to be fulfilled through living. Milton at the end of the Middle Ages gives us a classic description of this planned and delimited universe.

> He took the golden compasses, prepared
> In God's eternal store, to circumscribe
> This Universe, and all created things.
> One foot He centered and the other turned
> Round thru the vast profundity obscure,
> And said, "Thus far extend, thus far thy bounds,
> This be thy just circumference, O world!"

Men seeing apparent artifice and order in the world easily jump to the conclusion that these had been planned. The rabbinic legend taking advantage of this natural tendency presents the argument for design in a simple and telling form. "There is a story of a sceptic who came and said to Rabbi Akibah, 'Who created this Universe?' Said the latter, 'The Holy One, Blessed be He.' 'Prove it to me,' said the sceptic. He was told to come the next day. When he presented himself on the morrow, Rabbi Akibah asked, 'What are you wearing?' 'A cloak,' he said. 'Who made it?' 'The Weaver.' 'I don't believe you; prove it to me,' said the Rabbi. 'Why should I prove it to you, don't you know that the weaver made it?' 'And you, don't you know that the Holy One, Blessed be He, created His Universe,' responded the Rabbi. The sceptic went off. And the pupils (of Rabbi Akibah) asked, 'Where is the proof?' So he said, 'My children, just as the house implies a builder, the cloak a weaver and the door a carpenter, so does the Universe imply the Holy One Blessed be He, who created it.'"

The sceptic, as the story tells, goes off, though we may suspect that he remains unconvinced. Obviously, the students who should understand their teacher are not persuaded at first. Perhaps the difficulty all along has been that those dissatisfied with the old explanation had no other to offer in reply. What the theory of evolution has done is to propose a constructive suggestion concerning the genesis and development of our world, so that the sceptic need no longer be silenced for want of an answer. The new theory submits evidence that this wonderful scheme of things which seems to hang together so beautifully could have come into being without having been planned beforehand. It is now clearly realized that since the world is here, it had to arise in some manner; and that *any* process of events would seem, after the fact, as if it had been purposely planned to bring about what really had been the result of mere happening, if the process had at the same time chanced to culminate in a being like man who could look over and think about the course of development.[1] The conflict between Religion and Science has ended, with reference to the question of cosmogenesis, with such a complete victory for the latter that no thinker would to-day seriously suggest the simple assumption so universally accepted in former times.

Hand in hand with this dialectical dethronement of the King of Kings has gone an inevitable revolution in thought far more important than the irreverence of *lèse majesté*. Ideas of chance variation, of selection and survival by adaptation to circumstance have entered where before Immutable Purpose perfect and complete from the very beginning reigned supreme. Not only has the theory of evolution brought the notion of change and development into the explanation of forms and species; its contagion has spread and affected the conception of Truth, of Purpose, and of the meaning of the Universe.

---

[1] William James, *Pragmatism*, Chap. III, pp. 113–14.

These, also, if the Doctrine of Evolution be sincerely held and consistently applied are seen to be in the process of slow development with no "fixed first or final causes."[1] With this introduction of relativity into the sphere of philosophy the fundamental notion of value cannot escape restatement. Among the absolutes that have been banished is also the conception of absolute *values*.

The term 'value' is in itself a relative term and can have meaning only in reference to some definite point of view. What could we possibly mean by a good which could not be related finally to an existence for which it was considered beneficial? With Socrates we must agree that goods which are 'just good' and not good for anything in particular must be good for nothing. But a value may become an 'absolute' by being related to an existence whose good is in itself considered absolute. By serving a Being or Purpose or Good assumed to be absolute the ministering value too becomes absolute.

As long as there existed in men's minds an overshadowing idea of a Transcendental Master of the Universe it was easy to insist on absolute values without disturbing the logical sense. Some sceptic now and then may have questioned the basic assumption, but the prevailing notion not only of the masses, but of scholars, writers and teachers was permeated with the predominating conception. Accordingly when value or purpose or truth were spoken of, the mind did not immediately fly to the necessary logical question, *whose* or *what* value, purpose or truth; for it was tacitly understood that all realities were to be referred to God. So deeply embedded in the social psychology was the assumption of a conscious creator that the failure to mention the point of reference raised no problem at all; just as the omission of the word 'air' after 'to breathe' would disturb no one to-day. It was possible under the ruling conception of an Omniscient Creator to give to men's desires, aspirations, beliefs, laws and values, an eternal and absolute significance by ascribing their origin to the Almighty. Any interest, whether it had resulted from social experience and traditional practice or represented the desires of the powerful, received the sanction of a sacred value, if it could in some way be established that it had its origin in a revela-

---

[1] Dewey, *The Influence of Darwin on Philosophy*, Chap. I.

tion from the deity. Indeed, carrying this doctrine to its logical conclusion (which Samuel Butler tells us is very bad for any doctrine) nothing had value except as it was from God and in the degree that it served *ad maiorem dei gloriam.* "Man was swallowed up in the plan of God."

So when the Doctrine of Evolution spread, not only among the few philosophical, but to the more influential class of writers, poets, teachers and students, undermining the accepted assumption of a conscious creator, the whole system of absolute values and the notion of a teleological plan of the universe lost the powerful support of the established order. The transcendental sanction upon which it had been possible to rest the whole scheme of traditional values had to be given up and the logic of authoritarianism was called into question. Just that problem which had sunk into the level of unconsciousness under the anaesthetic influence of placid belief in God was roused by the new dynamic theory. From what point of view shall value be reckoned? The notions of change and development in our modern point of view make it so evident that there can be many worlds to which our ideas of value may be related. *The significant effect of the Doctrine of Evolution on the world of thought is its destruction of the possibility of maintaining with equanimity the conception of absolute values and purposes.*[1] We are harassed when we mention the word 'value' by the obligation of telling also the position from which we speak.

If we can no longer refer our values to a conceptual deity, has the Doctrine of Evolution given any other large impelling idea to guide the labors of men? Has it proposed any constructive notion which might serve as a criterion by which to judge 'the good'? One might be prompted to respond that in the idea of the "survival of the fittest" some standard might be found, but it is clear on second thought

---

[1] It is not the aim in these few paragraphs to prove the position of the relativists as against the absolutists. The writer assumes the relativist attitude as the only defensible position. All that is meant to be said above is that value assumed as absolute was a currency which would pass unquestioned formerly because it had the stamp of the established realm of theological thought, but that now with the overthrow of that regnant position, the coin will not pass—each one tends to ring it and to examine it with great care. It no longer serves adequately as a means for facilitating action and life's processes. It is, as James would say, a "dead hypothesis."

that the word "fittest" adds nothing to the idea of "survival." Whatever survives, that is the "fittest." Both very complex organisms sensitive to a variety of stimuli and simple inanimate substances are in the category of the "fittest" since both persist and have become "adjusted to the environment." A diamond maintaining the identity of form and substance even after the earth had cooled might be looked upon as more fit than a highly complex animal organism which needs a complex environment for its perpetuation. Evidently whether an organism is fit depends upon what its environment is, which in turn depends upon its own capability to react, which is indeed another way of describing the characteristics of the organism. The two relations are completely reciprocal. Everything that we find in the world must from such a point of view be considered equally fit.[1]

The evolutionary doctrine consistently considered has taken away the point of reference for our values, and has of itself been unable (on account of its very nature as a descriptive and not a subjective study) to substitute any new point of view. The total effect of the scientific teaching on the question of values has tended to be negative. The realization of the futility of such destructive criticism alone has begun to impress itself upon our thinking. As Santayana says, "There is unfortunately no school of modern philosophy to which a critique of human progress can well be attached. Almost every school can furnish something useful to the critic, sometimes a physical theory, sometimes a piece of logical analysis. We shall need to go to borrow from current science and speculation the picture they draw of man's conditions, his environment, his history and mental habits. These may furnish a theatre and properties for his drama; but they offer no hint of its plot and meaning. A great imaginative apathy has fallen on the mind."[2]

Into this situation of philosophic bankruptcy Democracy has come with a new vision of the drama of human life to relieve the world of the meaninglessness of an unevaluated universe. It is the new faith, the religious inspiration in which the modern man finds a unification for his experiences and aspirations. Though it is not yet clear in its

[1]Hobhouse, *Social Evolution and Political Theory*, Chap. I, pp. 7 ff.
[2]*The Life of Reason*, Vol. I, page 9.

implications or formulated into a complete system, men nevertheless feel that there is something of primordial strength and of immense significance in the new call. It has begun to be felt and even feared as the potent underlying creative force. Men envisage in it the Great Ideal which makes life worth living and for the attainment of which it is necessary to dedicate life. In this it comes not to destroy all other religious faiths but to fulfill. Its prime interest in the welfare of mankind makes it a completion not a negation of former religious aspirations.

More than its accompanying characteristics of unification of consciousness, its intensification of emotional attitude and its tendency toward universalization of outlook, Democracy becomes identified as a religious striving through its central interest in the life of man. All the great religions center about the salvation of man. Even when philosophic or theologic verbiage have so dressed up a religion as to make it seem that its central aspiration is for an abstract idea or to praise the deity, the fundamental interest of all religions, as the modern psychological reinterpreters of the value of religion have clearly demonstrated, will be found to repeat the prophetic message, "Seek the Lord and live."[1] Democracy like all religions makes man the hero of the universal drama. In this anxious concern for human welfare it repeats the central idea in all religions, the anthropocentric conception of the cosmos.

Every religion in addition to the deep interest in man's life has also a cosmology, its picture of the world theatre in which man plays the heroic part and a ritual or method of action by which the end is to be attained. While agreeing in their main aspiration for human welfare, it is in these elements of cosmology and ritual that religions are distinguished from one another. That is why when ceremonies are given up and cosmological setting changed—as, for instance, when the biblical account of creation is abandoned—men are perhaps rightly regarded as having forsaken their old religion. Democracy, the religion of the modern man, has a new cosmology—it takes for its background the picture of the genesis and development of the world which modern science and speculation have drawn for us, a

---

[1]See Josiah Royce, *The Sources of Religious Insight*, Chap. I.

picture far more gloriously imaginative than any of the ancient myths—and a correlated ritual, the mechanistic implications of the new cosmology which demands that we have methods which are verifiably efficient and that between cause and effect no mystic gap will enter. Democracy has the basic elements of a religion, an intense anxiety for the salvation of man, a cosmology in the broad doctrine of evolution and a ritual based on experience and on science.[1]

The implications of the new faith are, of course, as manifold as are life's activities and what the applications in any one field will be must occupy many men for many generations. It can hardly be said that the main principles have received formulation into a system. Nevertheless something of a positive and definite nature can already be said. The remaining portion of this chapter is an attempt to set down some of the basic meanings which the writer believes might be considered as making up a doctrinal test, so to speak, for communicants of the new religion. To trace out some of the fundamental notions of democracy through a consideration of the significances for the development of human life inherent in the cosmology of evolution and its biological connotations is our next problem.

III

THE QUINTESSENCE OF DEMOCRACY

Our first criterion of democracy is derived from the negative teaching of the doctrine of evolution to which reference has already been made above, namely, the denial of 'design' and the disintegration

---

[1]Perhaps the nature of Democracy's cosmology and so called ritual prevents our principle from being rightly called a religion. It is the use of magical methods, it may be said, that makes a process "religious"; and, since the implications here are scientific and mechanistic they cannot be considered "religious." But no sincere modern believer in religion will admit that religion must be "supernatural," must *violate* the known scientific laws. That would resemble the timeworn story of the Sunday School teacher who defined faith as "something we know to be untrue and which we believe in." It must be remembered also that former mythical methods were not considered so by their users. They were the most practical known in reference to the puzzling problems of human welfare for which they were utilized. So, too, methods which may seem practical to us, based on reliable experience, may in many instances seem fantastic and inadequate to a later and wiser age. We must never lose sight of the fact that our own methods, however efficient they may seem, are practical for ends whose value rests upon the assumption that man's life is supremely worth while—an

of the prevailing belief in a conscious creator which permitted discussion of values without mentioning their reference. One who speaks about values to-day must state openly the position from which he judges the world, otherwise he is taking the name of the Lord in vain and is a veritable scoffer who has no respect for sacredness of meaning. Even modern apologists of the absolutistic position must admit that value is in its meaning essentially relative and can become absolute only with reference to some assumed point of view.[1]

Since the points of view from which we may look upon the world are infinite in number, we must come to a pluralistic conception of value, truth, reality, etc., unless we arbitrarily assume some definite standpoint. The values and goods of the world are as numerous as are the possibilities of analysis into units of existence, or, in other words, infinite. Were we really impartial and did we look upon the world with no bias, every activity would be equally valuable for it could be conceived as furthering something. For the good would need to be considered not from any external point of view but from the immediate and internal aspect of the being concerned. Even processes which we call 'disintegrating' would seem proper if we were not in the least concerned. In accordance with the doctrine of the "survival of the fittest" anything existing at any particular time would need to be considered fit. A thoroughly naturalistic religion pressing its doctrine to the logical extreme would look upon all being as sacred and judge all values as absolute from their own point of reference (in opposition to the theological conception which considers things as worth while only from *one* fixed point of view). There would be, so to speak, a thoroughgoing democracy in the world, for all things would be regarded as free and equal.

Here indeed we have the clue that brings us to the quintessence of the democratic doctrine. The tendency to regard everything as an end in itself is the fountainhead from which springs the new view of the world. With far-reaching vision does Walt Whitman define Democracy. "The quality of Being in the object's self ac-

---

assumption that is based on desire, faith, and the will to existence. The analogy of Democracy with a religion is not necessary for the subsequent argument and should not be taken too strictly.

[1]Hugo Munsterberg, *Eternal Values*, Chap. I, p. 9; Chap. VI, p. 76.

cording to its own central idea and purpose, and of growing there-from and thereto—not by criticism of other standards and adjust-ments thereto—is the lesson of Nature."[1] The seer of Democracy, looking beyond temporary embodiments and manifestations, gives us his creed in the terms of its ultimate aspiration.

Were the world so harmoniously arranged that it would be possible to treat all beings both on the plane of the human and below it as if they were ends in themselves, we would not speak of such an aspira-tion as this in religious terms. But existences conflict with each other. The hypotheses of the universal presence of force at the foundation of all our evolutionary doctrine makes conflict an inevita-ble factor in our universe—a conflict out of which rise integrated forms and the struggle for survival including the struggle of desire with desire, of man with man, of species with species. Of these conflicts are born our ideals. Without this conflict we would have no philosophy and no religion, for these obviously are harmonizing principles, describing universes better than the one we live in, with the hope that the actual world will be brought somewhat nearer the ideal conception. In so far as it is a religion democracy does not describe a condition already existing; it reflects an aspiration. *Democracy finds its significance in the attempt to multiply the things in the world which may be considered as ends in themselves.*

This broad and general statement of the essential meaning of democracy is, however, to be considered a sort of Messianic hope, pointing the direction but not giving the limits of practical realiza-tion. The Universe cannot be saved all at once; in a practical and realizable program there are always limitations. It is with Man that we are most concerned. The prophet who dreams that the lion shall eat straw like the ox is in reality interested not in the animal kingdom but in the relations of men to men; and so democracy, too, has the human being at heart primarily. Walt Whitman's definition is meant above all to apply to men, and might be para-phrased, "The quality of Being inherent in the Self according to its own central idea and purpose and of growing therefrom and thereto,—

---

[1]*Democratic Vistas.* Though Whitman happens to use the word Nature in this sentence he has really set out to define Democracy.

not by criticism of other standards and adjustments thereto—is the teaching of Democracy." Whatever will be the aspiration of future epochs, in our own age the religion of democracy consists in the aspiration to construct a world in which it will be possible to live in accordance with the Kantian formula, to regard every human being as an end, not as a means merely.

Democracy assumes an anthropocentric world, which as noted above is a characteristic that it has in common with all religions. It should be noted, however, that the naturalistic origin of our creed has left its trace on the attitude which the democratic mind takes toward all values. Under a theologic conception the tendency is to look upon the world as condemned, and to find in it values only as they are seen to serve some accepted higher principle. In the democratic attitude, though we may reject the extreme of regarding everything as valuable, we are nevertheless left with a tolerant feeling toward all life even that which does not immediately concern us. In the one case, every activity stands condemned before the bar of thought unless it can show itself serviceable for aims which have valid precedents; in the other case, illustrating what is fundamental in a democratic mode of thought, the defendant must be considered as innocent until it can be shown that there is a definite violation. This difference of attitude is the crux of the whole matter and will be important in our discussion of diverging forms of culture and individuality. The difference is a fundamental one; the one mode of thought will tend to lead to a suppression of everything which diverges from the established, the other mode to that liberation of forces which is necessary for the creation of a fuller and richer life.

The democratic conception would look with tolerance upon all forms of life and would endeavor to understand them from their own point of view. With reference to human individuality democracy would go even further; it considers personality as absolutely sacred, and its exploitation as the worst form of sacrilege.[1]

This supreme belief in the person is perhaps in the last analysis like all else in human life based upon instinct and desire, a result of the will to live, a part of that assumption which places man at the center

---

[1] Cf. David Jayne Hill, *Americanism, What is it?* Chap. IV, pp. 133 ff.

of the Universe. Since human individuals are alone articulate, it would be strange indeed if this fundamental fact had not left its traces in our philosophy. If a man speaks sincerely he must reveal what in his own experience (which is in part a personal experience) has seemed valuable. Nevertheless, in addition to these natural causes there seems to be sufficient rational justification for emphasis on the human individual once we have agreed that democracy finds its significance in the desire to multiply the things in the world which may be considered as ends in themselves. The self-conscious nature of human individuality makes it worthy of this preeminent consideration.

In comparison with the whole plane of beings below the human, the human being is alone capable of realizing the significance of his own nature. Cows have no conception of the purpose that animates their breeding and do not suffer from the memory of the lot of their fellows or from a prevision of the end which overshadows them. The term *exploitation* loses its sinister connotation when applied to beings on a low plane of consciousness; for the realization that any control is external is the other side of self-consciousness and can exist only in direct proportion to the extent to which one's own nature is known. While wanton destructiveness and cruelty are repulsive to a humane nature, a too anxious solicitude concerning animal individuality and the integrity of natural forms would savor of sentimentality in a world in which the majority of human beings are not yet considered as living for themselves. Democracy, in a practical way, insists that the most sensitive organism above all must be saved from exploitation.

On the other hand, by comparison with existences which are superindividual, like the family, the state, society, etc., the exploitation of the individual alone would appear really cruel. Poetically, we can speak of these groups as if they were individuals and had souls, as it were. Actually, however, they lack a sensorium and must be directed in their action through individuals. The individual has purposes which it is true cannot be fulfilled except through living in a social world. But how could a group have values except through its constituent individuals and in the last analysis for their sake? By talking about society as if it were a single entity we are only too apt in our romanticism to commit to martyrdom the many individuals who are in reality self-conscious and for whom exploitation, therefore, is so malignant.

In the third place, even if our point of view were not anthropocentric and individualistic, but thoroughly natural and objective, it would appear to be the pragmatic thing to do (in a world which by hypothesis is not ideal) to set up first of all the self-conscious entities as the supreme ends of creation. Self-consciousness is no inner self-ebullition, but a knowledge of one's relationship to other human beings and to the whole outer world. A deeper self-consciousness means not an intensification of the ego, but a realization of how many other persons, things and ideas are necessary for the fulfillment of one's own life. Men must realize as they begin to understand their needs how dependent upon society they are. Thus it is that society as a whole is served by promoting the good of the individuals within it. Surely if the individuals in any society are satisfying their highest desires the whole society must be accomplishing its function. On the other hand a nation can still continue to exist while many of its citizens are killed or unhappy. And again referring to the plane of lower existences it is inconceivable that the lower animal or the plant should learn to understand what man's nature is and save it from exploitation. It is more reasonable to expect man to be able to understand the ends of lower beings and prevent them from exploitation. The self-conscious individual is the most complex being. Since he is dependent upon the world to the greatest extent he must learn to preserve more and more of the world. Comparatively speaking it is more economical to start with the self-conscious individual; for if the world has the ideal possibility of becoming a place where a great variety of beings may pursue their existences harmoniously then the chances for increasing the number of such self-determining entities are greatest when we begin with the self-conscious beings.

Self-consciousness thus provides a clear reason for centering our attention on the individual; it gives to the reality of the human individual an unmatched intensity, makes the idea of exploitation intolerably sinister, and assures us that Man must ultimately realize the necessity of a rich natural environment and of a complex social order.   While all beings in the world seem worthy of perpetuation, the human individual seems most worthy.   His survival more than that of any other being will lead to the conservation of life.   So, too, within the group of human individuals, those who are most self-conscious, i.e., who realize most truly their dependence upon nature, upon other human beings and upon social institutions, are most worthy of being preserved.   Maintaining the very doctrine that individuality is sacred, we must come to the conclusion that individualism in the sense of selfishness is an abomination.   Only those men who can live without exploiting others are desirable in a world in which all personalities are considered sacred.   To admit anything else would be to negate the basic assumption.   Like the God of Israel the God of Democracy is a jealous God, the one jealous for the principle of social justice, the other jealous for the creed of respect for personality.   That individual in the world is most worthy of preservation for whose fulfillment the free expression of the individualities of other men is also a necessity and for the upbuilding of whose life a rich world is the prerequisite.   He is the highly self-conscious individual who understands his dependence upon the world.[1]

Self-consciousness translated into terms of action becomes *self-determination*.   Forged through the greatest upheaval in human history to express the ideal of the democracies of the world this new phrase might well serve to convey the essential meaning of the Kantian doctrine and of the vision of Walt Whitman.   Self-determination is the quintessence of democracy.   Values must be related to the self if they are to be in truth goods and the individual must be regarded as his own end.

This idea will give us the orientation; but the term 'self-determination,' clear as it is in reference to intent, is still too vague to use as a standard; it does not imply the conditions of its own fulfillment.   The specific criteria of democracy will need to take into consideration the terms which limit the possibility of free self-development.

---

[1]For an excellent discussion of the significance of self-consciousness for individuality, see Warner Fite, *Individualism*.

IV

THE CRITERIA OF DEMOCRACY

UNIQUENESS OF EVALUATION

It is fundamental to remember that each individual is a unique specimen; human individuals are not copies of each other like so many buttons turned out by the same machine. Our doctrine of evolution would impress upon us the heterogeneity within each species and the tendency for greater individual diversification as the species reaches higher levels. This primary fact of individual differences must be taken into the first reckoning in our evaluation of the good. The unique nature of the particular individual involved must become the reference point if we are seeking a real benefit for him. The extent to which it is possible in any given society to understand each individual's good and to include it into the social good becomes the limit of democracy.

The traditional tendency has been to pass judgment on persons in accordance with some group in which they were classed. Race, sex, social class or church were for the most part considered to be the determining factors in assigning to the individual a place in society. The presumption was that difference in some characteristics carried with it similar differences in respect to the total character. Classification seems to have the result of investing a person with a sort of quality which makes him what he is. Against this attitude of mind the democratic conception would insist that the character of each individual should be directly examined in order to ascertain what he is. A person is what he is, because he is so, not because he belongs to a certain class.

This tendency in democracy, to approach the matter in hand directly, is matched by a similar development in the conception of cause. In primitive stages of thought when men sought the cause of a phenomenon, they did not seek it in the phenomenon under examination, but in some other object or process. To control, little interest or study was given to the matter to be controlled; the endeavor was to exert influence through something external which was considered as having a dominating potency. The disease which had come over a man was considered as quite separate from the man. It had entered into him. The ensuing activity, therefore, was to do something not to the man but to the evil spirits which needed to be expelled. In the cosmic scheme, God and creation were considered as quite distinct and the world was to be controlled not by mastering creation, but by appealing in some way to God.

In science to-day the tendency is to seek the cause in the very subject under consideration, not in the distant far-off external relationships. We find the 'cause' in the immediately preceding and surrounding conditions; i.e., we find it more useful from the point of view of control to know what immediately precedes and surrounds. We refuse to be satisfied with the intuition of a connection between this before us and that remote ultimate. Even if the ultimate can influence the immediate object at hand, it must be through intermediate connections which must in the last analysis be contiguous with the immediate object. So we begin with the matter at hand and seek to gain control over the nearby conditions.

Cause, therefore, is to be sought *in the peculiar organization of the specific instance in question*, not in any external fact or object, which on account of some overt similarity or some other process of association or some mystical connection is assumed to exercise potency over it. So closely have cause and effect approached each other in modern thinking that the use of these words tends to give a false connotation of disparateness, when in reality they have come to mean two aspects of or stages in the same process.

The mechanistic interpretation of the universe as against an idea of creator and creation; the attempt to get at heredity not on the basis of external resemblances of relatives, but through a study of the germ plasm; the explanation of human nature not by means of 'faculties', but in terms of the organization of the nervous system; the analysis of historical phenomena by examining the local and contemporaneous conditions rather than harking back to supposed 'origins'; and in philosophy the finding of purposes not in some external Authority or Law or Society, but in the functioning organism— all these seem to be products of working with intrinsic, immediately related conditions.

This attitude of seeking the 'cause' in the sphere of efficient condition, in the particular, immediate, internal, specific organization of the business in question rather than primarily in the realm of 'final causes' in the general, ultimate, external, mystical relationships, is the attitude to be borne in mind when we approach the task of understanding the nature of any individual.   To come as near home as possible, to endeavor to begin from within, is part of the democratic doctrine of self-determination.

Race, color, class, sex, social position are themselves at best only hints concerning the individuals to whom we wish to refer. They are not powers or spirits which enter into the individual and make him what he is.   To understand, for instance, what place a person who happens to be a woman ought to play in our social organization, it would be in the democratic spirit to ascertain just what she could do from an impartial test of her capabilities, rather than to assign a preconceived status, determined altogether by one factor, that of sex.   The movement of democracy is to get away from such prejudgments on the basis of one factor (a procedure which is bound to bring about a judgment by an external standard) and to get as close as possible to the actual individual, as near as possible to his own unique nature.   The same line of reasoning which forbids absolute values, related to a conceptual God, precludes values related to conceptual Classes.[1]

It is the unique person to whom values must be related. We fulfill the demands of our relativistic conception of value only in the degree that we give due consideration to the individual's nature involved. *In thinking about the good, the point of departure from which our reckoning begins must be the individual persons who are most closely concerned in the situation*—that is the first prerequisite of a democratic procedure.   Because we are incapable of realizing in its fulness and intensity the experience of others (we seem, too, naturally disinclined to do so) the practical application of democracy involves the setting up of machinery which will enable men to control the policies that

---

[1]The type of state outlined in Plato's *Republic*, for instance, with its threefold classification, is in effect an undemocratic conception.   While the individuals are classified supposedly with due respect to their natures, the assumption that there are only three types would give little scope to individuality.

govern them.   For this reason "consent of the governed" is regarded as the basic principle in political democracy.   Participation in the control of any activity which vitally affects the course of one's life becomes the safeguard of human liberty.   The word 'self-determination' expresses so happily the essential meaning of democracy because it implies that the ultimate judgment of the good and the final power over one's fate must rest with the living subject of experience.

Since the individual undergoing an experience is alone capable of realizing to the full the value of any experience, we might conclude (granting that he accords to every other individual the respect of personality which he demands for himself) that the individual himself must in the last analysis be the ultimate and only judge of the salvation which is in accordance with his own nature.   Such is perhaps the case, but it will be well to see in what important directions the validity of his judgment must be practically limited.

DIVERSITY IN THE ENVIRONMENT

We can speak of judgment on the part of the individual only when he has a variety of possibilities of experience from which to choose. When there is only one possible mode of responding either in act or in imagination there can be no judgment in the true sense.   In accordance with the biological conception underlying this discussion the individual is conceived as an organism responding to an environment and learning through the satisfactions and dissatisfactions accompanying his reactions to choose what for him is the good and to reject the evil.   There must be present a multiplicity of material and ideal objects to which to respond before a free choice becomes possible.

The removal of governmental and social restraints which prevent some from enjoying the benefits already conferred upon others is only the first step in the attainment of freedom.   For its full development it is necessary to create continuously new possibilities in the surroundings.   A richly diversified natural mental and social environment must be present before the individual can be thought of as reacting in accordance with his own nature.   America must be justly considered democratic even more because it is the golden land of opportunity than because it opposes privilege. The popular conception colored by the long, difficult struggle for equal rights naturally emphasizes most the personal aspect implied in the phrase *equality* of opportunity. But equality alone is negative and empty when not joined to a *multiplicity* of opportunity. "The troubles of the many —that is half consolation," so runs a Hebrew proverb. The individual human undoubtedy finds some measure of satisfaction in realizing that he is no worse off than his fellow. An intelligent and positive conception, however, will stress the impersonal condition of freedom—a manifold diverse opportunity. The presence of a variety of possibilities is the *sine qua non* of freedom, and defining from the point of view of the environment the only real meaning that the term can have.

The mere existence of objects and ideas obviously does not imply that all will react; to be present in the environment signifies also a potentiality on the part of the organism. Fundamentally important differences of instinctive endowment affect the possibility of response. Original nature, therefore, gives both the possibility of freedom and its limitations. So, too, the modifications upon the nervous system known as habit formation have their effect upon the possibilities of reaction. Habit, too, makes possible, but at the same time may limit freedom. The establishment of fixed modes of reaction permits the organism to engage the attention in new fields. Fixed habits are necessary to relieve the mind from the many harassing details of the daily routine of physical and social living. The number of situations into which we are thrown is so great that it would be impossible to consider in each case what would be the best type of reaction. In many cases nearly any mode of reaction would do nearly as well; in other cases age-long experimentation has evolved customs which have justified themselves in practice. In all such instances the development of habits serves freedom. The danger lurks when habits are established in reference to matters where freedom of choice is all important. For this reason individualists have often warned that the only habit to form is the habit to form no habit.

In any matter in which freedom is considered of great moment fixation of habit setting up an unalterable reaction amounts really to a limitation of environment. Habit formation can even be used as a means for the suppression of freedom. By bringing about an immediate and fixed response the organism becomes less able to choose, for as a matter of fact it no longer has the possibility of several reactions. When the series of habits acquired was originally contrived with little consideration of the person in whom the habit is later fixed and the process is calculated to further the interests of those who implant them, habit formation becomes indoctrination. Indoctrination limits freedom by closing the imagination to any but the ideas which have been indoctrinated. When one comes under the influence of only one language, one literature, one church or one school system, the tendency in a sense is toward indoctrination. A good illustration is the parochial school which takes all the child's time, sets up definite ideas as exclusively the true ones, and prevents the child from coming under other influences than its own. Similar, too, may be the effect of state control of the public schools, although in a different direction. If the public school demands practically all of the child's time, education can avoid becoming indoctrination only when the diversity and richness of the curriculum matches with the uniqueness of each child's nature.

An understanding of the organic nature of the individual would make us insist that greater diversification of possibilities to react to can alone lead to freedom. Since the organism cannot react to nothingness, it is only by offering additional ways of doing things that liberation from the necessity of reacting in one way can come. The mediaeval serf, whose slavery depended upon the fact that he was bound to the land, would not have received freedom if land were, so to speak, abolished; only by being permitted to move from place to place, i.e., to be in many lands, could freedom be attained. To be relieved from the hardship that expression imposes upon thought, it would be necessary not to become ignorant of all language, but to know more of the languages. To be a free thinker it is necessary to understand and at least in a sense believe in many religions, not to be ignorant and skeptical of all. Especially if we have in mind any

high degree of individual uniqueness, as we have in our conception
of the self-conscious individual, we must assume an environment
with diversified possibilities. Organic uniqueness and dependence
upon a diversified environment proceed together. The conception
of the individual as an organic entity must immediately lead us to
a positive conception of freedom, and to the insistence upon a diversification of environment as well as upon a uniqueness of evaluation.
In addition, then, to the necessity of regarding each individual as
unique, a second prerequisite of self-determination will be *an environment rich in possibilities of thought and act.*

The term 'organism' includes the ideas of an environment and of a
relationship between the organism and the environment. The distinctions, 'organism,' 'environment,' 'reaction,' are mental discrimi-
nations; in nature these three are aspects of one unitary process.
Any one of the terms must imply the other two, for they are all
correlative. It is the interest of the particular discussion that will
determine the standpoint from which to view the whole process. In
the discussion above, conceiving the process from the point of view
of the individual organism, we were led to emphasize the need of
each individual organism as unique. Taking the environmental attitude, it was shown that diversity of possibilities is necessary if the
organism is to have freedom to react. Our third criterion will be
developed by examining the question from the point of view of the
relating principle, the interdependence of organism and environment.

SOCIALIZATION

The first standard of democracy stressed the importance of the
realization of the uniqueness of each individual as basic to any
meaningful conception of value. This argument will have been
completely misunderstood, however, if the idea of uniqueness has
been confused with that of disparateness. Each moment in a lifetime is a unique experience, but time would be inconceivable if the
moment were regarded as separate and unrelated to the preceding
and succeeding moments. Each act and each thought, though unique,
has its background and its references, its 'causes' and 'results'. So,

too, uniqueness of the individual does not imply a separation from, and lack of relation to, other things and men. Quite the contrary. Uniqueness depends upon the peculiar organization of relationships, and no great degree of uniqueness can exist without a corresponding complexity of organization which of course involves a multiplicity and complexity of relationships. Organic uniqueness and dependence upon a diversified environment must proceed *pari passu* because they are in fact the same things. The individuality of a man consists in the relationship that he bears to the world; it is the world from his point of view.

Man's dependence is upon the whole of Nature—things, ideas and persons. The individual can exist neither physically nor as the figment of a conception without dependence in some measure on one or all of these three aspects of the environment. As his individuality develops, the dependence upon ideas and persons becomes of more significant importance. In so far as any individual at any moment recalls the relevant experiences of the past and foresees the references to possible future happenings, and in the degree that he realizes in true measure the dependences upon which his own individuality rests, he will be true to his own nature. Man does not live by bread alone; a complexity of social and spiritual relationships is necessary for his welfare. To understand that all relationships have significances wider than the present application and to assume the responsibility that they imply, is a part of democracy. Nothing in the world that we can discover is irrelevant to our existence, and nothing that we do or neglect to do can fail to influence ourselves and the world. *The extent to which the individual realizes his many interdependences* becomes the third criterion of democracy.

Democratic thought has in view especially our relations to other persons. A natural view of things unbiased by anthropomorphism, as we have noted earlier in this chapter, would regard all nature as sacred and all beings as ends in themselves. The democratic view, accepting this outlook, nevertheless assumes the prior importance of human life and insists on the sanctity of each person as the highest good. So also here, logically insisting on the importance of all dependences, the crucial interest of the democratic aspiration turns about mankind and on the relation of men to each other.

Our first doctrine of the sacredness of each unique personality already implies that each man must respect the personality of the other. If a conflict of interest ensues, an adjustment is necessary which will consider in equal measure all concerned, and which will avoid the exploitation of the one at the expense of the other. In addition to this, our concept of interdependence demands from the individual the responsibility to maintain those social relations and organizations upon which his welfare rests. To know that every action of his has reference to other persons and to consider the effect of his activities upon the social institutions is a duty which he must fulfill not only by virtue of the doctrine of the inviolability of all persons, but also because natural conditions make him dependent upon social life for his very existence.

It will be realized from this emphasis placed upon socialization that the need of unique evaluation does not imply selfishness or unbridled individualism. Undoubtedly danger lurks in the overemphasis of either of the two factors to the exclusion of the other—democracy is a balance of forces. We are entering upon a period in which socialization will for the time being be considered the more important factor in many plans of economic and political life. The change is from an emphasis upon rights to emphasis upon duties. Nor are we yet ripe for that exalted conception of 'mutual aid' implied in the theory of Anarchy. Evidently since all individuals have not accepted the responsibility of *noblesse oblige* involved in the democratic doctrine it will be necessary to have means of restraint to use against those who would attempt to violate the personalities of others. Furthermore, the relations upon which we are dependent are far from being obvious. It has taken hundreds of generations of human living to fully realize many of them and it may take a lifetime to rediscover them. Respect for social institutions and obedience to them until more adequate ones can be established will follow as a corollary from a realization of the individual's dependence upon social life. Here education has an important function in making explicit the significance and deep roots of social institutions. Moreover, since the dependences of man upon other men and upon nature are not of a definite and limited number but are really infinite, always multiplying in number and increasing in complexity, the social relation cannot be confined only to adjustment to existing institutions and traditions. Education has the additional function of extending the social idea in new directions to apply to wider and more complex societies and to find embodiment in new and more highly developed institutions. The process of socialization is never complete. In no sense is the individual to be conceived of as disparate, a law unto himself, self-sustaining and self-sufficient; at every point it will be seen that he must reckon with other forces and with other men, and with his future as well.

The unification of the individual with the World is an abiding thought in philosophy and religion. The longing to become merged with the All, to save oneself from the loneliness of a dissociated life, is at the heart of the notion of Salvation. The quest of life is a quest for the unification of the individual soul with the soul of the world. Born from the World, we are yet, so to speak, bound by an umbilical cord from the very center of our being to the womb of Mother Earth and we dare not break the bond without cutting off the sustenance of the nourishing mother.

Differentiation, a separating from the total matrix, never means an absolute separation from the body. It is as if with every diversification the bond that unifies us with earth undergoes a subdivision; a new finely spun thread appears with each differentiation. Never is the individual in reality cut off from the world from which he was born. The higher the differentiation, the more numerous are the bonds, the more finely spun, the more closely interwoven; they cannot be neglected or broken without hurt to the being. The full development of our personality depends upon retaining these bonds of union between our differentiated self and the Universe.

Our new outlook has not suppressed the deep human longing for unification with the world; but the conception of what constitutes union has been transformed. In the philosophies of the East the unification is to be attained by merging again into the Infinite from which we have sprung. Through a loss of consciousness we are to be unified again with the world of the unconscious. The whole work of evolution is to be undone and the self is to lapse again into

an undifferentiated state of unconsciousness. In accordance with
our own conception a complete life is possible neither when the bonds
are broken nor when they are merged into indiscrimination, but only
when the Individual becomes conscious of the myriad relationships
which join him with the World. The union of the self with the
World cannot be attained by falling back into the undifferentiated
state, by going back into the womb, as it were. Once born we must
continue to grow, that is, to become differentiated. Only one process
can save us. We must become *conscious* of the bonds that hold us
to the world; see clearly every relationship; discover more and
more how we are bound to the world. Our own notion of evolution
teaches us that the line of development is not in the attainment of
homogeneous undifferentiation, but of integrated diversifications;
not in a falling back to unconsciousness, but in the attainment of
self-consciousness. The progress of our salvation is in the continued
differentiation of each self and in the progressive, conscious realization of the bonds of union that the differentiating self bears to the
rest of the world.

To regard each individual as an end in himself; to know that he
is a growing organism and that the goal of his Being is already inherent
in his instinctive endowment; to understand that as he grows he
becomes more differentiated from his fellows and yet more dependent
upon them; to realize that consciousness of himself and of his relationships to the world is what keeps him whole—all these are of the
democratic doctrine which looks for the goal of the world not in the
fulfillment of any objective law or principle, but within man himself
to the fulfillment of his Personality.

In the endeavor to develop Personality three conditions must be
held in mind:

1. That each unique individual be regarded as the point of reference
     for value;
2. That the environment present a diversity of possibilities accessible
     to all;
3. That there be a consciousness on the part of the individual of his
     dependence upon the intricate series of natural and social
     relationships upon which his individuality rests.

Since these three conditions may exist in an infinite variety of degrees, we must realize that democracy is no one definite state but a tendency of development. We can, therefore, speak of democracy only in comparative terms. It is the direction of the movement which will define any condition as democratic or not. Where there is a *progressive consideration of uniqueness*, a *multiplication of diverse possibilities*, a *growing consciousness of man's interdependence*—there does democracy exist.

V

DEMOCRACY AND MINORITIES

Our main task, that of applying these criteria to the special problem of the adjustment of foreign ethnic groups, is part of the more general question of the democratic treatment of minorities. What attitude should a Democracy assume toward minority divergences? A consideration of this question will serve to make the foregoing analysis more concrete as well as to develop some important notions relevant to the subsequent discussion.

Democracy has often been completely identified in practice with the rule of the majority, as if this were the essence of our principle and not merely an expedient. Obviously, once admitting the correctness of such an identification, suppression of minorities would be in thorough accord with the ideal of democracy, even its avowed purpose, and not an evil made necessary by the practical limitations of the evolved political machinery. If the presumption is that the opinion of the majority and the right are one, then all divergences from the majority must be set down as evil. Our own basic principle, however, it will be recalled, demands that we tend to regard all things as good; suppressing alone is evil and can be justified only when it becomes necessary to avoid a worse evil. In accordance with our own notion divergences must be regarded as good until they are shown to be evil and must be permitted to exist until the effects of their activities are evidently detrimental.

Nevertheless, a tolerant attitude towards minority views and policies does not leave us without any criterion for judging when they should be suppressed.   Too often an artificial dilemma is proposed to choose between rule in accordance with the majority or license for minorities to do anything they please.   Such a Hobson's choice is quite unnecessary.   As is usually the case the dilemma is to be solved by analyzing other possible positions and by the introduction of qualifications.   Minority divergences are not of one kind and any wholesale statement in reference to them is bound to mislead.   For the purposes of our own discussion we may divide them into at least three broad classes.

CRUCIAL IMPORT

In the first class are the divergences which are not really crucial. Whether a person prefers greys or browns, whether he likes fish or fowl, whether he favors Shakespeare or Shaw, would not, generally speaking, be matters of great concern to the state.   Perhaps in discussing divergences we do not usually have such differences in mind. Yet it is of prime importance to remember constantly that there is such a class.   If we stop to think for a moment we shall admit that more matters than we commonly assume really fall in this class; perhaps it is the largest class.   There is a tendency—so universal as to lead to a suspicion that it may be instinctive—to regard differences from the majority or from the established order or from the conventional as being inferior.   To remember that there is a vast class of differences which really do not matter will certainly serve to improve our sense of humor and our spirit of tolerance.

OBJECTIVITY

On the other hand there is a class of divergence which can be objectively demonstrated to be malignant.   By an objective demonstration we mean one that would repeatedly convince men regardless of their race, creed, occupation or personal idiosyncrasies provided they were open-minded.   Science tends to deal with such matters as are capable of such experimental objective verification.   Whenever we know through scientific research that a certain condition is harmful, then the opinion of a contrary-minded minority need not be respected. There is a range of matters where such scientific conclusions are possible and generally accepted. Sanitation, for instance, calculated to safeguard the health of all regardless of creed, politics or nationality may be enforced even against the unwillingness of the unclean.

Academically it is possible of course to controvert this argument of objectivity by showing that objectivity is relative, not absolute. Whether a certain condition is really evil or not, it may be said, depends not only upon demonstration that it exists but upon a certain assumption of aims. If trance states and the seeing of visions are considered as in themselves good, starvation which may promote these abnormmal conditions may be transvaluated into goods. But we are not pursuing hairsplitting discussions for their own sake. Common sense will pragmatically accept the principle that in matters such as these there is no justifiable right to differ and no society will encounter any very great trouble in suppressing activities which scientific investigation concludes to be harmful for the human race as a whole. We may lay down the principle that in the degree that a demonstration of the evil results of a minority opinion approaches objectivity, in that degree is it democratic to suppress the diverging opinion.

Approaching the possibility of objective demonstration as a limit is a whole range of actions universally acknowledged to be evil. Here, too, drastic action is justifiable. Such matters as stealing, lying, adultery, against which there is a deep laid and universally widespread antipathy, may be forcibly suppressed without violating our sense of democracy. For even those who commit these sins will in moments when they are not engaged in the action admit that these are wrong in principle. The particular offensive action may be excused as necessitated by circumstances or as really not falling within the sphere of the rule broken; but the principle would be defended by all, even the doers of the mischievous deed.

Of the same temper as the objectively demonstrable and of the universally approved or disapproved is a range of matters capable of rational demonstration. Rational justification is really an extension of the two former positions. Through reasoning we show that the situation under discussion is really another instance of a position already assumed to be covered, where the same principle must apply. In the degree, therefore, that we attempt to reach rational conclusions we are approaching a democratic attitude. In essence, summarizing the three divisions of this second class, *objectivity of judgment rather than majority of judgment is the goal toward which democracy tends.* No majority rule should stand in the way of a position objectively or rationally demonstrable to be salutary, even in a democracy. Needless to say, neither has a minority in such a case a right to retain its private point of view.

SOCIAL INTENT

However, in the discussion of the treatment of minorities we generally have in mind not divergences which do not matter or those where there is a universal accord, but divergences which are of import and in reference to which there is a difference of opinion. This third class refers especially to those positions where the minority avows its social-mindedness, claims to be acting for the general good, but differs from the majority in its opinion of the proper means. It is the treatment of these instances which will be the test of whether democracy exists in a situation or not.

In these cases the plain rule of democracy is to strive toward tolerance; to permit the minority to be active even to the point of exasperation. It will be necessary to reckon carefully how crucial the situation is. When it is a case of survival or destruction, there is no other way but to fall back upon prejudice. The retreat from tolerance, however, must be with the face toward the unattainable position. Where objective proof is impossible, let us have a representative majority decision; where the majority cannot be trusted, we must as a last resort entrench ourselves in rash guesses, in prejudices, in instinct. But then democracy has been defeated. However, in less crucial situations democracy demands that we wait for the demonstrably evil results before we suppress. If the situation is really bad, the evil results will soon be seen. Suppression of minority views in situations where such suppression is not absolutely necessary is the antithesis of democracy.

In dealing with minorities it is necessary to make a serious intellectual attempt to classify the divergence under consideration with reference to its crucial import, to its social intent, to the objective demonstrability of the quality of its effect, and to decide upon the degree of tolerance to be accorded from its relation to these standards, endeavoring always to afford the greatest freedom compatible with the protection of all other freedoms. The application of these criteria demands knowledge, skill and good judgment; their analysis alone does not guarantee a correct application. Nevertheless, an earnest attempt to use them as guides will lead us out of the artificial dilemma of choice between the license of the majority and the license of the minority. The application of the rules laid down may serve as aids and as sanctions for our action.

The suppression of free speech, for instance, on the part of organs that were frankly opposed to the war would be seen from such a criterion to have been undemocratic. It would argue a great weakness in our cause and methods if a minority press, in spite of an overwhelming majority of pro-war opinion, could have influenced our mind to stray from the righteous cause. Reasoning about it, the chances are that a complete freedom would have redounded to the support of the majority idea. Suppression constantly adds to a bitterness that would be alleviated by talking. There is an insinuation that the arguments hidden are very powerful when in reality the mere statement of them might be their own refutation. Similarly no one would seriously maintain that humane treatment of conscientious objectors even in the apparently few doubtful cases would have led to an appreciable increase of those who feared possible death more than sure disgrace and cowardice. That would, indeed, be a frank admission of the lack of patriotism among the many or of the worthlessness of our cause. The arbitrary methods in both instances must be attributed not to the reasonable needs of democracy, but rather to the stupidity that comes with states of high emotional excitement. In the degree that an evil has been inflicted unnecessarily on divergent minorities such mode of action must be regarded as undemocratic.

But even when the objective consideration leads to the conclusion that the minority is in the wrong and must not be permitted to continue a certain activity, suppression by means of force should be avoided wherever possible. Coercion is the antithesis of everything democratic; it imposes an external will upon the subject; it acts always by limiting the alternative possibilities; it leaves no room for the development of that feeling of responsibility which is the *sine qua non* of a moral life. Democracy's method is the word, not the whip. The means of social control in a free state is education—the bringing of people together into communication, a free press, free speech, free schools, the dissemination of knowledge,—these are the means of influence that a democracy should use in an endeavor to convince of what is reasonable. Whenever it is necessary to substitute some kind of physical force for mental persuasion, some element of democracy has somewhere been left unfulfilled either on the part of the subject (who may not be reasonable enough) against whom it is exercised, or, more often, on the part of the agent exercising it. Whenever it is possible to use any other method, the use of force becomes reprehensible in a democracy. It can only be justified as a lesser evil. "Force without stint" is the last resort when every other method has proved unavailing. Democracy exists in any situation to the extent that force is unnecessary. When we speak of the recent war as a democratic war, and the incidental activities, such as the draft, the limitation of free speech and free press, the curtailment of freedom for those who happened technically to be enemy aliens, as being democratic in their nature, we are in reality not saying what we mean. These activities had to be carried on, not because they were democratic, but because external conditions made democracy impossible within; i.e., because the world is not yet safe for democracy.

This basic notion of tolerance, with its implication of the need of objective demonstration, of careful judgment, of reluctance to use coercive methods, gives the keynote of the treatment in the following chapters which deal with the place of ethnic minorities in the state. As civilization grows more mature—as in the life of the individual— a realization comes upon us that we can afford to be far more tolerant than we ever imagined without really disturbing anything vital, and even with greater chance for success and happiness. Toward our individual likes, toward our children, our wives, our neighbors, toward our own actions, those of our friends and even of our enemies, a liberality of spirit is the only possibly justifiable rule of life. This enlightened confidence in the good of divergence rather than the primitive suspicion of differences is the temper with which it is necessary that we approach the problem of the relation of ethnic minorities to the state.

THEORIES OF ETHNIC ADJUSTMENT

CHAPTER II

THEORIES OF ETHNIC ADJUSTMENT

I

INTRODUCTORY:

THE JEWS—A MINORITY ETHNIC COMMUNITY

In discussing the place of the Jewish group[1] in America we are dealing with one particular kind of minority divergence. The question is not merely one of homogeneity vs. heterogeneity, as is often implicitly assumed in such discussions, and our problem cannot be so easily disposed of by pointing out that divergences are necessary for progress. Even within the homogeneous nation differences of individual character and intelligence, of locality, of economic conditions, of political affiliation, of education, will lead to a diversified opinion in reference to the important political, industrial, educational, social and moral problems of the day. The question before us relates not to differentiation as such, but rather to the particular kind of differentiation due to the retention of ethnic loyalties. The problem that faces us is whether ethnic distinctions are to be tolerated in America.

The supreme difference from our point of view between the ethnic

[1] In speaking of the Jewish group as an entity, one must be warned against conceiving the Jewish unity as homogeneous or compact—a frequent error among those who do not know the Jews intimately. From any point of view that one might measure the Jews, their economic or social status, synagogue affiliation, attitude toward religious, educational, social problems and even toward the important question of the perpetuation of their own group identity, a great range of divergences will be found. Even the purity of the race so often taken for granted may be questioned. Far from being closely welded together, they have no central organization, and no ecclesiastical unity. There are, indeed, many examples of coördinated activities, such as the federations of charities; and there are certain bodies of national scope, like the American Jewish Committee, the Joint Distribution Committee, and the Zionist Organization of America. Such unified activities, however, represent voluntary attempts at centralization and coöperation for specific purposes and are for the most part recognition of the superior efficiency of coördinated effort. These societies have no official or authoritative power such as a government or a church organization might have. The Kehillah (Jewish Community) of New York City is an attempt to organize New York Jewry so that there may be the machinery to evolve a representative public opinion

group and the other classifications such as political parties, economic
classes, geographic sections, mentioned in the previous paragraph,
is that the former is foreign and the latter are indigenous.   These
ethnic distinctions—Jew, Italian, Pole—were formed under the
conditions of other times and other places.   Shall these associations
made in the past and in other territories persist to-day and into the
future in the new geographic area and under the new governmental
unity; or shall all groupings within the nation be the result of conditions in our own country and of the present period?   Further, if
these foreign groups are to persist, under what limitations may they
do so?   How shall we answer these questions in the light of the
principles formulated in the first chapter?

Although our main interest centers about the Jewish group, whatever is said in the following pages concerning the fundamental
method of adjustment is meant to apply equally to any ethnic minority in America which is desirous of maintaining its group identity.
Great care will need to be observed, however, in applying the main
principles to take into consideration the differences between one group
and another and to introduce the relevant qualifications.   For
instance, the fact that political allegiance has been an important
element in the German's ethnic loyalty—at least until very recently—
while it is negligible in the case of the Jew, suggests immediately
that the practical application will be limited by practical differences.
Nevertheless, general principles there are and the manner of adjustment proposed for the Jewish group as harmonious with the democratic conception is considered as an example of, not an exception
to, a general mode of assimilation.

In treating of the Jews as a foreign ethnic group coördinate with
other immigrant national groups such as the Italians or the Poles,

---

that could make itself felt upon all general Jewish problems.   Although the form of
the organization already exists and a certain amount of good work has been done
through it during the last ten years since its inception, its aim to become a body
recognized by the Jews as representative of the community as a whole is far from being
an accomplishment.   Underlying this disunity and heterogeneity, however, it is
undoubtedly true that there exists a certain unity of consciousness, perhaps almost a
feeling of family kinship.   This is well evidenced in a number of striking ways: for
instance, the tendency to marry within the group; to become awakened in the face of
what may be regarded as common dangers, pogroms, blood accusations, slander of
the Jewish name; to organize readily for the relief of Jewish suffering.

the writer has not failed to realize that some objections might be raised against such a classification. It may be that all Jews are not immigrant in the same sense of the word. In addition to the interesting but incidental fact that the Jews played an important part in the discovery of America and that the first white man who set foot on the soil of the New World was in all likelihood a Jew, it is true that the settlement of Jews in America dates from the earliest period.[1] There have been three important migrations of Jews, the Spanish Portuguese up to the close of the eighteenth century, the German Jews from 1772–1870, the Eastern European Jew[1] from 1881–1914. Jews played an important part in the War of the Revolution and fought on both sides during the Civil War.[2] Therefore, some Jews residing in America are native in any sense that the term might be used of white men in America. On the other hand, of the three million Jews[3] living in America over 85 per cent are either recent immigrants of the 'new' migration or the children of such immigrants. These are the so-called Yiddish-speaking Jews[4] who hail from Russia, Poland and Galicia. These Eastern European Jews, who are thus the overwhelming majority, present the crucial problem of adjustment, for the Jews of the older migrations have through intermarriage and through complete taking over of the customs of the land (with the exception sometimes of a formal religious adherence) so adjusted themselves that the divergence between them and the general population is hardly to be noted. It is the Russian Jew who particularly impresses himself as a Jew. Coming as he does from the ghetto, he comes from a *milieu* as distinctly Jewish as the social conditions from which the Italian hails are distinctly Italian. He presents a type diverging from the American in physique and personal habits; he is unacquainted with English and with the law and usages of the new country. He presents a problem of Americanization similar to that presented by an Italian, a Pole, or a Czech. Moreover, he has lived under the influence of the development of the national movement and the renascence of Hebrew literature, which has inbred

[1]Article, "United States," in the Jewish Encyclopedia.
[2]Peter Wiernik, *The Jews in America.*
[3]*The American Jewish Year Book*, 1919–1920.
[4]i.e., Jews who can speak or understand Yiddish. In the second generation they usually speak English.

him with a national consciousness. The numerical strength of the recent migration, furthermore, is of great influence in aiding to keep alive the group spirit.   It is, therefore, the Eastern European Jew of the recent immigration who presents by his peculiar characteristics and his highly developed national and cultural consciousness the problem of adjustment which faces us and gives to our question also the character of a problem of assimilation.

In the second place the Jew does not owe an allegiance to the nation from which he has emigrated in the same way that a German or an Italian might; the Jews do not come from their own land. This does away in a measure with the apprehension of a double political allegiance. Like the Pole, however, he has a potential double political loyalty, in the event that a Jewish state be reestablished in Palestine.[1] Here, too, there is a qualification. The Polish State was destroyed only in comparatively recent times, and most Poles who live here were born on Polish soil. It is two thousand years since the Jews have had a state, and the Jews that we have in mind were born on other than Palestinian soil. Since there are fifteen million Jews, and Palestine can accommodate only three million, the mass of Jews living in America will never experience a double political allegiance. Moreover, the Palestinian State will in all likelihood be reestablished under conditions which will make the question of a double political allegiance academic. However, in spite of the improbability that the Jews will ever be involved in a dual political allegiance, a discussion which would neglect even this possibility would hardly deserve to be considered as adequate.[2]

To treat the Jews as forming a religious group parallel with Protestants and Catholics would certainly not be sufficient. Even in the case of many other nationalities it would be a mistake to fail to recognize that religion plays a large part and is often synonymous with the national spirit. Yet in no case is religion coextensive with nationality as in the case of the Jews. While all Poles are Catholics, not all Catholics are Poles. There are very few Jews, however, who

---

[1] This sentence, as well as most of this book, was written prior to or during the Peace Conference.
[2] See Chap. V.

are not Jews by birth; and Jews by birth even when they are not positively affiliated with any synagogue are seldom professedly members of any other religious denomination. The intimate connection between ethnos and religion in the Jewish group will not be without its effect upon the discussion of our problem. However, to consider the Jews as forming only a church would conceal the fundamental issue in our problem.

Such procedure would fail to take into consideration what is of most importance to hold in mind, that we are dealing with a *community of men* who have characteristics diverging from the general population, not merely with divergent doctrines. The Jews have an identity of race, a community in history, social traditions, religion, language and literature, a consciousness of these common possessions and a hope and possibility of being reestablished as a nationality in Palestine.[1] Our problem rises from the desire of the Jews to maintain their identity and to live the life of Jews in the midst of the social conditions of a divergent environment.

Although the purpose is to propose a solution to this problem harmonious with principle, the plan must be more than a theoretical conception. We are confronted with a practical need, not merely with an academic issue. An analysis will be made of the various types of adjustment already suggested in current practice and literature with the view of determining which of these will fulfill in the greatest possible degree the demands of our democratic criteria. This method is in agreement with the attitude that looks upon democracy as relative. We must accept the adjustment that has a possibility of being translated into a realizable program. No "counsel of social perfection" is premeditated, but a plan which with full regard for the circumstances and conditions recommends itself as a liberal solution.

The modes of adjustment are usually in these discussions pictured as representing two possibilities: either total assimilation or complete retention of the group identity. Such a broad division suggests the

---

[1] It has been frequently pointed out that the *consciousness* of race and ethnic unity is more important than actual identity. The psychological force is what motivates. Thus the purity of race may not be actual, but merely assumed; the language may be spoken or merely waiting to be revived; the land may be possessed or merely loved.

vital issues involved. Nevertheless, it leaves room for so many unanswered questions and disturbing implications as to make discussion unprofitable. A closer examination of current thought and practice will reveal that there are at least four possible broad methods of adjustment, two which look toward absorption and two which in some form or other provide for the perpetuation of the individuality of the ethnic group. The analysis into four instead of two theories is important; it serves to make clear the objections and limitations which are obscured by the more general treatment. Too often each position fixes its attention and bases its opposition on those considerations which the other side would immediately concede were they presented unequivocally. The juxtaposition of the several possible modes of adjustment will bring out clearly the issues really at stake and narrow down the discussion to the questions which are in fact relevant. The carelessness in the analysis of the question has been in a great measure an obstruction to a satisfactory solution of this intricate problem. What is necessary in order to reach an acceptable settlement is not so much persuasive arguments calculated to induce a change of heart as a more discriminating treatment that will show what is as well as what is not involved.

The four theories the criticism of which will constitute the analysis of our problem are (a) the 'Americanization' Theory; (b) the 'Melting Pot' Theory; (c) the 'Federation of Nationalities' Theory; (d) the 'Community' Theory. The names with which the theories presented have been captioned are phrases of common usage chosen because they immediately suggest the central tendency if not all the implications. Indeed, it may at times seem that the interpretation is too strictly literal and the proponents of a certain theory may claim that they never meant to imply so much. The actual number of theories no doubt is equal to the various modes of procedure and there are times when it would be difficult to classify any particular instance definitely within one class. Obviously, however, the very purpose of formulation is to bring distinctions into clear relief and to make explicit considerations which are usually forgotten or underemphasized.

The present chapter will deal with the first three of the theories—with those which are considered inadequate from the point of view of the principles developed in the foregoing analysis of democracy. The 'Community' theory and its implications will receive separate consideration in Chapter III.

II

THE 'AMERICANIZATION' THEORY[1]

According to this position America is pictured as already populated with a fairly homogeneous type, which both in race and culture has Anglo-Saxon affiliations. Even if these, say the proponents of this theory, who are conceived to be the 'real' Americans are not actually in numerical majority, their type ought to prevail nevertheless. The main point is that all newcomers from foreign lands must as quickly as possible divest themselves of their old characteristics, and through intermarriage and complete taking over of the language customs, hopes, aspirations of the American type obliterate all ethnic distinctions. They must utterly forget the land of their birth and completely lose from their memory all recollection of its traditions in a single-minded adherence to American life in all its aspects. The kind of life proper for America is regarded as a matter to be decided altogether by the Anglo-Saxon and by those who have become assimilated.[2] The foreigners must mould themselves into the ready-made form. They must do all the changing; the situation is not to be changed by them.

This point of view is often illustrated in the attitude toward what is called the 'new' immigration. In the 'old' immigration from 1820 to 1880, the North Europeans predominated. It was made up mainly of Swedes, Norwegians, English, Irish, Scotch, and Germans. This immigration is in current text-books regarded as superior because the immigrants approximate in physical type the early American pioneers

---

[1]For writings which exemplify this attitude wholly or in part, see Ross, *The Old World in the New;* Grant, *The Passing of the Great Race;* Woodruff, *The Expansion of Races;* Brandt, *Anglo-Saxon Supremacy.*

[2]Of course, it is not only those of Anglo-Saxon lineage that hold to this theory; one is as like as not to find those whose families have lived longest in America liberal toward the foreigners. Indeed, it very often happens that an insistence upon complete obliteration of foreign characteristics comes from those who have been Americanized comparatively recently and who, not being so sure of themselves, perhaps, must necessarily demonstrate their Americanism.

and show in language and culture a close kinship.   On the other hand
the new immigration since 1880, of Southern and Eastern Europeans,
is regarded as inferior and even dangerous, on account of the divergence from the stocks of the older immigrants.   These latter are
brachycephalic, small in stature, dark-eyed and dark-haired, and
odious comparisons are drawn with the northerners, who tend to be
dolichocephalic, tall, blue-eyed, and fair-haired.   Virtue and the good
are seen to be in direct relation to the type represented by the original pioneers, and divergence from this fixed standard is conceived of
as an inferiority.

So untrue to the facts and so inconsistent with the spirit of democracy does such a scheme of 'Americanization' seem to the reasonable mind that the question may be raised whether such an idea is
really anywhere entertained; whether in reality it is not an exag-
gerated statement of a very reasonable demand to have the foreigner
acquaint himself with the existing American institutions and adjust
himself to the new life with a regard for the purposes and ideas of the
American people.   Unfortunately, however, the opposite is rather the
case.   'Americanization,' in the sense defined here, is the accepted
current theory and practice so far as most of the important agencies
dealing with this problem are concerned, and it is to be feared that
with the intensification of feeling resulting from the war this tendency
will receive an added impetus.   The following instances will perhaps
suffice to show that the foregoing is no mere academic analysis.

Most striking from the point of view of the particular problem
before us, the task of assimilating the Jew, is the work of the Educational Alliance, the largest Jewish social settlement in this country.
It was founded over twenty-five years ago and was one of the first
to recognize the importance of the problem of the adjustment of the
immigrant to the new life in America.   Situated in the heart of the
East Side, in the midst of a district densely populated with immigrant
Jews, it conceived its problem to be the complete de-orientalization
of the Russian Jew, the ironing out of all those characteristics which
stamped him a foreigner.   Although the neighborhood in which it is
situated is the centre of the 'intelligentsia' of the ghetto, and represents in many ways a high status of literary culture, the Alliance

has remained completely oblivious to the possibilities of cultural and spiritual contribution inherent in the life of the people. A great deal of valuable work has undoubtedly been done, in the teaching of English and civics, in the industrial classes, and in the provision for recreation. But to Jewish things, the attitude has been negative. A 'religious school' and Sabbath services for children have, indeed, been conducted, but in the manner and spirit antagonistic to the conceptions of the Russian Jew for whom the institution was created.[1] Whatever was most vital and spontaneous in the neighborhood received no support, and often as far as lay in its power was suppressed in the single effort to make 'good Americans' out of the Russian Jew.

Naturally, the confidence of the Russian Jews was never gained and a rift of misunderstanding has always existed between the Educational Alliance and the East Side. It has never ceased to be regarded as an institution from the outside world condescendingly philanthropic. Thus it missed a wonderful opportunity for working out a democratic scheme of assimilation and for helping a neighborhood full of cultural forces and idealistic tendencies to find itself in American life and to contribute to it. Even from its own point of view of Americanization it has not accomplished its function, for it has been only an incidental force in the inevitable process of the Americanization of the population of the East Side. It has failed to add

---

[1]As a matter of fact, though the Alliance exists *for* the Russian Jew, one is led to suspect in reading the annual reports that it was not *his* benefit solely that motivated the activities. The institution was not an expression of neighborhood feeling, but was the creation of those Jews who lived uptown, partly it would seem for their own protection. These Jews who had come to America between 1850 and 1870 had risen to position in American life, and had become at least in their own eyes thoroughly assimilated. They feared that the peculiar ways of the newcomers might reflect upon them since all Jews are generally regarded by the non-Jewish community as "being responsible one for another." Consequently the Educational Alliance was founded, to educate the immigrants out of their old ways so that they might not disturb the peace and good will that the older inhabitants had attained. In this they meant no unkindness, perhaps. They knew that they had been successful in their own struggle for a place in American life, and threw themselves wholeheartedly into the task of making the immigrants as closely as possible according to their own image. One must, of course, recognize that on the part of some there was a real humanitarian (though perhaps not intelligent) motive; but the feeling of need of self-defense stands out too clearly and moulds the character of the work only too evidently. See *Annual Reports*, 1893–1908, especially Dec., 1896, pp. 24–16; Jan., 1898, p. 34 ff.; 1901, pp. 36, 37; 1903, pp. 79–80–8; 1906, p. 52.

to the general Americanizing influence of the social and educational environment what it might have added—and what alone could have justified its existence as a Jewish institution—a finer interpretation of Americanism in the light of Jewish thought and an enrichment of American life through a utilization of the spiritual forces inherent in the life of these foreign-born Jews.   Perhaps its saddest contribution is its influence upon other institutions.   In its lack of sympathy and at times antagonism to things Jewish it struck a false note which was reechoed in many subsequent attempts.   Since the Alliance came first, is the largest institution of its kind, and had an unusually powerful backing, it was naturally followed by other institutions, with the result that Jewish social work has received an impetus contrary to the ideas of sympathy, tolerance and respect for expression of personality so necessary in the democratic ideal.[1]

The New York public schools offer another example of an unexampled opportunity for intelligent work with immigrant people wasted through lack of understanding.   In no city in the country is the problem of greater importance than here, where the majority of

---

[1]After careful consideration the writer believes that these strictures are necessary to state the plain truth.   Nevertheless, the following qualifications are equally necessary to avoid a false impression.   The criticism is against the Americanization policy of the Alliance which it regards as its essential work.   There is no desire to imply that the Alliance has not been useful in furnishing certain excellent activities such as its various classes, its reading room, its gymnasium, etc.   Furthermore, not all the directors are at one in regard to the policy.   There are some liberal influences and in recent years these have tended to multiply.   The *Twenty-fifth Annual Report* shows a delightful change in attitude toward the immigrant from the monotonous unvarying indictment of the reports from 1893 to 1908.   It is for the first time discovered that Jewish and Hebrew conceptions have much in common with American ideas and that assimilation of the Russian Jew to the ideals of America ought not to be very difficult (see speech of Justice Greenbaum); while in all the previous reports the Russian Jews are pictured as unfortunates coming from a benighted country whose government is so different from our own, etc.   The change can be traced to certain very definite factors.   I am informed, however, from authoritative sources that the old forces still have considerable potency and that it is too early to conclude that a real change of heart has come about in the controlling policy.   Finally, it is important to note that the workers of the institution have not all or at all times reflected the opinion of the directors, and much of the good work of the Alliance was done in spite of stubborn opposition.   The tragic struggle and martyrdom of David Blaustein, a man who had an unusually fine insight into the problem and whose dream of a "People's Palace" might be regarded as the bridge between the older humanitarian conception of the "Settlement" and the modern democratic notion of the "Community Centre," is perhaps too well known to need recounting here (see *Memoirs of David Blaustein* by Miriam Blaustein).

the population are foreign-born or the children of foreign-born. The Jewish children alone represent over forty per cent of the general school population, while in some neighborhoods they number over ninety-five per cent.   There are many examples of kindly sympathy and understanding on the part of individual teachers and principals, but the attitude of the official system is intolerant.   The following reply given recently by the Superintendent of the New York Public Schools to a query as to his conception of Americanization reflects the official attitude: "Americanization is a spiritual thing difficult of determination in mere language.   Broadly speaking, we mean by it an appreciation of the institutions of this country, *absolute forgetfulness of all obligations or connections with other countries because of descent or birth.*"[1]   There is a realization here that the problem must be seen through the positive terms of a loyalty to the new life, but the negative attitude toward the past of the immigrant's life is still conceived of as being an essential part of the process of assimilation.

An attitude even more disappointing is represented by the "Americanization" policy suggested in Professor Cubberley's *Changing Conceptions of Education.*[2]   It is quoted at length, because it is such a clear and full statement of the position, and because it offers an excellent basis for a critical analysis of this theory of assimilation.

About 1882, the character of our immigration changed in a very remarkable manner.   Immigration from the north of Europe dropped off rather abruptly, and in its place immigration from the south and east of Europe set in and soon developed into a great stream.   After 1880, southern Italians and Sicilians; people from all parts of that medley of races known as the Austro-Hungarian Empire; Czechs, Moravians, Slovak, Poles, Jews, Ruthenians, Croations, Servians, Dalmatians, Slovenians, Magyars, Roumanians, Austrians and Slavs, Poles and Jews from Russia began to come in great numbers.   After 1900, Finns from the north, driven out by Russian persecution, and Greeks, Syrians and Armenians from the south, have come in great numbers to our shores.

These southern and eastern Europeans are of a very different type from the north European who preceded them.   Illiterate, docile, lacking in self-reliance and initiative and not possessing the Anglo-Teutonic conceptions of law, order and government, their coming has served to dilute tremendously our national stock, and to corrupt our

[1]Italics mine. *The Evening Post*, August 9, 1918.
[2]Riverside Educational Monographs, 1909.

civic life. The great bulk of these people have settled in the cities of the North Atlantic and North Central states, and the problems of housing and living, moral and sanitary conditions, honest and decent government, and proper education have everywhere been made more difficult by their presence.   Everywhere these people tend to settle in groups or settlements, and to set up here their national manners, customs and observances. Our task is to break up their groups or settlements, to assimilate and amalgamate these people as a part of our American race, and to implant in their children, so far as can be done, the Anglo-Saxon conception of righteousness, law and order and popular government, and to awaken in them reverence for our democratic institutions and for those things in our national life which we as a people hold to be of abiding worth.[1]

These complacent statements were not intended perhaps for careful analysis or discriminating examination and it may be inconsiderate to subject them to undue scrutiny; especially since the new situation has given us changed prejudices that will no longer permit us to mention all of these various peoples in one breath of denunciation and to hold up the hyphenate *Anglo-Teutonie* conception of law, order and government, for universal admiration.   But, while names may be changed, unfortunately enough the underlying attitude toward the foreigner remains the same in most that goes by the name of Americanization.   It is of utmost importance to point out the fundamental errors in this mode of approach.

In the first place we would be suspicious of the lumping of some twenty-five various groups together on the basis that they are not North Europeans and then following the argument on the assumption that they are pretty nearly alike in reference to a few chosen qualities. As a matter of fact the differences between certain of the specified peoples and others will be found to be greater in reference to some or all of the particular qualities mentioned (conceptions of law, cleanliness, literacy, initiative, etc.) than is their difference from the average American or from the older stocks.   It is, of course, not true that every one of these groups is, generally speaking, inferior to the older stocks in all of the qualities mentioned;   in reference to certain qualities some of the stocks would seem to be decidedly superior! But apart from the facts at issue, what is most objectionable is the prejudgment of hosts of men on the basis that they do not belong to a

---

[1]pp. 15–16.

certain favored group. Not only do these groups differ one from another, but the individuals within each group vary.

Apart from the dubious assumption of the superiority of one race over another, whatever evidence we have should utterly refute the idea that knowing a man's race you could know very much about his mental and moral characteristics. The variability amongst individuals of the same race and the overlapping of one race with another are so great in the measurement of any trait in original nature, that 'race' becomes a useless criterion for determining an individual's place on any scale that one might choose to measure. The one fact of racial origin (at any rate, with reference to all white races) means nothing. This is the scientific testimony[1] which together with a democratic faith in the value of all human personalities might have led to a more tolerant attitude. Such wholesale condemnation runs counter current to the first requisite condition of democracy, that the unique make-up of individuals be taken into consideration.

It is erroneous to fly to the conclusion that the inferiorities and evils when they do exist are caused by the 'race' of the immigrant. What is more probable is that social and governmental conditions in other lands are to be blamed. In that case our theory of amelioration would certainly be affected. Indeed, it is also possible that some measure of the evils of crowded tenements and poor sanitation are to be traced to our own failure to deal adequately with the problem and perhaps even to our desire to exploit the immigrant. To throw the entire blame on the vague 'race' of the immigrant often serves merely to obscure the real causes and to hinder an adequate solution. It tends to shift attention from the true evils involved and from the reforms really required. Sociological theorists are only too often innocent supporters of what are in actuality the prejudices and interests of the classes.

America, it should be remembered, does not exist for the benefit of any one class of persons, whether we consider the grouping economic, political, or racial. The idea that the predominating stock of the inhabitants of the United States is Anglo-Saxon is a myth. The

[1]Thorndike, *Educational Psychology*, Vol. III.

composite American is a multiform hyphenate: Scotch-Irish-English-German-Spanish-Polish-Jewish-Italian-Russian, etc., etc. All of these are represented in fair numbers in the new "Galilee of the Nations." To conceive of America as belonging exclusively to one race, because priority of habitation has given it a divine right to possession of the land, is a notion contrary to democracy. Indeed, this minority, due to its priority and to the undoubted excellence of native gifts, has stamped its culture ineffaceably upon American life, its language, its political organization and spiritual aspirations. The influence of this group outweighs, justly, that to which its numerical strength would entitle it. To say, however, that American institutions and forms of life have once for all been fixed by the fathers of our country and that the newcomers, the majority, must mould themselves into these forms, is itself contradictory to the principle of freedom upon which these forms are built and of which they are but a particular and perhaps inadequate expression. Our newcomers had no voice in the formation of these institutions, and to force them upon the immigrant without regard to his consent and without permitting his own personality to modify them in the least is an arbitrariness suggestive of tyranny rather than democracy. Many of these foreigners fleeing from religious, cultural, and political oppression come to America to seek the spiritual freedom which the constitution grants but which an interpretation in accordance with this line of thought completely abrogates. Of what significance is the opportunity of economic advancement, if it must be bought at the price of suppression of individuality? Even under the conditions of Russian persecution the Jew was permitted to speak his own language and to live in many senses an independent cultural life. But if a conception of Americanism as here outlined is to be followed, such rights would be taken from him, in this country whose distinct and peculiar excellence lies in its gift of freedom. The result of such a program of Americanization is a tyranny over the beliefs and minds of men worse than the economic and political slavery from which they fled. Those who would put the immigrant into an American straight-jacket may be superficially American in that they attempt to adjust to the established forms of American life; they are not true to the fundamental spirit of American life and American institutions, which is to liberate and not to suppress the individuality of men.

Thus again this conception of Americanization fundamentally transgresses the first doctrine of democracy, that the unique individual must be taken into account in considering the end of his own development and the standard of his own good.   The theory under discussion implies the unquestionable superiority of one group, of the Anglo-Saxon race and culture, and proceeds to judge the value of the other groups by their approximation to this standard.   There is no question here regarding the desirability of institutions and conceptions objectively demonstrable to be beneficial to the generality of men.   Cleanliness and righteousness must be enforced because they are universally admitted to be good, not because they are peculiarly Anglo-Saxon virtues.   Obedience to these cannot be regarded as an external criterion, for they serve for the good of all men.   Perhaps it is even necessary in practice to go a little further and to maintain— although this may not be altogether rationally defensible—that priority of occupation does give a certain preference to the established group apart from or in addition to any inherent excellence.   But the tendency to believe that America exists solely and exclusively for the type of life represented by one particular group, must be challenged.   The assumption of total and exclusive superiority on the part of one group amounts to the imposition of an external standard which does not reckon with those concerned and savors of a theocratic or of an aristocratic state rather than of a democratic one.   No room is left for taking the nature and personality of the immigrant into consideration; his physical characteristics, his individuality, his ideals and culture are contemptuously ignored as unworthy of consideration.   The most profound feeling in American tradition is violated, the fundamental intuition upon which American institutions and political organizations are based, namely, *a decent respect for the worth of personalities which are not altogether like ours and a sincere faith in their potentialities.*

But not even in a democracy, one might say, are all individuals to be tolerated and every inclination permitted to have its way. Perhaps the tenor of the argument even thus far will carry the conviction that no individualistic position is proposed here and more will be said later explicitly on this question. The point urged, however, is that no neglect of interests or suppression of personalities is permissible in a democracy without some definite demonstration of the evil effects. Even criminals cannot be convicted without due process of law and in accordance with democratic notions they are to be considered innocent until proved guilty. In the face of the fact that the United States is richer, more powerful, more highly cultured, and its moral outlook as lofty as it was in the days of the fathers of our country, in spite of a continuous stream of immigration, positive evidence would be needed to prove that our fundamental institutions are being threatened. Problems have been created; but who can say that even these problems have not within them the seed of a contribution? The evil result is often due to the lack of understanding in meeting the new problem presented rather than to something inherent in the situation. The difference between the democratic attitude and the autocratic one would be just this: *the democratic attitude would have faith in the worth of a personality until positive proof of its inferiority were presented; the autocratic would condemn without proof. What is America if not liberal and generous? Not that which is the least, but that which is the most compatible with its integrity must be done.*

III

AMERICANIZATION AS LIKEMINDEDNESS

The emphasis on homogeneity which characterizes the Americanization theories undoubtedly finds justification in the need for national unity. If the citizens of the state are to act upon their affairs with reference to each other's interests and for the common good of the whole community, a certain degree of likemindedness must undoubtedly exist among them. Without common interests crystallized into common purposes, without the means of communicating these purposes and the relevant facts and ideas through a common language, without opportunity for general discussion of common problems and for participation in common tasks the democratic ideal of government by the people remains impossible of attainment. More than this the nation may fall prey to dissension from within and present a weakened front to inimical forces from without. Apart from the cultivating and humanizing influence that the inculcation of any great tradition may have, Americanization finds its irrefutable defense in the need of likemindedness to safeguard the very existence of the state.

However proper in its motives the current 'Americanization' theory with its connotation of "breaking up communities," of "ironing out differences," of casting the immigrant into the mould of a standardized American is false in effect, not only because it does not give consideration to the personality of the immigrant, not only because its method is psychologically indefensible, but especially because it fails to grasp adequately the basic principle of its own purpose, that of creating likemindedness. Its conception of likemindedness is superficial and primitive. It is the application of a primitive idea of what 'like' means to a complex modern social situation that makes the 'Americanization' theory, as ordinarily understood and advocated, so tragically erroneous.

The hiatus between the means applied and the results expected, which is so striking to the civilized person when he observes the manipulations of magic among primitive men, in all likelihood does not at all disturb the savage. No feeling of a gap is present in his mental reaction toward these ceremonies. According to his mental categories likeness of sense and emotional appeal gives the impression of complete similarity, and similarity somehow has a causative potency. To make an effigy of the enemy and stick daggers into it, is felt to be 'like' doing the real thing, and is accompanied by a feeling of satisfaction and accomplishment. A discriminating intellect, intent upon the practical outcome, would not feel such an action as relevant to or 'like' the real task. When it seems apparent even to the primitive mind that the two actions are not identical, there is attributed to the similar action a potency which causes the desired action to occur. It is vaguely felt that the dagger piercing the effigy in some way causes the destruction of the human object of hatred. Similarity to senses and emotions assumes a causative power.

Whenever a new problem occurs in a highly emotional situation, undiscriminating minds will tend to respond in the fashion characteristic of primitive men. Burning and burying the Kaiser in effigy undoubtedly gave those who participated in such ceremonies a feeling of satisfaction, as if they had really accomplished something. What is satisfying to the senses and the emotions tends to be totally satisfying even when the rational end of the action is not fulfilled. Naturally such emotional and sensory responses often prevent the attention from centering itself upon the real work to be done.

The conception of likemindedness underlying the current 'Americanization' theory partakes of the primitive notion that 'like' means similar to senses and emotions and that it implies causative potency. The attention centres upon outward conformity, which is conceived as likemindedness and as being productive of unity. Men are thought of as being alike when they look alike, when they dress alike, when they speak the same language, and these external similarities seem to be considered sufficient for bringing about an inner national unity. Differences in manner, speech and dress have a disturbing effect upon the attention, and if only these distinctions could be eliminated, it is felt, what harmony there would be! Hence the tremendous anxiety to have the races fuse, to do away with dissimilar customs, to abolish foreign languages. If all Americans could be made to seem alike, unity would be assured. Similarity will bring about unity somehow, even if in itself it is not unity.

This desire for conformity, an emotional response in a situation which is felt as dangerous, is increased further by the apprehension of public opinion. It is good to be able to *demonstrate* Americanization. Directors of social settlements and principals of schools are anxious to be able to *show* that those in their charge are American. To permit or promote differences is not quite safe; they may imply divergences not in harmony with a one hundred per cent patriotism. To level down to an accepted standard which everyone can recognize and no one question is the easiest and the most practical plan.

There is a third force, perhaps, in addition to a primitive psychology and the apprehension of public opinion, that tends to stress the importance of conformity, namely the American aptitude for standardization. Machinery has been standardized; clothes, food, school buildings, handwriting have all been standardized. Why not standardize personalities? And educational thought forthwith busies itself with the standard American, to be produced with the minimum of effort and most quickly by the appropriate educational machinery.

A conception of likemindedness which identifies it with conformity is both inadequate and erroneous. It permits outward resemblances to hide inward disunities; it crushes inner unities for the sake of outward conformities. In accordance with such a notion the unscrupulous politician and the exploiter of the social good may be considered the best Americans, and the foreign-tongued social reformer, even were both his theory and practiced plan valid, would tend to be considered un-American.

A more adequate conception of a true Americanization policy will appear if we scrutinize somewhat more carefully the word 'likemindedness.' 'Like,' if it is to mean anything, must signify not a vague general resemblance, but similarity in reference to the specific interest. Sticking daggers into an effigy is not 'like' killing the man, because in reference to the essential purpose there is no resemblance. Were we interested in race likeness, language likeness, or dress likeness the current Americanization notion might satisfy. But what we are interested in is *likemindedness.*

The word 'mindedness' implies a likeness not alone in reference to means. Mind signifies purposeful action, and the term 'likemindedness' when used as a justification of Americanism must direct itself to a unity of social aims, beyond all else. In so far as likemindedness requires conformities in manner and language as prerequisites, it will be necessary to insist on these. But sheer destruction of divergences without reference to the ultimate purpose cannot be defended on grounds of 'likemindedness.' What the promotion of unity implies is an emphasis upon the deep-lying purposes of American tradition rather than an exclusive attention upon its instruments or upon the negative task of the elimination of possible disturbances.

Americanization is a positive task, not a negative one. *Forgetting* other languages and other traditions, *destruction* of other spiritual allegiances is not an essential part of it, or if it is truly seen any part of it at all. Americanization is a constructive work of developing knowledge, ideas, social attitudes; conceptions of law, order, government; interpretations of duty, freedom and the meaning of life. It implies above all the creation of a psychological attitude of willingness to serve the nation rather than the self, the family, the class, or the group exclusively. How inadequate is that notion which identifies training for citizenship with 'coaching' on the answers to questions which will be asked of the applicant for citizen papers! How meagre is the plan which looks only to conformities in dress and speech. But even more objectionable is the current 'Americanization' theory, which regards the uprooting of foreign tradition as a necessary antecedent to true assimilation. If Americanism has to do with social ideals, is it not quite possible that it will have kinship with other traditions? May not understanding of another tradition be an aid rather than a hindrance ?

A little thought would reveal that not only is there a possibility of common elements in two traditions: there is rather a necessity. Any social tradition which has lived for some time embodies institutions, customs, ideas which promote the living together of men. These may have reference to local conditions, to particular periods, to certain types of men. But it would argue a disparateness which is untenable in human affairs, to maintain that all of these are sectional and particularistic and that there are not some which embody elements of the universal. With the length of a tradition and with the breadth of its experience, the chances for possibility of wide application become greatly increased. Undoubtedly there will be found elements in the European traditions which can be of service in the upbuilding of American life. For Americanism itself is not exclusive and sectarian; its ends are broadly human. A sympathetic and constructively minded statesman or educator with insight into the nature of social tradition would immediately recognize that every foreign system has within it possibilities of interpretation in terms of American life. The most stupid thing in the 'Americanization' program is the failure to recognize that the morality, folkways, ideas and aspirations of the immigrant groups could be utilized for the development of true Americans out of immigrants.

With contemptuous neglect, often with direct opposition, the current 'Americanization' theory has tended to break down deep-laid traditional social attitudes of respect for family, for kin and for the ethnic community; for the ideas of duty, service and self-restraint that such loyalties involve. The public school system has not succeeded in implanting equally deep-rooted conceptions of service; it has not realized how interwoven with the integrity of the family, and of the "consciousness-of-kind" groups, is the loyalty to the state and to society as a whole. The assumption was that breaking down a loyalty of seemingly smaller range leads of itself to a wider loyalty. It does not, necessarily. More often it leads to license and to individualism in the bad sense of that word. The notorious increase of criminality in the American-born second generation is due to the breach made in the social tradition of the family. Very often the foreign system of traditional morality breaks down not because it is inferior in aspiration but because it cannot adapt itself to apply to the new conditions. In such cases it should be the policy to reinterpret and apply in reference to the new conditions, not to destroy it or to permit it to disintegrate in the transition from one environment to another. Once morality and idealism have been implanted these attitudes may be transferred from one social situation to another much more easily than they can be developed altogether anew. Much of the lofty idealism and exalted loyalty among Americans of foreign near-ancestry are attitudes transferred from their ethnic tradition to the new life. It is possible to speak of justice, duty, service and loyalty, of law, order and government in other languages than English. Yet too often does the 'Americanization' theory imply that righteousness is Anglo-Saxon exclusively and that foreign languages ought therefore not to be tolerated. If the concept of likemindedness be carefully borne in mind it must lead to the realization that Americanization will be served very often by a conservation of social ideals even when they are foreign rather than by a destruction of them.

If we turn our attention from the objective aspect—ideas, aspirations, purposes—implied in likemindedness to the inner personal organic common feeling connoted in the phrase, "to be minded alike," the need for a sympathetic attitude toward the foreigner again becomes clear. The immigrant must be made to feel American; it is not sufficient that he strive in an objective way or mechanically for ends which can be identified as American. For it is such whole-hearted emotional identification with the body of citizens which is at the basis of a lasting allegiance. Now the current 'Americanization' theory, which contemptuously places the immigrant outside of the group and gives him a share in the people's heritage only when he divests himself of his most significant characteristics, is not calculated to promote that feeling of common ownership and responsibility which is the *sine qua non* of the community spirit. How can the immigrant feel himself part of the people when those who are recognizedly of the people place him outside? Such a course must drive the self-respecting among the immigrants to a heightened self-consciousness which divides his group, in heart, from the American people. This attitude taken towards the immigrant acts like anti-Semitism toward the Jew, impressing upon him a feeling of separateness from the general body of citizens.

The more the immigrant is permitted to retain and to develop his own type of life, when these are not detrimental to the general good, the more likely will he be drawn to feel that this really is his country. The splendid loyalty that immigrants have shown toward America and their heartfelt reverence for the new Promised Land are the result of no 'Americanization' program, but of living under institutions which by their very nature permitted economic advance, educational opportunities, and individual freedom in a degree unknown to them in the lands of their birth. It is the excellence of American tradition working indirectly and spontaneously which Americanizes, not the direct application of strict methods. The general work of the public schools, giving the individual a better start in life, permitting him to make more out of himself, has in all likelihood done more for the inculcation of a desire to maintain these institutions than any direct teaching could have done. High-handed artificial methods negate the natural effect of democratic American life which is to identify the good of the individual with the good of the state. If the immigrant is to attain to a whole-hearted allegiance and undivided loyalty to America, he must be regarded as kin with the other citizens, i.e., as a man whose personality must be respected, not as an inferior being whose individuality must be obliterated.

In yet a third way can the term 'likemindedness' help to a better conception of what proper assimilation means, namely through a consideration of the educational method that a developing mind implies. In the development of mind, it is necessary to start with the present mental situation, with the apperceptive mass of ideas, interests and associations. In general education it is the pupil that furnishes the method; in the Americanization of the foreigner, the latter is the starting point. The teacher must understand the tradition and past experiences of the immigrant if he is really to develop his mind. He cannot neglect these and get his own thought across. The process, too, requires patience, and will be slow and developmental rather than hasty and forced. The terms 'break up' and 'iron out' should be expunged from the vocabulary of assimilation. These are not words which are congruous with the ideas of growth, implied in the living mind. They savor of the methods of Russification that used to be practiced by Russia and of Prussianism that used to be practiced by Germany, rather than of the technique of democracy in education. Were Americanism conceivable as a completed doctrine, handed down through generations by authoritative interpreters, it would be easier to think of Americanization as conformity to a certain fixed type or standard. But, since the democratic faith looks upon the living forces in human nature as primary and respects personality above all else, standardization of men must be recognized as the cardinal sin.

Weighed in the balance of our first and fundamental criterion of democracy—respect for personality—the 'Americanization' theory must be found wanting. The tendency to interpret Americanism as the culture of one definite race, something well established to which the newcomers must completely conform, falls into the category of an absolutistic conception which assumes beforehand what is good without relation to the persons affected. By tacitly, if not expressly, denying the right of the immigrant to modify and contribute to the development of Americanism, the 'Americanization' theory violates that notion which is the quintessence of democracy, namely that the person involved must be considered as the end. Neither is the second criterion of democracy—a diversity in the environment—fulfilled by the 'Americanization' theory. It idealizes a fixed type of culture as against a diversified culture enriched by the tradition of many peoples. By the elimination of foreign ideas it would indoctrinate the tenets of a nationalistic cult. True liberty is served by the enrichment of possibilities, not by the establishment of uniformity. Lastly the conception of socialization in the 'Americanization' theory is faulty. It breaks down loyalty to the immediate family and to the cultural institutions—language, customs, etc., with which it is affiliated. It fails to realize that much of what the man's character is depends upon the integrity of these relations. To cap the climax, it fails in relation to the problem of affiliating with the new social life. Its stress is so negative, constantly emphasizing the danger of the old associations, that too little attention is given to the positive task—and a task it is—of building up on a firm and profound basis the culture of the new land.

Thus the public school graduate grows up to know that he must despise his parents with their poor knowledge of English, that he must be thoroughly conversant with the batting averages, and that he must possess a large quantity of Americanism—100 per cent at least! But how shall he know the profound quality of America? Whether from the point of view of democracy (which may be considered idealistic) or from the point of view of efficiency, the current 'Americanization' theory fails to qualify. Neither reason nor practicality can justify it. It can be explained only by an emotional hysteria which bids us do *something*, by the superficial intelligence which confuses the uniform with the unified, by the will to mastery which sometimes makes us brutally intolerant.

IV

THE 'MELTING POT' THEORY[1]

The 'Melting Pot' theory agrees with the 'Americanization' theory in that both look forward to a disappearance of divergent ethnic strains and cultures within the unity of American life. Both would sever the loyalty to the past lived on a foreign soil. But while our first theory tends to look upon Americanism as essentially bound up with Anglo-Saxonism and would give the recent immigrant no part in the development of American culture, the second theory welcomes the contributions that the new racial strains make to American life and looks with favor upon the addition of new cultural elements. Americanism is conceived of as in the making; something representative and growing out of the people that live here rather than a definite completed doctrine; something much more of the future than of the past. Americanism is a new life to which all can contribute. Out of the present heterogeneity of races a new superior race is to be formed; out of the present medley of cultures a new, richer, more humane civilization is to be created; out of the present ferment a new religion will develop representing the spiritual expression of the new people, a religion more relevant to modern conceptions of life than the historical creeds and more tolerant of the differences among humankind.

"America is God's Crucible, the great Melting Pot where all the races of Europe are melting and reforming!—Here you stand good folk, think I, when I see you at Ellis Island, here you stand, in your fifty groups, with your fifty languages and histories, and your fifty blood hatreds and rivalries. But you won't be long like that, brothers, for these are the fires of God you come to—these are the fires of God. A fig for your feuds and your vendettas! German and Frenchmen, Irishman and English, Jews and Russians, into the Crucible with you all! God is making the American! . . . The real American has not yet arrived. He is only in the Crucible. I tell you—he will be the fusion of all races, perhaps the coming superman. . . .

[1]For writings indicative of this attitude, see Israel Zangwill, *The Melting Pot;* Francis Kellor, *Straight America;* Mary Antin, *The Promised Land;* Walter E. Ravage, *An American in the Making.*

Yes, East and West, North and South, the palm and the pine, the pole and the equator, the crescent and the cross, how the great Alchemist melts and fuses them with purging flame! . . . Here shall they all unite to build the Republic of Man and the Kingdom of God. Ah, what is the glory of Rome and Jerusalem, where all nations and races come to worship and look back, compared with the glory of America where all nations come to labour and look forward!"

This theory which Zangwill evolved as the vision of the ultimate goal of American life many have formulated on the side of method from their experience with the process of Americanization. Those who have themselves been immigrants, like Steiner and Ravage, social workers with sympathetic insight, like Frances Kellor and Jane Addams, and many gifted teachers who have taught the immigrant have realized the inadequacy of the method prescribed by the Americanizationists even when they agreed in the ultimate hope of converting the foreigner into an American. They saw too many examples of elevated character and superior ability to remain contemptuous; they were close enough to the immigrant to see him as an individual person, not merely as one of a congregate of "sheenies" or of a horde of "wops." So it became clear to them that the social and psychological "apperceptive mass" of the immigrant had to be taken into consideration, that it was necessary to start from the point where he was when he came to our shores, and to work slowly, not hastily. This is keener insight into the nature of the immigrant and better understanding of the process involved in the making of an American.[1]

The 'Melting Pot' theory has a greater respect for the facts involved and a better conception of the true psychological method. The dubious assumption of the Anglo-Saxon character of the population and of the inferiority of types in the measure that they diverge from the North European is not made the basis of a drastic attempt to mould all newcomers into the form of the hypothetical American. The careless assumption that there is a 'typical American' easily identifiable and distributed in great numbers among the population has permitted the easy belief that a stamping out of foreign charac-

---

[1]Israel Zangwill, *The Melting Pot.*

teristics would of itself make a person an American.   There has, therefore, been a far greater anxiety concerning the elimination of differences than careful thought in reference to what is American and how to attain it.   'The Melting Pot' theory, less sure that the complete and typical American has already been evolved, tends to be more constructive in its policy.   It is seen clearly that such emphasis upon uprooting the tradition as is implied in the 'Americanization' theory may lead to the the acquisition of a new culture, but merely to the destruction of the old.   It understands that a loyalty is not to be built upon a disloyalty.   To make a good American is a positive task; it does not mean to make a bad Italian.   It is apprehensive of lack of culture much more than it is of a diversified culture, and is, therefore, not so quick to condemn the old heritage which the immigrant brings with him.   It tries rather to preserve the old while the new is being formed.

The 'Melting Pot' theory differs accordingly in the technique of the process of assimilation.   A lowering of the morale of the immigrant is to be avoided.   Pride in his past and in his people is to be encouraged, for our new American must have self-respect.   The process is to be gradual, taking into consideration the language, customs, and social environment of the pupils, and building up from these.   Old cherished memories and old ideals are not to be forsaken in the anxious endeavor to teach the new.   The tragedy of disintegrated families, with a consequent loss of social control is to be avoided by keeping the children faithful to the old life while bringing the parents nearer to the new.   Whatever has been learned concerning the psychology of the developing mind is to be applied to the process of assimilation.   The 'Americanization' theory speaks *de haut en bas*, the 'Melting Pot' theory is democratic.   Not one race is singled out as the standard; all the races that play a part in American life are conceived of as having a contribution to make.   A better understanding of the foreign groups, a spirit of humane toleration, and a notion of the dynamic nature of society pervade the Melting Pot idea.

The standards which have been laid down as the criteria of democracy would seem to be fully satisfied by the second mode of assimilation. The 'Melting Pot' theory has a profound respect for the Person. He is seen to be the central fact in the situation. Americanism is regarded more as a cultural and spiritual expression of the community of men who live in America. The citizens of America all participate in the creation of the common civilization and have a part in its modi-fication. The ideal is here related to the *persons* whom it is to serve. The realization of the heterogeneity of our population leads to an understanding that the uniqueness of each individual must be considered. The enrichment of American culture, through the contribution of the many peoples, supports the idea of a diversity in the environment which forms our second criterion. Finally, its conception of socialization bears in mind the actual social relations of the immigrant and reckons with these in building up the loyalty to the new life. From all angles the 'Melting Pot' theory is seen to be superior to the 'Americanization' theory and to fulfill adequately the several criteria of the democratic idea.

However, self-annihilation is the price that the 'Melting-Pot' theory demands while permitting the foreign groups to contribute to the life of the new country. It is by losing their own corporate existence that the foreign groups are conceived of as becoming part of the new nation. The new strains of blood are mingled with the old stock through intermarriage; new folkways to make a new 'cake of custom,' new ideas are conceived of as enriching the American spiritual heritage. But always the community which has made the con-tribution itself perishes as it gives forth the products of its own life. The 'Melting Pot' theory is adequate only for those groups which are willing to give up their identity completely in becoming incorporated into the life of America. It is no solution for those who wish to participate in American life and yet retain their ethnic identity, at least in some manner. These wish to make their contribution perennial, not merely a once-for-all contribution. For such groups the 'Melting Pot' theory, notwithstanding its superiority of method, is quite as inadequate as the 'Americanization' theory, for, in the essential, the right to maintain the ethnic identity, both theories are ultimately alike; they both lead to complete absorption.

"But does a group, which needs to be preserved forever, really have a contribution to make?" is the doubting query. "If the ethnic group really has a contribution to make, why not make it and have done? Why continue its existence interminably?" The answer of the ethnic groups is implicit in what they wish to preserve—namely their *culture*. 'Melting Pot' theories usually stress the contribution in terms of *race*, for the physical heredity remains a potent factor even after amalgamation, entering as it does as a strain in the make-up of the individual. The contribution in culture made by completely absorbed groups is almost negligible. Few words, customs, or ideas are added to the dominant culture by dying immigrant peoples. If the factor of culture is to become an ever present force, it is necessary to maintain the social atmosphere in which they live. The racial element is transmitted and preserved through the germ plasm even after intermarriage, while the perpetuation of culture requires social organization.

Physical heredity transmits itself, so to speak; social heredity, language, thought, ideas, etc., which are acquired characteristics need institutions to transmit them. This idea becomes even more apparent if we draw the important distinction between the two meanings of the word 'culture,' the cultural products of a past life and the cultural life itself. The objection raised above can apply only when we interpret contribution in terms of specific products of past life, a word, a doctrine, a social custom. It needs no answer when it is interpreted (as of the ethnic groups who wish to retain their cultural identity) in terms of the life of a cultural nationality. We may as well say, concerning any great man, "Let him give his contribution and have done. Why prolong his life?" But it is easily seen that any man is more than a single statement of his ideas. We recognize that as long as he lives he will continue to interpret and offer his ideas in new ways and continue to develop new ideas, the products of a continuous experience of his personality with situations. So, too, the nation must be looked upon as an ethnic personality, whose existence is not an idea, but a life. The longer it lives, providing it does not stagnate and retrogress, the more it has to contribute. Not only the crystallized products of a past life are conceived as being transferred and added to the culture of the new land.   The ethnic groups are seen as living and growing communities, fruitful in cultural influences, as long as the community maintains its vital existence.   Not separate, fixed, and abstracted ideas and dissociated customs are to be contributed, but a unified life expressing itself in language, social atmosphere, literature and religion. It must be carefully borne in mind that it is a life, not the products of a life, that these ethnic groups wish to perpetuate for themselves and to contribute to America.

For those ethnic groups which wish to maintain their cultural identity neither the 'Americanization' theory nor the 'Melting Pot' theory can be offered as a solution.   Both these theories deprive the immigrant groups of the right to perpetuate the group heritage. In accordance with them the immigrant groups buy their freedom at a cost of suppressing what many may consider of highest worth, their distinct cultural and spiritual life.

Were all foreign groups desirous of fusing and none anxious to maintain their ethnic and cultural identity, such a method of assimilation as our second theory implies would meet the demands of a democratic platform.   The whole discussion began with the assumption, however, that some groups desire to maintain their identity and do not want to obliterate themselves.   What shall be our attitude toward a group that has a conscious desire to maintain its historic identity and sets about to organize its life here in accordance with this desire?   Must such groups be suppressed, as the 'Americanization' theory would imply, in order to insure the unity and perpetuity of American life?   Or is there a way compatible with the best interests of America of preserving freedom for the immigrant group to maintain its cultural identity?   The following two theories offer solutions which look to the retention of ethnic and cultural identity of foreign immigrant groups in contradiction to the theories already presented which lead to total fusion.   How do they propose to make the adjustment to American life, and do they square with our criteria of democracy?

V

The 'Federation of Nationalities' Theory

Instead of eliminating totally or limiting in some degree the influence of the ethnic grouping in favor of a racial and cultural homogeneity, the point of view underlying the 'Federation of Nationalities' idea would make the ethnic group paramount and permanent in its influence on American life. The ethnic groupings are to be the basic groupings; they are regarded as comparatively stable. The purpose of the political organization is to promote and in no way hinder their distinctive integrity.

The basis of this theory rests on the assumption that the ethnic quality of an individual determines absolutely and inevitably what his nature is to be. "Self-hood . . . is ancestrally determined."[1] This motivating idea is put dramatically in the phrase referring to the immigrant, "Whatever else he changes, he cannot change his grandfather"; and more fully, "Men may change their clothes, their politics, their wives, their philosophies to a greater or lesser extent; they cannot change their grandfathers." Since 'race' is such an ineradicable and all determining element, it is the central fact of any man's life. Government performs its function of freeing human capacities only when it exists for the purpose of freeing ethnic expression. Its special function is to permit free development of the ethnic group, for the individual's happiness is "implied in ancestral endowment."

Consequently, the proper form of government for America in accordance with this underlying concept is a "Federal republic; its substance a democracy of nationalities, coöperating voluntarily

---

[1] These quotations, as well as those following on pp. 79–80 are from "Democracy versus the Melting Pot," Horàce S. Kallen, *The Nation*, May, 1915.

The articles by Randolph Bourne in *The Menorah Journal* and *Atlantic Monthly* and other newspaper references are in all likelihood inspired by this article. Dr. Kallen has elaborated upon the ideas of nationality implied in this article in his recent book, *The Structure of Lasting Peace*, which applies the concept to the general world situation. Without going into greater detail at this point it is suggested that the notion is more applicable to the international relations of European peoples, where distinct peoples are discernible occupying definite territories. In America there are no distinct nations holding definite territories in the same sense. The "Poale Zion Yiddishist Nationalists" have this conception of nationality as the background of their philosophy. See Zhitlowski, *Gesammelte Schriften*. See also Zimmern, *Nationality and Government*.

and autonomously in the enterprise of self-realization through the perfection of men according to their kind." No very clear idea of the limitations of such a government is given, but it is emphasized that the unity of America should be of a politico-economic nature. English, too, is to be a common language, in the sense of a *lingua franca* necessitated by the politico-economic unity. For the expression of its cultural and spiritual life, however, each group will depend upon the ethnic language, literature, social life and religion, for it is only through some ethnic form corresponding to the ethnic original racial endowment that true culture and spiritual life can exist. From this it may be implied that education should be controlled by the ethnic group, and this is the idea tacitly held by some of the Yiddishist protagonists of the national-culture idea. Throughout the scheme proposed prevails the analogy of a federation such as is found in Switzerland where three nationalities with distinct languages and cultures are joined harmoniously under one government. "American Civilization is to be conceived of as the unified resultant of the separate cultures existing side by side as distinct entities."

"Thus 'American Civilization' may come to mean the perfection of the coöperative harmonies of 'European civilization,' the waste, the squalor, and the distress of Europe being eliminated—a multiplicity in a unity, an orchestration of mankind. As in an orchestra every type of instrument has its specific timbre and tonality, founded in its substance and form; as every type has its appropriate theme and melody in the whole symphony, so in society each ethnic group is the natural instrument, its spirit and culture are its theme and melody, and the harmony and dissonances and discords of them all make the symphony of civilization, with this difference: a musical symphony is written before it is played; in the symphony of civilization the playing is the writing, so that there is nothing so fixed and inevitable about its progression as in music, so that within the limits set by nature they may vary at will, and the range and variety of the harmonies may become wider and richer and more beautiful."

In this conception of coöperating but distinct cultures the proponents believe themselves to be representing a line of thought which is in harmony with the progress of democracy. They point out the close connection between religious beliefs and cultural ideals, and argue that the modern formula *cuius regio huius natio* is as arbitrary and as oppressive as the eighteenth century *cuius regio huius religio*. They plead that freedom to develop one's own culture is as primary a right as is freedom to believe in the doctrines of one's own church. It must be remembered that these nationalists always interpret nationality in psychological, not political terms—in desire to promote literature, art and beliefs. They do, however, maintain that there is between birth and culture a definitely relevant relation and tend to look upon culture as national in its character.

The 'Federation of Nationalities' theory has undoubtedly served a purpose in offering a striking challenge to the easy-going assumptions of the total assimilationists. It brings to the fore considerations which the first two theories have failed to reckon with. However, whatever may be the final conclusion with reference to the desirability of maintaining the identity of the ethnic group within the state, the grounds upon which such a conclusion is to rest must be other than what is implied in the scheme of thought underlying the 'Federation of Nationalities' idea. The theory is based on the assumption of the ineradicable and central influence of race. That race in the sense of ethnic affiliation is the all important and predestinating fact in the life of the individual, or that it ought to be if the individual is to fully realize himself, cannot be upheld either from a logical analysis of what the term 'race' can mean or from any examination of the facts at our disposal of the influence of race on the life of the individual.

What lends the color of plausibility to such statements of the prime importance of race as is implied in the expression, "Selfhood is ancestrally determined" is a vagueness and equivocality in the meaning of the word 'race.' Sometimes it is used in the sense that the biologist or psychologist most often employs it, in the sense of actual heredity, i.e., the original nature of individuals as against acquired characteristics. In this sense the word is abstract and has no plural. At other times the word is used in the sense of the anthropologist denoting a group of human beings classified together on the basis of some physical resemblance in stature, head shape, eye color, etc.

There is indeed an assumption that the general outward resemblance
hints at some common origin; but it must be remembered that the
classification is made on the basis of the physical resemblances;
nothing is really known of the actual origin.   In this sense the word
is concrete and has a plural and in fact can only be thought of in
connection with the possibility of differentiated groups.[1]   Now,
saying that heredity in the sense of the original endowment of the
nervous system is far more important than environment (in reference
to some things and in some ways) is a different thing from saying
that the ethnic group to which one belongs, according to some anthro-
pologists, should decide absolutely for each individual what place he
shall hold in society.

[1]This error of double and equivocal usage is excellently illustrated in a recent work
on the importance of the Nordic race for European civilization, and the calamity that
awaits us because (as the author claims) it is passing away.   (*The Passing of the Great
Race*, Madison Grant).   A special preface explains the importance of the book in that
it is an interpretation of history in terms of 'race'.   "European history has been written
in terms of nationality and of language, but never before in terms of race; yet race has
played a far larger part than either language or nationality in moulding the destinies
of men; race implies heredity and heredity implies all the moral, social and intellectual
characteristics and traits which are the springs of politics and government.   Quite
independently and unconsciously the author, never before a historian, has turned this
historical sketch into the current of a great biological movement, which may be traced
back to the teachings of Galton and Weismann, beginning in the last third of the nine-
teenth century.   This movement has compelled us to recognize the superior force and
stability of heredity, as being more enduring and potent than environment."   Evidently the writer of the preface used the word 'race' in the sense that a biologist or a
psychologist would use it, in the sense of heredity, i.e. original nature of the individual
as against acquired characteristics.   The author of the work, however, throughout
the body of the book carries on the discussion of the term 'race' in the sense that the
anthropologist would use it.   The author, holding for the most part consistently to the
anthropological usage, tacitly assuming an inevitable relationship between the two
meanings of the word 'race', nevertheless in one place patently commits the fallacy of
the double meaning within the scope of a single paragraph.   "This something which we
call 'Genius' is not a matter of family, but of stock or strain, and is inherited precisely
in the same manner as are the purely physical characters.   It may be latent through
several generations of obscurity and then flare up when the opportunity comes.   Of
this we may have many examples in America.   This is what education does for a
community; it permits in these rare cases fair play for development, but it is *race*,
always *race*, that produces genius.   An individual of inferior type or *race* may profit
greatly by good environment.   On the other hand a member of a superior **Race** in
bad surroundings may and often does sink to an extremely low level."   Where the word
race has been put in italics (which are mine), it is used in the sense of heredity; in the
last case, placed in bold faced type, the author by introducing the indefinite article a
has easily slipped into the meaning of a group of men supposedly with the same origin.
Throughout the book the author assumes that there are superior races and that to be a
member of them is the very significant matter.   Most of the arguments about race
superiority have at bottom committed this fallacy.

Now the proposition that race is more important than environment, or that it is important at all, would depend for its truth upon the sense in which the term 'race' is used. If race here means an ethnic group, it is in all likelihood false; if race means heredity it is with limitations true. All that biologists mean when they say that heredity is more important than environment is that seeing an eminent person we should ascribe that eminence to some gift of original nature rather than to some process of training or to circumstances alone, i.e., put another man through the same course of education and the same environment and he will not become eminent; on the other hand take an individual with good original endowment and put him anywhere and he will become a somebody in the minds and opinion of his fellows. Few would maintain that a man's vocation is determined wholly by original nature and even fewer perhaps that the language a man speaks and the church with which he is affiliated are determined by his original nature. The proposition does not mean that two individuals of the same heredity will not be vastly different, absolutely considered, whether they are born and develop in Germany or in the United States. It does not mean that a genius brought up among savages will in absolute achievement equal the average man in a highly civilized state. In this sense and with such limitations it is true that race (i.e., heredity, original endowment) is more important than environment.

In the other sense, of a group with identical or closely related ancestry, the statement that race is all important in determining the status of the individual in all likelihood is false. Every serious study has demonstrated[1] that variability within one race and overlapping between races are so great that one can prophesy nothing with any degree of certainty about the original endowment of an individual from the one fact of his ethnic origin. There are differences, but the similarities are far in excess of the differences to such a degree that among European peoples the mass of each group is in original nature

---

[1]For the relationship between race and culture, see Robert H. Lowie, *Culture and Ethnology;* Franz Boas, *The Mind of Primitive Man;* Gustav Spiller, in *Sociological Review,* "Science and Race Prejudice; Franz Boas, *Changes in Bodily Form of Descendants of Immigrants;* Gustav Spiller, *The Interracial Congress;* Edward Thorndike, *Individual Differences,* Vol. III in *Educational Psychology.*

indistinguishable from the mass of any other group. While the influence of the near ancestry, i.e., the family, seems to be potent, the influence of the remote ancestry is practically negligible in determining the gifts of the individual. Thorndike, summing up the evidence on the influence of remote ancestry (race) in reference to education, expresses the relations as follows: "Calling the difference between the original capacity of the lowest congenital idiot and that of the average modern European 100, I should expect the average deviation of one pure race from another in original capacity to be below 10 and above 1, and the difference between the central tendencies of the most gifted and the least gifted races to be below 50 and above 10. I should consider 3 and 25 as reasonable guesses for the two differences. Even if the differences were far larger than these, the practical precept for education would remain unchanged. *It is, of course, that selection by race of original natures to be educated is nowhere nearly as effective as selection of the superior individuals regardless of race.* There is much overlapping and the differences in original nature within the same race are, except in extreme cases, many times as great as the differences between races as wholes."[1]

It is not difficult to understand why this great variability within each race and overlapping between races exist. If each human being had only one trait and each race was differentiated from every other race in reference to that one trait, then, granted that such was the case at the beginning of things and that no intermarriage has taken place since, every individual of one race would possess the trait in the form appropriate to his race. Every member of a race A would have trait A and every member of race B would have trait B, no member of race A could have trait B and no member of race B could have trait A; and granting further that a trait could exist only in one amount or one degree, there would be no divergences within the race group. The traits, however, which we have in mind are very numerous, the degrees in which they are present highly variable. Even if at the beginning of things there were pure races[2] intermarriage has taken place among all races that now inhabit Eurasia and there are

---

[1] Thorndike, *Educational Psychology*, Vol. III, Chap. X, p. 224 (italics mine).
[2] It would of course be going far to assume that the various subdivisions of the white race had separate and distinct origins.

no pure strains. Even such a comparatively pure race as the Jews are supposed to be[1] is undoubtedly a highly mixed race. They intermarried in Biblical times and throughout the diaspora with proselytes to Judaism and thus the racial elements entering into any modern Jew are highly complex.[2] Even in the case of the Jews, then, it would be very surprising to find a definitive line of demarcation between all Jews and all non-Jews. One would expect to find, as is certainly the case, no mutual exclusiveness in the original nature of Jew and non-Jew.

It may be argued, however, that the important differences are those of emotional reaction and desire, and that the conclusions cited above are the results of experiments on other than these characteristics. Separate measurements of simple mental traits, it may be urged, are not adequate for the determination of what the large important total reactions may be, and no adequate experiments have as yet been made in reference to these more complex functions. On the other hand, it should be noted that no experiments have proved the contrary, namely that the members of a race resemble each other very closely in some things in which they are very much differentiated from other races. Discounting for environmental influences, whatever evidence we have will insist on a great divergence within each race in reference to any point that one might measure, be it virtue or vice, riches or poverty, intelligence or stupidity; business ability, musical ability, manual skill; vocations, politics, pleasures. Whatever special tendencies there are among various ethnic groups can far more easily be traced to social pressure or environmental circumstances or to a slight racial difference.

On the other hand, the contention here is not that racial distinctions do not exist at all or that being small they are not very important for the development of any group as a whole in comparison with another group as a whole. In all likelihood, racial differences have played their part working through environmental and historical forces

---

[1]On good grounds because intermarriage is forbidden by religious laws and is contrary to the social opinion. In addition those who intermarry generally cease to maintain the Jewish tradition; those who are Jews are thus the selected non-intermarried Jews.

[2]Arthur Ruppin, *The Jews of To-day*.

to create distinctive cultures and to give some nations superiority over others.   However, differences of habitat, of vocation, of political institutions, of the 'zeitgeist' and social atmosphere also have great influence in deciding the characters of men in a profound way.   Tribal origin is at most only one of the many factors which combine to form the personality.   *It is the conception that ethnic differences are the basic matters in the life of each member of the ethnic group, that the ethnic differences are primary, ineradicable because natural, while all other differences, those of environment and acquired, are secondary and changeable because artifacts, which the argument opposes.*

It must be recalled that the differences between one culture and another when both are on a high plane of development are after all differences in quality or degree.   The distinction between Jewishness and Anglo-Saxonism is a difference comparable to the difference between Russian music and Italian music rather than to the difference between music and no music.   Let us imagine that a band of children, the offspring of gifted musicians are transported to a country in which no music exists; their musical souls would in all likelihood remain unsatisfied until they had created some music to live by.   Had the band been transported from Russia to Italy, rich in musical tradition, the children would have been none the wiser, and would have had full latitude for self-expression.   Indeed some rare genius of the Russian soul, it is conceivable, if he had happened to be among them, would have broken the chains of the foreign tradition and have revealed his primordial origin.   The average, however, would have taken the forms and spirit of the new nationality. So, too, the average Jew, brought up in an Anglo-Saxon environment, would have ample opportunity for self-expression, no matter what one assumes the Jewish genius to be, money-making, abstract religion, mysticism, or a passion for social justice.

But he would not have reached his full self-realization, one might urge.   Such an objection, however, takes for granted two matters which are open to question.   In the first place, such a conception takes for granted that every Jew is a Jew, i.e., that every person born in a Jewish family has the peculiar original endowment which makes Jewishness the only ultimate and complete satisfier. By original nature probably most Jews can fit into one culture as well as into another culture just as most men are not born to any vocation but fit equally poorly or equally well into a number. There are some men who are born to be musicians, or artists, or lawyers, or statesmen; but these are the exceptions, the men above the average. Most men have no special vocation; perhaps nearly all men can adjust themselves equally well within a certain type of work. The majority are mediocrities and nondescripts. So, too, most Jews are mediocrities and nondescripts in reference to their Jewishness. They can turn to any environment within the range of European civilization with equal facility. In fact their facility to adapt themselves is as proverbial as their ethnic tenacity. Those whose Jewish spirit is like a "fire burning within their bones" are few and far between.

In the second place, granting that there is a Jewish 'genius' and that most Jews possess at least a spark of it, is it necessary to assume that the present Jewish religion and culture, the evolved institutions of the Jewish spirit, comprise the true Jewishness? There are and have been many kinds of Judaisms. Since all historical expressions of a people's soul are of necessity only compromises with certain environmental circumstances and historical happenings and the true embodiment is continually developing and growing, whatever Jewishness we have to-day is inevitably imperfect. May not, therefore, another culture, say Americanism, though itself no complete expression of the tendencies which have created Jewish life, be a better embodiment than any of the particular forms which the force of historical circumstances has permitted to the Jewish genius? Certainly, some aspects of American life many would agree are more in accord with the spirit of the Hebrew Prophets than some aspects of traditional Judaism.

Before a doctrine of ethnic predestination can become tenable, it is necessary to hold that each member of the ethnic group possesses the ethnic genius, so that no other form of culture can bring him salvation, and, secondly, that the historical expression of the ethnic culture is more in accord with the ethnic soul than any other culture to which the individual may attach himself. The only way the former could be proved would be by permitting the member of the ethnic group to come into contact with more than one type of culture and to learn to which he tends to gravitate. The latter can only be demonstrated by watching the development of the ethnic group under conditions which guarantee social autonomy. Of the two, the writer believes the first to be relatively untrue and the second relatively true. These two large social experiments will be tried out in the coming generations; the second in Palestine if the Jews are restored as a self-governing people; the first in the diaspora, and especially in America, as will be the endeavor to show in the discussion of the 'Community' theory of adjustment presented in the next chapter. The conclusion that race in the sense of ethnic affiliation is no inevitable determinant of individual character would prevent us from fixing conditions in this country in such a way that the ethnos should have a predominating influence.

Perhaps the foregoing long argument is unnecessary to show that the epigram, "We cannot change our grandfathers," is but a sophism. A moment's reflection would show that we can "change our grandfathers," and in two specific ways. In the first place, when a man forgets who his grandfathers were and neglects their traditions, i.e., fails to retain the characteristics which marked his grandfathers and adopts other models, to all intents and purposes he "changes his grandfather." Our grandfathers are psychological as well as physical. What we are depends not only upon our original nature but also upon its interaction with the environment. To think of the nature of an individual as something independent of his environment is to be guilty of an impossible dualism. Since beliefs and traditions and manner of social life are part of the environment, any change in these from the standards of our grandfathers is in reality a "change" of our grandfathers. In the second place (since we are considering groups) grandfathers can be changed through intermarriage. Any individual who marries outside of his group is thereby changing the ancestry of his children. To what degree intermarriage is going on is a matter that needs to be ascertained through study; but that it is a possibility is open to no question.[1]

---

[1] Dr. Arthur Ruppin statistically proves the increase of intermarriage in Europe with the removal of social-economic deterrents. Julius Drachsler has shown

The contention of ethnic stability does not seem to be borne out either by the theoretical discussion or by the facts in so far as they have been ascertained. Wherever one ethnic group of the white race tends to remain separated from another, cultural, political and religious factors are the impediments, not racial characteristics. The objection to a scheme of organization like the 'Federation of Nationalities' theory rests, however, not only on the conclusion that its hypothesis of racial predestination is false, but also on the ground that such a scheme of organization would fail to satisfy in full measure our democratic criteria.

To regard every individual of an ethnic group as having primarily the characteristic nature of that group, as if affiliation with it invested him with a particular kind of ethnicity which then determined his nature, is contrary to the doctrine that each individual structure is primary. To assume that he is what his group is, and that solely or even primarily, is to apply to him something in the nature of a transcendental standard. If, indeed, after permitting him freedom of action, the individual shows tendencies that align him with his ethnic group, he can be rightly conceived of as sharing in its nature. To take for granted that he does so share the character of the ethnic group and to proceed to mould his life from that point of view solely is to apply to him an external standard. Undoubtedly an individual may be influenced by the character of his remote ancestry. But before governmental organization can be permitted to make ethnic origin the central consideration, there must be overwhelming proof of its importance. Otherwise such a scheme of government cannot help but artifically make race a greater factor than it deserves to be, leading to a repression of the individual, a lessening of the possible opportunities of a variety of type of living and an insufficient realization of his responsibilities to the larger group of which he is a part.

Now, undoubtedly, a member of a foreign ethnic group within the United States has interests which cross the boundaries of his

that the rate of intermarriage is very great for all groups in New York City except in the case of the Jews, that all the foreign ethnic groups are breaking down with the exception of the Jews. Even in the case of the Jews intermarriage is on the increase in the second generation. Both are at one in the conclusion that social and economic forces and acquired habits are between the white groups the only barriers to intermarriage. The race element is ineffective.

particular group, and which he holds in common with members of other ethnic group. In his economic activity, in his politics, and even in his general outlook on life, he has relationships with a wider range of persons than those which comprise his own group. He is as likely as not to be at variance in some of these matters with other members of his own ethnic group. To make the ethnic group the main basis of organization within the larger unit would in a sense make all of these other factors subservient to the ethnic consideration. For with autonomy of the ethnic group would have to go partial segregation and power over the school system. The free play of divergent currents, which the community of interests in America should demand, would be interfered with. Such an organization, a federation of ethnic groups, would lead to sectionalism, a condition in which a group decides issues affecting also other groups mainly from its narrower group outlook. Here sectionalism would be ethnic. The ethnic relationship would limit the view, as does the territorial alignment in local sectionalism.

Another way of saying this would be that ethnic automony would lead to indoctrination. A man's ethnic groupings would determine, fix, also his other relationships to the other members of the State. One factor in a man's life must certainly influence, but should not determine the other factors. Democracy is essentially opposed to determinism, either by physical force or by any other extrinsic or not fully related fact of life. Democracy does not oppose (as indeed it cannot) the influence of heredity, or church, or economic class; but it asserts that these must not have undue influence made possible by artificial organization of society. Since life is wider than any one of these factors, the rights of the individual in society must not be altogether determined by any one of these. So, too, when we would segregate our children in the schools on the basis of nationality, we would tend to make one factor in the complex situation determine all other relationships to their fellow American citizens. In effect, the possible opportunities of coming in contact with divergent currents would be artificially limited.

Furthermore, wherever unities of an economic and political nature do not lead also to cultural unities, to participation in a common spiritual life which rises out of the community of natural conditions, the most significant thing has been irretrievably lost. In the real human sense, all common economic and political activities are significant only in so far as they lead to a finer insight into, and finer appreciation of, life. To earn one's livelihood here and to vote here may be fair rewards for American citizenship. The great opportunity will be missed, however, of learning the significance of human life as it reveals itself in the activities and in the thought of a great country, rich in natural resources, heterogeneous in its racial composition, tolerant and open-minded toward life.

But is it not possible, one may protest, to conceive of the new conditions leading to growth by modifying the traditional ethnic culture? Indeed, this is so; but such a conception assumes the past of the race to be the Law, and the new experience mainly its illustration and sometimes its amendment. The democratic idea of culture demands that the significances spring out of the physical and practical life of the day, and that the function of history is secondary. Life is the author, history the interpreter, not vice versa. The notion of the hegemony of the ethnic group tends too much to bend the present life to a standard created by the past.

The simplest and therefore most telling objection to this type of governmental organization for the United States is the recognition that it is a notion imported from foreign conditions without realizing that the very considerations which make it valid there are totally different in this country. The analogy of a Federation of Ethnic Groups within one state is directly inspired by the situation in Switzerland, the British Empire and the old Austria. In all of these as in the United States there is a heterogeneity of ethnic types, with one set of essential differences. In these other countries each ethnic group is fairly well defined and attached to *particular localities*. The land was in all cases possessed by the ethnic group before the government came into existence. Together with this common ancient possession of the soil goes a community of language, social life and nearly always a common religion. The language of general social intercourse and the language of the street are the folk tongue. *The function of the Federal government which has come after the distinct existence of these groups promotes intercommunication and common action between groups hitherto separated and sometimes at variance with each other.*

In America conditions are quite different. The phenomenon of attachment of the various ethnic groups to certain definite localities from ancient times is altogether missing. Even where there is the gathering of groups in certain spots, we must remember the important distinctions. In the first place, it is not tenure of land that holds the group together, but certain psycho-social forces which in their nature of acquired characteristics tend to disappear with intercommunication. In the second place, one ethnic group will be found to have colonies in many places; it is not settled in one centre. The populations tend to be rather mobile and move from place to place. Even in the specifically foreign quarters the second generation tends to use English and not the ethnic tongue as the medium of expression. The children in the streets play in English. In order to have a Federation of Nationalities in America it would be necessary to separate the various nationalities and then organize them on the basis of the ethnos. Such a procedure would, in reference to the conditions in the United States, illustrate a tendency directly in opposition to that involved in federalization in the case of the European countries named. It would tend to impede impenetrability rather than to further it. In reference to the position already attained such a movement would be a step backward and not forward in the process of democratization. The analogy to European federations does not hold in reference to the central and relevant consideration. The conditions in America have no exact analogy and the solution cannot, therefore, be merely a copy of a ready made pattern. The task is to create an adequate mode of adjustment which will be harmonious with the novel conditions of thought and life presented here.

The 'Federation of Nationalities' theory has been treated at perhaps greater length than its practical import merits. Even among the Jews who are most keen in their desire to maintain the group identity this theory, especially in the literal form presented here, would find comparatively few advocates. Its strength lies rather in its negative criticism of the prevailing theories of assimilation than in its positive suggestion. Its proponents have given it undue force through excellent theoretical presentation; but it must be regarded as a doctrinaire solution, not as a practical plan.

Both the 'Americanization' and the 'Federation of Nationalities' theories assume too much. They fix to an unnecessary degree the end for which the individual nature exists. The 'Americanization' theory regards the life of the country to be fairly well determined and insists that the individual must bring himself within the limits of the evolved and dominant type. What the individual should be is predetermined altogether by the conditions of the geographical present. The 'Federation of Nationalities' theory would predispose, but in the opposite direction; the individual's race predetermines his end. Since the term 'race' here really signifies the traditions of his ethnos, it in the end amounts to giving the past of the tribe a vested right to determine the future of the individual. In both cases the cloth is to be cut in measure with some preconceived pattern. The theory to be offered as the constructive suggestion, while admitting the validity of both these forces, would endeavor to avoid exclusive control by either. To permit the greatest number of possibilities for the individual, to give an opportunity to all of these factors to function, to keep the future as flexible as is compatible with the integrity and stability of the total society will be the underlying purpose of the 'Community' theory of adjustment.

THE COMMUNITY THEORY

We perceive a community great in numbers, mighty in power, enjoying life, liberty and the pursuit of happiness; true life, not mere breathing space; full liberty, not mere elbow room; real happiness, not that of pasture beasts; actively participating in the civic, social and economic progress of the country, fully sharing and increasing its spiritual possessions and acquisitions, doubling its joys, halving its sorrows; yet deeply rooted in the soil of Judaism, clinging to its past, working for its future, true to its traditions, faithful to its aspirations, one in sentiment with their brethren wherever they are, attached to the land of their fathers as the cradle and resting place of the Jewish spirit; men with straight backs and raised heads, with big hearts and strong minds, with no conviction crippled, with no emotion stifled, with souls harmoniously developed, self-centered and self-reliant; receiving and resisting, not yielding like wax to every impress from the outside, but blending the best they possess with the best they encounter; not a horde of individuals, but a set of individualities, adding a new note to the richness of American life, leading a new current into the stream of American civilization; not a formless crowd of taxpayers and voters, but a sharply marked community, distinct and distinguished, trusted for its loyalty, respected for its dignity, esteemed for its traditions, valued for its aspirations, a community such as the Prophet of the Exile saw in his vision: "And marked will be their seed among the nations, and their off-spring among the peoples. Everyone that will see them will point to them as a community blessed by the Lord."

—ISRAEL FRIEDLAENDER

CHAPTER III

THE COMMUNITY THEORY

The 'Community' theory[1] which is proposed as the constructive suggestion is in reality the formulation of a process already shaping itself among some of our immigrant groups as a result of the confluence of the ethnic will to live with the conditions of American life. To the writer the suggestion has come from the experience of the Jewish group; and, although there are many indications of this scheme of organization among other immigrant nationalities, the Jews have undoubtedly gone furthest in its development. In fact, it may be regarded as the response of the Jewish group to the problem of adjustment. While many among the Jews would differ with our proposal or with some of its features, the tendency of Jewish institutional development would indicate that the 'Community' theory is the acceptable mode of adjustment for the Jewish group as an ethnic entity. Confidence in the validity of this plan should be the greater because it represents the resultant of many intricate social forces working slowly upon each other under democratic conditions. It will be apt to escape the basic unsoundness of an *a priori* plan built upon the interest of certain classes, the undiscerning emotionalism misunderstood as patriotism or the romantic imagination of sociological litterateurs. The formulation presented below comes after the process and is an attempt to build a consistent theory out of dissociated methods to the end that the further course of adjustment may be guided more directly in line with the ideal. Drawn from Jewish life, it will undoubtedly apply most closely to Jewish life. Nevertheless, it is hoped that the Jewish experience may form the basis of a

---

[1]See Horace J. Bridges, *On becoming an American;* Julius Drachsler, *Democracy and Assimilation.* Such an attitude is perhaps also implied in "Nationalizing Education" by John Dewey (in *N. E. A. Addresses and Proceedings*, 1916); and *Newer Ideals of Peace,* by Jane Addams. The underlying philosophy of Jewish life upon which this theory is based has been propounded by Ahad Ha'Am; though he does not develop it with special reference to the theory of adjustment in the lands of the Diaspora. That has been done with special reference to America by his disciple and exponent, the late Professor Israel Friedlaender. See *Past and Present, A Collection of Jewish Essays,* especially Chaps. XV, XVI, XVII, XVIII, XIX, XXVI.

theory of adjustment which will be applicable to all groups which
desire to maintain their ethnic identity in the conditions of democratic
life in America.

Like the 'Federation of Nationalities' theory, our position insists on
the value of the ethnic group as a permanent asset in American life.
The 'Community' theory differs from the 'Americanization' and 'Melting Pot' theories in that it refuses to set up as an ideal such a fusion as
will lead to the obliteration of all ethnic distinctions.   Furthermore,
it regards a rich social life as necessary for the development and
expression of the type of culture represented by the foreign ethnic
group.   There is, however, a fundamental difference in what is
conceived to be the ultimate sanction for maintaining the identity
of the foreign ethnic group.   In the 'Federation of Nationalities'
theory the assumed identity of race is pivotal; the argument is made
to rest primarily upon the proposition that "we cannot change our
grandfathers."   The 'Community' theory, on the other hand, would
make the history of the ethnic group its aesthetic, cultural and religious inheritance, its national self-consciousness the basic factor.
This change of emphasis from race to culture brings with it a whole
series of implications rising from the fact that culture is psychical,
must be acquired through some educational process, and is not inherited in the natural event of being born.   The 'Community' theory
is to be understood as an analysis of what is implied for the theory of
adjustment by considering culture as central in the life of the ethnos.
Community of culture possible of demonstration becomes the ground
for perpetuation of the group, rather than an identity of race, questionable in fact and dubious in significance.

The distinction between race and acquired characteristics shows
itself in a greatly overemphasized form in the logomachy which has
for many years been carried on between the extremists of the Reform
Movement and the Modernist Radical-Nationalists.   The Reform
position maintains that "the Jews are a faith, not a race."   Perhaps
most Jews would subscribe to such a pronouncement if the term
"faith" were made broad enough and interpreted to mean a kind of
life.   The followers of Reform, however, anxious to become as near
as possible to the nations of the West, adopted Western customs and

modes of life wholeheartedly and made of Jewishness a formal creed
to which one might maintain a sort of verbal adherence without
changing in any important respect the content of life or thought.
The movement toward divesting Jewishness of all social background
and leaving it a bare, attenuated doctrine finds its extreme logical
development in the conception that Israel has been dispersed amongst
the nations providentially, for the purpose of teaching "God is One."
The crystallization of Jewishness into a phrase permitted the growth
of the illusion that one could live any type of life and remain a Jew
by giving a lip allegiance to words.   Orthodoxy,[1] as it develops in
Western countries among German Jews and Jews who have lived in
America for some length of time, shows a similar tendency toward
formalization.   But instead of becoming crystallized into abstract
ideas, orthodoxy has been codified into religious ceremonies whose
meaning and relation to life are little understood.   Thus the 'orthodox'
Jew can become assimilated to Western modes of life quite as much as
the Reform Jew while he saves his soul by the mechanical performance
of the Jewish ritual.   Since actions and customs are more noticeable
than phrases kept in the mind, differences of ceremonial, as for
instance the keeping of the Dietary Laws, often impress themselves
more readily on the non-Jewish mind.   These external peculiarities,
however, only too frequently are not accompanied by any distinct
cultural or spiritual life.   They are merely social conventions.
There is, however, an element of fundamental truth in the tendency to
associate Jewishness with 'Religion,' and that is to insist that Jewish
life must have a spiritual justification.   The error in both Reform
and Orthodoxy seems to be that the conception of 'spiritual' is formal,
sentimental, and abstracted from social life.

    The modernist Radical-Nationalists, impatient with codified
formulations of the spirit and aspirations of a people, especially since
these formulations had been embodied in 'religious' practices and
terminologies on account of historical circumstance, were seeking for
something underneath and below these crystallizations of custom
which had become encrusted on the Jewish organism, for something

[1]Orthodoxy as a creed is meant; not the social life of the Russian ghetto, which is
often called 'orthodox' Judaism.

motivating and spontaneous, some life force which could be conceived as manifesting itself throughout history in a variety of embodiments.   They did not blindly worship the Western World.   They had confidence that the Kingdom of Heaven was within them too. Looking for some inherent Protean potentiality rather than for completed excellence, and within themselves rather than in the environment, they fell back on the term 'race.'   Such a conception of identity in race leaves room for progress and new embodiments, though it tends to minimize the importance of history and what has already been acquired.

Jewish tradition and with it the Jewish masses speak in terms of neither 'race' nor 'religion.'[1]   Both of these terms are imported from the Western world and are foreign to the Jewish spirit as terms description of Jewishness.   The central idea in Jewish life is Torah. In legend and in literature, it is for the sake of the Torah that Israel was called into being; it is for the sake of the Torah that Israel has been spared annihilation.   Torah is a word of many connotations, ranging from the usual designation of the Pentateuch to the whole spiritual life.[2]   It was the Torah that was revealed from Sinai.   It was for the sake of the Torah that Israel entered the Promised Land. It was because Israel sinned against the Torah that he was exiled. It was for teaching the Torah that Akibah was flayed alive by the Romans.   It was the Torah that was burned during the persecution in the mediaeval dark ages.   It was for the Torah that the youth of the Russian Jewish ghetto gave up all worldly interests in a single-hearted devotion to learning.   It is the Torah ultimately that is to go forth from Zion, and bring about Peace and the Messianic Age for the nations of the earth.   Torah is the basis and the goal of Jewish life.   Interpret it as narrowly or as broadly as you please, the central idea is Torah.   It is Jewishness, the spiritual life, and Godliness, ישראל ואורייתא וקודשא בריך הוא חד הוא.   (The Holy One, Blessed be He, the Torah and Israel are one.)

In the writings of the Cultural Zionists, devoted to the renascence of Hebraic life, this traditional emphasis upon Torah has been made

[1]Israel Friedlaender, *Past and Present*, essay on "Peace and Religion."
[2]Solomon Schechter, *Some Aspects of Rabbinic Theology*, Chaps. VIII, IX, X, XI.

the central thought. The idea of Torah has been broadened to include cultural and aesthetic values as well as those which popular usage identifies as 'religious.' The fundamental notion, however, that the aspiration of Jewish life is spiritual remains the underlying conception in this philosophy. The term 'history' is sometimes used in the profound sense of "Philosophy teaching by example" as the interpretation of events through the experience of the human race with reference to human aspirations.[1] Torah, we may say, is History in this broad sense, as it manifests itself in the life experiences of the Jewish people: Culture as it expresses itself in the rich inheritance of the Jewish people; Philosophy and Religion as they become embodied in the social and spiritual ideals of the Jewish People. What brings Jews together is the significance and power of Torah, i.e., Jewish History, using the term in its richest sense.

This conception which identifies the Jewish people with its cultural and spiritual aspirations comes very close to the view that nationality is essentially a psychological force, a view held by many of the protagonists of 'national' autonomy for the smaller nations of Europe. When the Serb representative at the Hungarian Diet of 1848 was asked, "What is a Nation?" he replied, "A race which possesses its own language, customs, culture and enough self-consciousness to preserve them." This definition of nationality in cultural terms gives the clue to the solution of our problem of harmonizing two nationalities dwelling side by side. The essential distinction between physical and spiritual goods lies in mutual exclusiveness of the former and the permeability of the latter. Two individuals, however close their proximity, cannot enjoy the possession of the same physical good. A man cannot eat an apple and give his friend the apple. If they desire to share, each must give up a part. Two men cannot have possession, in the strict sense, of one piece of land; both of them cannot build a house on the same spot. Spiritual goods, however, have an opposite character. Many people can listen to one musical composition, admire one picture, read one book. Indeed, such sharing normally enhances for each the enjoyment which each derives from the use of the good in question. Thus a group which has as a common pur-

[1]Woodbridge, *The Purpose of History*, page 23.

pose the acquisition of economic goods, may be in great danger of coming into conflict with neighboring groups of like mind. If, however, the group purpose is expressed in terms of spiritual aspiration (unless, indeed, it believes that it is necessary to impose its own culture upon other groups by force) there is no innate necessity of conflict in the ordinary physical sense; rather mutual coöperation and exchange would be the logical outcome. The spiritualization of the purpose of nationality is the most important factor in the adjustment potentiality of groups to one another. It points to a possibility for the preservation of individuality by other means than segregation, and reveals a way of retaining loyalty both to the cultural life of the ethnic group and to the life of the total group in all its aspects. Cultural divergences are not incompatible with allegiance to a common culture. Two cultures have possibilities of harmonization which two political or economic independences would never have.

Accordingly, the 'Community' theory of adjustment makes culture the *raison d'être* of the preservation of the life of the group. The School[1] becomes the central agency around which the ethnic group builds its life. In accordance with our theory, the Jews are conceived of as living in no one isolated locality but scattered throughout the country and living amongst other nationalities. Together with other nationalities, they engage in commerce, in political and social life; they take advantage of all opportunities for educational and cultural development offered by the state, they fulfill whatever responsibilities citizenship implies even as understood by those who have no other loyalty than to the American ethnos, and they contribute in whatever way they can to the development of America, in all phases, economic, political and cultural. Over and above this participation in the common life of the country, wherever Jews live in sufficient numbers to make communal life possible, the Jews are conceived of having their own communal life organized with a view to the preservation of that which is essential in the life of the Jewish people—the Torah.

---

[1]The word School is used throughout to signify an educational agency much broader than the classroom (see Chap. VI).

Consistent with this conception the תלמוד תורה (Talmud Torah), as the Communal Jewish School is called,[1] becomes the central agency of the community, the institution around which it builds the social life and by means of which it transmits the significant culture of the ethnic group. Working hand in hand with the public schools the Talmud Torah provides that education which the ethnic community alone is capable of transmitting. It selects from the inheritance of the group those things which are of abiding worth. The loyalty which the school demands is not to the past for the sake of the past nor to characteristic customs and ceremonies when these are trivial, but to what is sublime, significant and beautiful in the history of the ethnos. The philological meaning of Torah, which is "Instruction," enforces the idea and gives the key to the method as well as the aim of the preservation of Jewish life. Torah, Jewishness, is not attained through revelation or maintained through racial persistence; it is essentially study and must be acquired by means of the educational process.

The function of the complementary schools, as is also the function of the communal organization of which the schools are the agency, is to transmit the culture of the ethnic group and thus to enrich the life of the individual Jew and through him that of the total group. If these schools have something to contribute to the citizen that will induce him to remain in loyal adherence to his ethnic community, his allegiance and the perpetuation of the community are justified. The ethnic group cannot demand the loyalty of those to whom the cultural life of the ethnos offers no inspiration, whether these have not the emotional and aesthetic faculties of appreciation or whether they regard the ethnic tradition as being too separatist. Those foreign groups which have no cultural heritage cannot remain segregated on account of some assumed racial identity. Our theory requires neither proof nor assumption that a group has an identity of race which is significant or a culture which is particularly excellent. It endeavors to provide conditions which will permit these factors to play—to determine whether they really do exist and are important—without at the same time minimizing the duties and possibilities which rise out of

[1]See A. M. Dushkin, *Jewish Education in New York City*, p. 68. The words תלמוד תורה mean "Study of the Torah."

living in America. By making the educational agency central and the fundamental means of perpetuating the group, we have chosen the instrument which is directly relevant to what we wish to preserve, namely, the cultural life of the ethnic group.

The attempt to promote Jewish identity by local segregation and autonomous government, as is implied in the 'Federation of Nationalities' theory, would introduce a force making for separation which would gather its strength from other sources than the value and the appeal of the ethnic culture.   Such organization would load the dice, so to speak, and bring to the support of the ethnic solidarity an aid in reality extrinsic to the nature of that which is considered valuable. It is necessary to be careful in pressing this point to avoid a dualistic position, for, undoubtedly, education cannot be given apart from some type of institution which involves the living together of men, community organization and some governmental guarantee that this free association will not be disturbed.   But it must be clearly borne in mind that whatever segregated communal power exists must be directly derived from the necessity of the educational process itself, sanctioned in so far as it can preserve what seems worth while in Jewish life, not from the mere fact of living together, nor from the assumption of a common heredity.   The sanction for Jewish organization must rest on its culture.

On the other hand, culture must have support in social life and adequate expression in communal institutions.   The religious idea with the synagogue, conceived as a place of worship primarily, as the central communal agency offers too narrow a concept to include the full range of Jewish spiritual life.   In the recent tendency to define religion in broad terms, making it practically synonymous with the spiritual and social aspiration, we have an attempt to regain for religion that wide province of control which it has lost through the transition from a theological to a scientific and political stage of social organization.   Nevertheless, there is an element of plausibility in this reinterpretation, for religion when it becomes elevated and ideal attaches itself to the profound, the eternal, the universal.   The error comes when this idealistic definition of the ultimate aspiration of religion is identified with the historical religions which have found expression in the temples, churches and synagogues, and these are presented as the central agencies for the development of social and spiritual life. But, obviously, the synagogue (or church) is only one agency with a limited sphere of influence. The synagogue even in religious ages included secular elements; it was the House of Study and the House of Meeting as well as the House of Prayer. In modern times, with the shift of emphasis to secularism, the Jewish conception, always tinged with anti-clericalism, must tend to emphasize the realistic interests of social life rather than the sentimental outlook which centers about prayer. The culture of the Jewish people, including as it does a language, a literature, and a profoundly spiritual social outlook, cannot be confined within the walls of the synagogue, where the erstwhile living thought is embalmed in liturgy, aspiration petrified into prayer, and social life fossilized in ceremonies. Not the particular form, but the vital longing for spiritual life is primary in Jewish life, and this finds embodiment in every age in that phase which for the time is most significant for social life. Jewish life, deeply spiritual, can be conceived of as cultural and political as well as religious and ecclesiastic. Only the combined force of formalized traditionalism, unwittingly abetting the anti-Jewish environment driving to denationalization, can reduce the richness of the Jewish cultural heritage to the attenuated doctrines, superstitious sentimentalisms and ceremonious practices which remain the content of 'religion' for the many.

Philanthropy can even less be considered as an adequate binding force between Jews, even though it will long continue to be an outstanding element in Jewish communal life. Charity is a public not a private function. When a man is ill or stricken with poverty it matters little whether he is a Jew or a Bohemian; the efficiency of the whole community is lowered and the public health endangered. So, too, the problem of recreation facilities, social centers, etc., is a public not a private function. There is no essential reason why the circumcized and the uncircumcized should not exercise together; the same rules of hygiene apply to all. The coming together of Jews merely because of their consciousness of kin is the most reprehensible form of clannishness. For it is not justified by spiritual products which should result from coming together. It is a strange paradox that those Jews who proclaim, "Americanization" most loudly and who are generally deemed assimilationists should be the very ones to promote the sectarian recreational settlement while often decrying the promotion of Jewish teaching and Jewish culture! Until the State realizes to the full extent the importance of providing for the abnormal and learns to understand the relation of ills and their cure to the social psychology of various peoples there is undoubtedly room, even absolute necessity, for private philanthropy along sectarian and ethnic lines. The Jewish leaders in New York City who have built up an excellent system of eleemosynary institutions have, to be sure, rendered invaluable service both to the Jews and to the community at large. Undoubtedly in the beginnings of communal endeavor the abnormal aspects had to receive first attention. But in the ultimate sense these are not permanent or essential Jewish tasks. Certainly, they are not the only Jewish tasks.

In so far as the ethnic group is organized for political purposes and through political means, its activity is a menace. In so far as it is organized as a philanthropic agency, it is performing a valuable function although one not essentially its own, but rather that of the state. But in so far as it exists to perpetuate the spiritual and cultural heritage of a community it is performing a task relevant to what sanctions the existence of such a community, the possibility of enriching the life of the nation by its own cultural inheritance.

The 'Community' theory, then, would seem to make full provision for the requirements of American life, while aiming to contribute to America the finer elements in the ethnic tradition. On the other hand, the question may be raised whether such a method of adjustment will be adequate for preserving the foreign ethnic group from extinction. Constantly subject to the play of forces from without, is there any hope that the ethnic group will be able to maintain its identity and to develop its culture in new and creative ways? In accordance with the 'Community' theory it is the clear consciousness of the worth of the ethnic heritage, implying the power of comprehension and appreciation in great degrees, upon which the perpetuation of the ethnos must rest in a democratic land. Are the many, usually unreasoning, fashioning their lives through force of instinct, personal habit and social pressure, capable of being held and directed by a spiritual heritage, which must be transmitted in great part through books and language; especially when this heritage is not supported by economic, political and social interests?

The danger of disintegration is undoubtedly real, especially if there is more than a formal religious adherence in mind.   To some thinkers[1] the fate of the Jews in democratic countries, wherever they form a minority of the population (and they do so practically everywhere) is inevitable extinction. The analysis presented here, suggesting a way, consistent with democratic notions, of maintaining the identity of a cultural nationality even when it is a minority, is presented not as the necessary outcome of a *laissez-faire* policy, but as a possibility of accomplishment through conscious and intelligent endeavor. Only when the minority cultural community is self-conscious of its purpose and deliberate in its method can there be hope that the school will be effective in counteracting the forces of disintegration.

In estimating the possibility of maintaining the ethnic identity, two factors of extreme importance must be borne in mind, the rate of intermarriage and the influence of a 'home' country where the culture of the ethnic group is predominant.   The integrity of the family will determine the physical stability of the group; the 'home' country will serve as a reservoir from which to draw forces of renewal.   The validity of the 'Community' theory will depend in great measure upon its implications in regard to both these factors.

THE FAMILY

From the point of view of the *raison d'être* of the preservation of the ethnic community, the school becomes the central institution because it reproduces that which is essential to the group as a community—its cultural life. From the point of view of physical perpetuation, which is the condition of any other kind of life, the family is basic. Intermarriage, with rare exception, leads to a total obliteration of the culture of the ethnic minority.   Unless the family preserves the ethnic affiliation, the child will never have the opportunity of coming under

---

[1]Arthur Ruppin, *The Jews of Today.* J. Welhausen, *The History of Israel and Judah.*

the influences of school and synagogue. The integrity of the Jewish family, therefore, becomes *sine qua non* to any preservation of Jewish life, and intermarriage tending to disrupt the group becomes logically impossible for those who wish to preserve the cultural values of the ethnic minority as vital living forces. The 'Community' theory, therefore, presupposes marriage within the group only as the general practice. What local autonomy and territorial boundaries would accomplish in the 'Federation of Nationalities' theory would be assured in our own view through family solidarity. To bring about the ethnic 'purity' indirect and intrinsic influences are conceived as functioning. The sanction for intermarriage would rest in the recognition that the ethnic group is of spiritual significance, not primarily on religious basis or communal pressure. Marriage within the group would be the result of free choice to preserve the cultural inheritance, not the impulse of racial clannishness or the dictates of a superstitious tribalism. Our theory, moreover, does not propose absolute non-intermarriage either as possible or as desirable. Wherever the ethnic affiliation has lost its significance, either because the individual is too gross to appreciate it or because a universal cause, such as science, music or art has become a religious enthusiasm and displaced other loyalties, intermarriage may take place without social detriment. In the one case, no cultural value exists anyway; in the other case, we may console ourselves that new spiritual values have been substituted. It is when the ethnic loyalty is obliterated without providing something equally akin to the nature of the person and equally elevating that a loss has been sustained. Once assuming the value of the ethnic group, a nucleus of family solidarity becomes necessary. Intermarriage dare not proceed to the point where it threatens the life of the community. This the community must prevent, not by religious ban or social ostracism, but by providing the educational influences which would lead the individual to cherish the cultural and spiritual values of the group.

Such exclusiveness may seem at first inconsistent with the free interchange of forces that the democratic idea demands. But the right to preserve the identity implies also the right to preserve those institutions which are basic. The process of mutual interchange

cannot proceed to the point where one of the bodies involved is
destroyed, for that would prevent a further exchange of forces.   The
Jewish family must undoubtedly be open to influences of American
life and be modified by them, but it would not be necessary for, or
really consistent with, our theory to destroy it.   Upholding in theory
the right of free immigration and favoring the resulting interchange of
forces, one may still counsel restriction when the volume of immigration threatens to swamp America and its quality to undermine our
institutions.   There must be a balance in the elements of give and
take to preserve the entities.   In the 'Community' theory the family
is the keystone of the social situation; if it should be destroyed the
whole would crumble.

ZIONISM[1]

It is to be understood that the 'Community' theory is not offered as
a total solution of the Jewish problem, the problem of freedom for
the Jewish People to live and to create in harmony with the spirit of
its history and its genius.   The theory presented purposes only to preserve Jewish life for the Jew living in America and through him for
America.   In the task of solving the larger Jewish problem the writer
is in thorough accord with the Zionists who maintain that an autonomous Jewish community with a territorial basis in Palestine is necessary
for the free development of the Jewish cultural and spiritual life.
Indeed the Zionist idea becomes even more urgent in view of the type
of adjustment, admittedly precarious for the ethnic group, demanded
by the democratic conditions.   Even the possibility of maintaining a
vital ethnic culture in the diaspora is dependent upon the existence of
a cultural center to serve as a source of spiritual replenishment and to
prevent the ethnic spirit from becoming the petrified relic of an ancient
grandeur.   The 'Community' theory becomes a hopeful solution only
if there will be established an autonomous Jewish center in Palestine.

---

[1]Theodore Herzl, *The Jewish State, Altneuland, Zionistische Schriften;* Leo Pinsker,
Auto-Emancipation; Moses Hess, *Rome and Jerusalem.*
   Ahad Ha'Am (Asher Ginsberg) *Al Parashat Derachim,* 4 vols.; *Selected Essays,*
Translated from the Hebrew by Leon Simon; Horace M. Kallen, *Constitutional Founda-
tions of the New Zion;* Richard Gottheil, *Zionism;* Jessie E. Sampter, *A Guide to
Zionism.*

Our theory, then, becomes part of an international conception.   The Jewish community in America is regarded as one of many sister communities throughout the world, each adjusted to the social and political conditions of the land of habitation, bound together by its cultural-religious inheritance and by the spiritual inspiration of the Palestinian center.   It is completely in accord and really an elaboration of the Culture-Zionist theory formulated by Ahad Ha-Am. Involving as it does an affiliation with a foreign land it will be necessary to make clear what is involved in such a loyalty.

In the first place, even an elementary understanding of the character of the Zionist movement should prevent us from setting up a bugaboo to frighten us into believing that here lurks the monster of a dual political allegiance.   The aspiration for the return to Palestine is essentially spiritual, resting upon the prayerful longing for the Shechinah's return to Zion which animates the Jewish liturgy.   There enters into the Zionist hope, no doubt, a complex of unfulfilled desires, the counterpart of two thousand years of political, economic, and social repression; and the modern leaders who created the machinery of Zionism often looked upon their movement as a means of obtaining equal rights for Jews.   Nevertheless, the thought of cultural freedom is central.   The political idea enters only in so far as it is seen to be prerequisite to cultural self-determination.   Especially in the formulation of Ahad Ha-Am which has now become widely accepted among Zionists the cultural idea becomes predominant.   In harmony with a rationalistic trend of thought Ahad Ha-Am gives Zionism a broadly cultural rather than religious atmosphere.   He does not minimize the importance of political and practical plans.   In fact he goes even further than former writers in demanding practical insight and thorough logic.   He has pointed out, nevertheless, that Palestine can be no ultimate solution for the problems of economic and political exploitation of the Jew and of social anti-Semitism, if for no other reasons than because Palestine is not large enough for the settlement of a large majority of the Jews.   It might, indeed, serve incidentally as a refuge in times of particular stress in some countries and might become a source of influence for the general amelioration of conditions.   But these benefits must be considered incidental.   The problem of the equality of political and civil rights must find its solution, even if slowly, with the humanization of Western civilization. Palestine is not the solution of the problems of the Jews as individuals. But it can become a haven for the Jewish soul, a place where Judaism as a national culture may be perpetuated and attain a full and unhampered development. What is being threatened is Jewish civilization which needs its own social background and atmosphere for free growth; above all it is a spiritual slavery from which the Jew must be emancipated. This thought has undoubtedly become the central idea in the modern Zionist philosophy.

In thinking, then, of a Jewish nation in Palestine, and of the relation to it of the American Jewish Community, it must be borne in mind that to the Zionist the words 'nation' and 'national' have a predominantly cultural (i.e., psychological) connotation, more familiar perhaps to English readers when the term 'nationality' is used.[1] They want a place where those Jews who so desire may follow their own customs, speak their own language, attend their own schools and live in accordance with their traditions and ideals. In this conception of nationality they follow that school of nationalists, disciples of Mazzini, to whom group individuality is justified not by its power to dominate but by its ability to serve. Nationality is conceived of in terms not incompatible with, but helpful for the good of mankind.

The allegiance that the Jew in America may offer to Palestine in accordance with the 'Community' theory is a spiritual allegiance to a cultural center. In his economic life he must by force of circumstances be subject to the conditions of the country in which he lives. In his political life, he must by virtue of the duty that his oath of citizenship implies, give a complete allegiance to America. In the event of any political differences between the two countries, although the Jews might do their best to avoid an open break, ultimately each citizen must side with the land of his habitation. His spiritual attachment, if we speak honestly, cannot be forced either to Palestine

---

[1]See *War and Democracy*, Chap. II. When an American says 'nation,' he thinks of government. When a cultural-Zionist (or many of the representatives of small nationalities) uses the word he thinks of language and literature. It is important to note that most of the confusion in reference to Zionism comes from an equivocal meaning of the word 'nation.'

or to America. It will go to both if the life of both are inspiring, provided that both are open to him. Living in America and attending the public schools insures contact with American life; the family and the Jewish school provide an opportunity for learning the significance of his people's history.

It must be borne carefully in mind, then, in urging the value of the retention of an ethnic loyalty that a clear distinction must be made between the political and cultural aspects of the term 'nation.' Indeed, it is possible even to feel friendly towards or even lend aid to foreign governments as we do to allied governments. In case of a conflict, allegiance is due solely to the land of one's citizenship. Cultural loyalties, however, since they partake of the nature of spiritual goods, need not conflict with each other. Thus even during the war all but the chauvinists realized that a distinction was to be drawn between the literary, artistic and spiritual products of the German people and the government of the German militaristic clique. In all thinking on the question of national privileges and rights of self-determination this important difference between a cultural and political allegiance must be borne in mind. It is explicitly understood that a cultural not a political allegiance to Palestine is involved in our conception, and that this cultural loyalty is compatible with an allegiance to the culture of America. The political allegiance is single and to the land of citizenship.

Such an organization of a people as is here contemplated, international in its scope, must itself become a force anxious to maintain the integrity of international relationships. It is one of those factors the multiplication of which makes surer the possibility of a League of Nations bound not only by verbal and legal agreements but also by a common good will and community of interests. It is one of those bonds which must make keener the realization that all modern wars are civil wars. While not in the end interfering with a wholehearted, complete allegiance to particular states, there is here a force working in the direction of mitigating and ultimately displacing that danger which is ever present in the current emphasis on economic nationalism.[1]

---

[1]See Chap. IV.

Variability in Retention of Ethnic Allegiance

It becomes apparent if we bear closely in mind the cultural nature of the allegiance proposed by the 'Community' theory of adjustment, that individuals will vary greatly in the degree and kind of their loyalty. Even when we are thinking primarily of political loyalties there is a great range of variation in the manner and readiness with which the citizen is prepared to perform his duties. But, granted that he performs them, we must in a practical sense count him among those who serve the country. When a cultural loyalty is involved the range of variation is surely wider, for there is no legally established minimum for spiritual allegiance. In addition to this the multiplicity of cultural forces assumed to play upon the individuals in any ethnic group will surely tend to increase the individual variability in retention of the ethnic attachment. It must be remembered, then, that in urging the perpetuation of the ethnic group through cultural forces we can never expect every individual within the group to retain allegiance or that all should retain it in equal degree. The range would vary through small and graded differences from the individual whose knowledge, ethnic consciousness and loyalty equalled that of an educated person in the homeland to the individual who had intermarried and severed all relations with the group in which he was born.

The following estimate of the maximum expectation for retention of the ethnic loyalty among the Jews may help to make more concrete the idea of variability in type of allegiance contemplated in the 'Community' theory of adjustment. For the purposes of our discussion the Jews may be conceived as being divided into six classes, as follows:

Class A. *Cultural Allegiance.* In this group would be included those upon whose personality the culture ideals and aspirations of the ethnic group have a shaping influence. Within the group there would naturally be variability, for the variations are conceived as individual. The maximum attainment would be such a knowledge of the language, literature and social life of the ethnic group as would be expected from an educated person in the homeland of the ethnos. The minimum would be a sufficient knowledge of the language and life of the ethnic group to make possible an appreciation of the literary culture of the group. Together with this knowledge and appreciation would generally go a desire to maintain and to perpetuate the type of cultural life represented by the ethnic group. Needless to repeat, such a complete ethnic loyalty is regarded as altogether compatible with an equally complete allegiance to America. Intellectual capability and education, not an exclusive spirit, will develop class A.

Class B. *Synagogue and Ceremonial Allegiance.* In this group would fall those whose main center of gravity lies not in the cultural life itself but who maintain contact with the spiritual productions of the Jewish people through its religious institutions. The religious institutions, it might be said, represent a selected, crystallized and attenuated form of the products of the Jewish social life and of the Jewish mind. Undoubtedly when the shell of religiosity is broken and the inner meaning realized these institutions represent the most significant products of the Jewish past. The prayer book, much of the Biblical literature and some of the Talmudic writings may be acquired in this manner. For this class Jewish life and thought still function to some degree in a significant national cultural way. This type of adherence is usually maintained through orthodox or conservative synagogues where the service is mainly in Hebrew and approximates the traditional.

Classes C and D. *Formal Non-Functioning 'Religious' Adherence.* In these classes would fall those who regard their Jewish allegiance as 'religious' in the conventional sense of the term. The Jewish practices are regarded as a variant form of religion, coördinate with Protestantism and Catholicism. In these groups would fall the great majority who follow out of force of convention and social momentum. An element of ancestor worship and superstition prevents them from abandoning "the faith." Jewishness really contributes nothing to their lives which another religious practice or ceremonial could not do quite as well. These individuals have not the energy or interest to make something out of their allegiance and yet lack the initiative to break away and to adopt a new "ism." The formal religious adherence, however, would still tend to prevent intermarriage.

In Class C can be included those who still maintain part of the Jewish ritual and ceremonial and who attend either an orthodox or a conservative synagogue on the Holy Days. In Class D can be included those who have given up Jewish ceremonial practices and who attend a 'Reform' synagogue (i.e., one in which the service is mainly in English and which in many respects resembles the service in certain of the Protestant churches rather than that of the traditional Jewish synagogue).

Class E. *Social and Philanthropic Connection.* In this group would be included those to whom the cultural allegiance is meaningless and even the formal religious adherence secondary, but who maintain distinctly Jewish associations through the social set with which they usually mingle or through their interest in Jewish philanthropy and Jewish affairs. All the groups preceding this one would tend to marry only within the Jewish group. The individuals in this group may be considered as not unwilling to intermarry.

Class F. *Severance of the Ethnic Relation and Intermarriage.* In this group would be included those who have practically severed all connection with Jewish life and whose origin is the only distinguishing mark. Accident rather than desire would decide whether these would intermarry.

The classification is offered as neither an exact nor a complete description of Jewish types but merely as a means of holding in mind the broadest differentiations. The groups are not sharply divided nor mutually exclusive. It will not be necessary, futhermore, for an individual to go through all the stages before reaching intermarriage, though that may be the tendency. Classification in relation to cultural allegiance does not imply a similar degree of religious piety nor, on the other hand, the opposite. Many individuals in Class A will be indifferent or avowedly opposed to established religion while many ignorant of Jewish culture in any real sense of the word may be deemed "orthodox." Among the intermarried, furthermore, one occasionally finds both learned and loyal Jews. With these precautions in mind we may say that under normal conditions, provided immigration is not unduly accelerated by untoward political and social conditions in other lands and provided an adequate school system implied in the 'Community' theory of adjustment has been functioning, the maximum expectation would be a distribution something as follows, graphically:

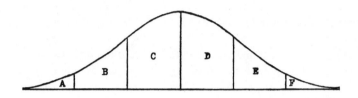

and in percentages:

    A. Cultural Allegiance.......................... 10% per cent.

    B. Synagogue and Ceremonial Allegiance 15%

C. and D. Formal Non-Functioning 'Religious' Adherence .. 50%

    E. Social and Philanthropic Connection........... 15%

    F. Severance of Ethnic Relation and Intermarriage .. 10%

Summarizing, twenty-five per cent would in some manner be influenced in a positive way by the ethnic culture, twenty-five per cent would be on the road to complete fusion and fifty per cent would in reality not be affected in a significant way by the ethnic culture though retaining the ethnic allegiance as a formality.

The estimate of ten per cent for the group in Class A is at present only an ideal. The percentage of American born children whom it would be possible to classify under A would be far below *one* per cent. The estimate for the group in Class F of those who have severed connection and are prepared for intermarriage, is very close to if not above the percentage given. It is evident, therefore, that the forces of the environment are considered by the writer as on the whole disintegrating to a significant Jewish loyalty on the part of the majority. The highest to be hoped for from such a scheme as is presented in the 'Community' theory of adjustment is to retain a

small proportion of those born within the group attached in a significant cultural way to the group. Even such success as is implied
here is doubtful and if attained at all will be only through the expenditure of directed thought and conscious action.

To those who are deeply concerned for the perpetuation of the
national culture and identity such an analysis may seem disappointing to the hope for retention of the subsidiary ethnic groups. Nevertheless, the type of adjustment sketched in the 'Community' theory
seems to be the only one compatible with the notions of democracy.
To restrict the free flow of currents of life from the general environment in such a way that some particular tradition may be artificially
protected, would not harmonize with the basic idea of freedom for the
development of individuality which is the main plea. In view of the
fact that the type of adjustment demanded in the democratic countries
in which the Jews live provides for only a limited and doubtful
perpetuation the necessity for a cultural center in Palestine becomes
all the more urgent. The Zionist idea is an important factor in this
whole scheme of adjustment. By insuring the Jewish future in
Palestine it permits the Jews in the diaspora to adjust themselves in
harmony with the principles and conditions of each land without
becoming guilty of the destruction of their people. This international conception of the organization of Jewish life leaves the individual most free in choosing whether he should continue in the life to
which he was born and also in what manner and in what degree.

SUMMARY

The 'Community' theory endeavors to meet all the justifiable
considerations presented in each of the other proposals. It seeks
especially to avoid such a scheme of adjustment as would tend to
force the individual to accept one solution as against another. It
leaves all the forces working; they are to decide what the future is to
be. Both the 'Americanization' and 'Federation of Nationalities'
theories presume too much to 'fix' conditions; the one would make
the citizen conform to the nature of a mythical Anglo-Saxon, and the
other to harmonize with the soul assumed to reside in the ethnos.
The contention of the 'Community' theory is that neither of these

facts can so easily be taken for granted, and urges that all forces be given a just opportunity to exert their influence. If these conditions are granted and the ethnic group perpetuates itself, only then does it become justified to the reason. On the other hand, if the ethnic group finally disintegrates, the 'Community' theory really resolves itself into the 'Melting Pot' theory, accomplishing the fusion without the evils of hasty assimilation. Its essential merit is that it rejects the doctrine of predestination; it conceives the life of the individual to be formed not in accordance with some preconceived theory but as a result of the interaction of his own nature with the richest environment. In this it satisfies the basic notion of democracy that the individual must be left free to develop through forces selected by the laws of his own nature, not moulded by factors determined upon by others either in the interest of themselves or in accordance with an assumed good.

So, too, a comparison with our three criteria, the unique individual, enrichment of environment, and dependence upon social institutions, finds the 'Community' theory the most adequate solution. It provides in greatest measure for conceiving the individual as creator of and participant in the culture to be evolved, and allows at the same time for a great degree of individual diversification. It strives for a culture enriched by the contributions from many cultures and thus multiplies the possibilities of varied experience. It intensifies the idea of duty and responsibility to social life and institutions by adding the ethnic group and all the significant institutions connected with its history to the burden of civilization that each developed citizen must bear. It offers the greatest opportunity for the creation of a free, rich and lofty Personality.

THE VALUE OF ETHNIC GROUPS

CHAPTER IV

THE VALUE OF ETHNIC GROUPS

I

The Basis of Evaluation

The defense of the right of the ethnic group to preserve its identity is usually based upon a claim to unique cultural possessions. This is well illustrated in the tendency to seek in Judaism peculiar values, a mode of thought, a theology or a moral code. Jewish apologists and protagonists both go about the task with the implication that Israel may continue to live only if it have a unique contribution to make different from and superior to what might be made by another group. Such an approach is altogether indefensible. The ethnic group is not a system of ideas but a nationality, a community of persons; it is a living reality related, indeed, to thought, but still flesh and blood and desire and no mere pale abstraction. In considering whether a person is worthy of living or not, we do not require that he be indispensable for the conduct of the nation or of the world. We do not seek in him a virtue which no one else possesses in any degree or a faculty that is unique. Were such a test applied to each individual, perhaps all men would be morally bound to commit suicide. Even geniuses are not indispensable. It is enough that each one is unique and serves along with the rest. In any case each man's individuality, even though unique, is made up of common human qualities and aspirations. So, too, every nation[1] must be conceived as a personality unique but not altogether different; serving but not indispensable. Some nations are greater, some more gifted, some have longer and richer traditions—but they are all nations and each has the same right

---

[1] It is sometimes objected that the analogy between individual and nation is not correct, that it is not necessary to justify the life of the individual because instinctive forces keep him alive, while the life of the nation depends upon habits and attitudes which have been acquired and need to be perpetuated. This argument might indeed be to the point had we in mind to create new peoples or to resurrect dead ones. But we are discussing living peoples with a desire to maintain identity. The will to live is the fact which must be reckoned with, whether it is innate or acquired.

to live.   It is not necessary to show that each nation has certain characteristics, without which the world would not get along, or which no other nation has in any degree.   It is not necessary to prove that if it should perish, either liberty, or justice, or religion, or the ethical life would perish from the earth.   However great its contribution in these fields may be, it cannot have a monopoly in these things, nor should that be expected.

Our own argument for the perpetuation of the foreign ethnic groups in the United States has been based not upon any demonstration of the value of the cultural contribution that any such group might make but upon the right to life and expression of personality inherent in the nature of the individual.   Incidentally, indeed, it has been assumed that some of them, at least, will contribute to the development and to the enrichment of our own culture.   But throughout the whole discussion the fundamental position has been that in a democracy no demonstration of value is needed precedent to permitting either an individual or a group to live.   The validity of an experience cannot be demonstrated to any one who has not undergone, either actually or by sympathetic imagination, a similar experience. There is no reason, furthermore, why it should justify itself to anyone else except where it also affects another person in an appreciable degree.   Music does not justify itself by an appeal to those who have no ear for music, but by the opinion of the musicians.   Philosophy, too, is justified because, for the philosopher, the unthinking life is not worth living.   So the ultimate judgment of the value of the ethnic group must be in the experience of the person who has lived the life of the ethnic group.   Life justifies itself.   It is the suppression of life that needs justification.   Indeed, if it is clearly shown that the presence or activities of any particular group cannot be continued except at the expense of other groups or of the total group, then its activities must be restrained within just bounds, or altogether eliminated when there is no other way out.   However, when no impartial demonstration of the evil effects of the presence of any group is possible, then 'tolerance' must be Democracy's rule; the further assumption being that any such 'tolerated' group, which has no contribution to make, must of itself become disintegrated under the influences which are bound to play upon it in the presence of the free interchange of currents of thought and life characteristic of a true democracy.   The burden of proof always lies upon those who would curtail an activity, especially when such action implies the negation of the aspirations of persons.

Such a position is the logical conclusion of our democratic assumption which maintains that the subjects of experience are the primary judges of life's values.   Nevertheless, a reasonable person, not too much concerned with the conclusions of logic, may feel unsatisfied with such a strict position, in spite of the rational assent which he may feel forced to give to the line of argument.   Granting to the ethnic group the right to maintain its identity, one may still wish to know why it should avail itself of its right.   While still maintaining that the ethnic life needs no *a priori* defense, this chapter dealing with the value of the ethnic group has been included to add to the formal, intellectual consent the force of a moral conviction.   In this it is not the intention to return to the position of the apologist who lays claim to a unique superior virtue for his people.   We shall not expect an explication of a superior religion, ethical code or *Weltan-schauung*.   All that will be done will be to point out several ways in which the ethnic loyalty in general and the Jewish loyalty in particular may be of human significance.

Needless to say, the member of the ethnic group is not necessarily motivated in a conscious manner by such significances.   If grasped at all, they are gathered from fragmentary experiences.   What keeps the individual loyal to his group is a complex of daily lifelong associations whose satisfactions are intimate and subtle.   In any case it would be difficult to transmit the meaning of a melody, of a witticism, or of a ceremony and when these are interwoven with the life and history of a foreign group, the task becomes well nigh impossible. It would require learning the literature and social life not only objectively but through living in the society of the people.   Undoubtedly it is these bits of "eternity in the narrow span of a song," the satisfactions which reside in the very living and daily contact, which build the desire to perpetuate the ethnic associations rather than the very conscious humane values which will be described below.

But here, too, we find a parallel with the life of the individual. Unconscious, unmoral forces make him persist.   And yet out of the flux of life can be gathered certain values which are of humane significance and which make life worth while.   The attempt here then will be neither to recount the rich, individual experiences which in reality furnish the motive forces for group persistence nor to elaborate a theory calculated to convert, but to point some values which raise the ethnic loyalty from the plane of the merely satisfying to a moral, ideal experience.

II

SINCERITY OF OUTLOOK

When Socrates, disillusioned but still courageous, ventured on the quest for truth, he determined that his primary task was to know himself.   For all knowledge in the sense of wisdom is a knowledge of the relationship of one's own self to the rest of the world, to the many persons, ideas and things.   To understand how each event which we have experienced or caused is connected up with numberless past events and to know the possible effects that it may have on all the rest of the world and upon ourselves in the future, is knowledge.   To understand who we are, we must understand our relationship to the many possible things in the world.   To understand the world is the same thing as to understand the relations of all things in the world to ourselves.   To understand the world on the hypothesis that one is something else than human is as impossible as to conceive of movement in a spaceless world.   The two notions are correlative.

One's nature and one's every act is the point of reference for true wisdom.   It makes no difference whether the events that we are concerned in are the result of our own doing or not; the same responsibility of assuming the obligation of the relationship is involved.   One may vainly cry that he did not ask his parents to give him birth; but he must still take the responsibility of his own needs and of his own life.   Happening to be, we must understand our relations to other beings who happen to be, and the moral responsibility rests upon us to gain deeper and deeper insight into the complexity of the relationships.   To close one's eyes to any fact in one's life and refuse to face the consequences is to court not only practical destruction but also moral and intellectual disintegration. Some facts are so important for our physical well-being that to neglect them is to hazard death; other suppressions may lead to abnormal psychoses. Even when these obvious abnormalities are not the result, a failure to realize possible significances means failure to be intelligent. Every event can be constructed into a universe, and to do less than one can with the events of one's own life is to be in a sense morally derelict.

Now a part of the circumstance of every one who is born of a foreign ethnic group is just this fact. Just as he was born human, and of the male sex, and in New York, he was also born, let us say, a Pole. His extraction is an event which must be reckoned with as every other event, i.e., he must recognize its significations. He may ultimately choose to continue or to sever this association, but the necessity of reckoning and understanding the fact is basic. Whether his "consciousness of kind" is the result of a certain racial composition, or whether it is the result of habits formed in the early stages of life through association, the effect is the same. The man knows himself as a Pole. To suppress this fact in his life in order to satisfy convention or public opinion is similar in its effect upon moral integrity to the suppression of instinct. The sound, virile person finds such prudery and hypocrisy odious and impossible. It makes a breach in his character. The sincere person must go about the world recognizing and assuming responsibility for what he is. Then he may hope to get somewhere.

The importance of recognizing the ethnic origin is enhanced if we grant that there is a possibility of connection between the race and the individual soul. Our own discussion has not assumed that every person born of a foreign ethnic group can find his salvation only through that group. No such inevitability of connection can be taken for granted. But there is the possibility, even the likelihood, that some can find their highest expression of happiness only in the culture of the ethnic group. It is reasonable to suppose that in a family of musical reputation some of the children have musical genius. It is their right to receive at least the elements of a musical education to determine whether their bent lies that way. So, too, unless an opportunity is given to the citizen of foreign extraction to know his people, we cannot be sure that we have not violated or crushed what is most significant in him. The core of truth in the dictum, "A man cannot change his grandfathers," might be paraphrased, "A man dare not fail to know who his grandfathers were." Especially when one belongs to the Jewish group does the necessity of reckoning with the fact of origin present itself. A Jew must be conscious of himself, not only because he wishes to, but also because the world whether in malice or in curiosity singles him out and makes him so self-conscious. The Jew, too, has played and still plays such a part in the world that the possible significances are unusually varied and complex.

To teach one to forget his ethnic connection as is proposed by the 'Americanization' theory is to make a breach in the moral foundation of one's character. An experience may be surpassed or understood; but to forget it is not moral. Of all the immoralities in the world lack of memory and lack of imagination are the joint parents. Our educational system can never mean much unless it realizes that wisdom must be based on understanding of experience and instinct. What a tragically superficial insight is revealed in the failure to understand that the welfare of the nation is bound up above all with sincerity of character!

The knowledge which men have, if it is to remain true, cannot consist of collections of memorized phrases conceived of as universally applicable. If a man is to remain whole, there must be an integration in his character. His instincts must be related to his experience, his former habits to his later associations. The various phases of his environment must be related to his growing self. A complete unification of character is attainable, in the midst of our complex and rushed environment with its abrupt transitions, by comparatively few. And for those few it is attainable only through a sincere recognition of what they are. To one who has been born in a relationship to a foreign ethnic group such an integration of character is not ultimately possible without a full realization of the significance of this connection.

III

LOYALTY TO A MINORITY

To the thoughtful member of a foreign ethnic community loyalty to a minority becomes a severe mental and moral discipline. His mode of life, his religious views, his evaluations are all called into question by the presence of the dominant current of thought. He must answer not only to the satisfaction of his neighbors but also (what is spiritually even more difficult) to the satisfaction of himself. His life is brought up from beneath the psychological threshold to the plane of conscious understanding. He must justify his ways to himself. If he survives in his loyalty, his life must be more highly self-conscious and rationalized than it need be for him who accepts current ways and modes of thought which are socially approved. He cannot follow the ethnic tradition blindly for it is constantly subject to criticism by the standards of the new life. He tends, therefore, to select and to perpetuate only those elements in the group culture which are of significance.

Likewise his loyalty to America tends to be raised from the level of easy acquiescence with the established order and the majority and from a purely emotional chauvinistic support to the plane of criticism by standards and rational appreciation. Forced to find worth and beauty in his own people's life to sanction his loyalty he carries over the same habit of thought in thinking of the new culture. America makes him ask himself, "Why is the heritage of my people worth preserving?" In finding a reply he cannot fail to begin to compare and to seek to understand what is truly profound and spiritual in American life. For his loyalty is not to the land as such, he has not lived here long enough; nor to its people, he does not know them well enough; but primarily to the ideal America about which he has thought and dreamed. Trained to seek below the surface of his own tradition, he will tend to look for what is exalted in American life and to base his loyalty upon a conscious realization of the significance of America.

In a deep sense he learns that the right is not always with the mighty. Perhaps the greatest obstacle to liberalism and a progressive civilization is the fact that men still believe in their hearts that might makes right in spite of their professed belief in the religions of righteousness that have sprung from the East. But the member of the minority group has it borne in upon him through his personal experience that the majority may be in the wrong, may fail to understand, may be spiritually obtuse. His sympathies are extended to the struggle of minorities all over the world and he gains insight into the life of peoples who are not of the politically dominant races.

IV

Multiple Cultural Loyalty

Those who have broken with the group usually consider themselves 'broadminded.' The loyalty to a minority ethnic group is often conceived of as narrowing. When the allegiance had been given blindly and exclusively to the family tradition, this may be true. But when it is given intelligently and with discrimination, without yielding the allegiance to the State and culture it represents, the double loyalty becomes a powerful force toward humanization.

The knowledge of another language, another history, and another point of view, is in itself a liberalizing influence. All additional knowledge is protection against indoctrination—a freeing of the mind. Knowledge of other peoples is not necessarily an allegiance. One may know very much about German philosophy and literature and yet not approve of them. Nevertheless, in the literature and culture of every developed nation humane elements will be found—interests and thoughts which conceive of life not from the narrow nationalistic point of view, but from the broadly human, universal outlook. Knowledge of these brings with it an appreciation which is psychologically an incipient loyalty. In so far as we have a love for foreign and ancient literatures and languages, we have the beginnings of an allegiance towards them. When this appreciation reaches out into the plane of action, when in addition to the intellectual and aesthetic appreciation there is involved also the emotional appreciation imperative to further these activities, then a loyalty has come into being. When the notion of duty enters, then the allegiance has been pledged. And it is here, where emotions and actions are involved, that a multiple loyalty becomes especially significant.

For emotions and actions are subject to conflict, and conflict tends to be resolved into harmony. The need of furthering two distinct cultures must lead to an elimination of those elements which are mutually incompatible and to the emphasis upon those elements in each which have a universal interest. Each group culture contains within it elements of an international character, and attention must be centered upon these if both loyalties are to be retained. As in the individual, the variety of conflicting instincts and emotions must lead to a process of elimination, modification and development resulting in the creation of a rational philosophy and mode of life, so, too, allegiance to more than one social group must lead to a larger view of life because it brings more knowledge and appreciation, but especially because the loyalties are under the necessity of rationalization.

It was not because they had a double allegiance that hyphenated Americans were odious. It was because in their case the hyphen was a pretense or considered to be so, and used in order to hide the actual fact of a *single* rival allegiance to a foreign government. Had they been true hyphenates, owing equal allegiance to both peoples and really equally interested in the welfare of both, they would have been led to judge not from prejudice, but from the rule of right. And from the moral viewpoint at least, there could be nothing better. It is just the presence of true hypenates, men who loved other nations as they did this, that gave our purposes in the war aims more truly human and less selfish than could otherwise have been possible.

The significance of a double allegiance, it should be noted, is greater than twice a single allegiance. Double here means multiple. The knowledge of an additional language and culture and the understanding of another people means not only a personality richer by so much. It means rather what an additional dimension does in spatial relations. It gives perspective. It opens up the mind to a new concept; there are other nations than one's own. The change of view is of significance not only for the additional nationality for which the interest is aroused but for the whole mental outlook. It prevents the mind from falling into the natural tendency of imagining that one's own culture is the only culture worthy of the name, and one's own countrymen, the only real humans. Interest in another nationality must go far toward giving one an international, as against a provincial outlook. Differences are seen more readily in their proportion; it is understood that humanity can speak in other languages, express itself in other cultures, exist in other physiognomies.

True universalization, colloquially called 'broadmindedness,' can come only through the multiplication of loyalties, not through the suppression of them, just as true spirituality comes from the addition of interests which must be harmonized, not through suppression of instincts. This is especially true in the present condition of society. There is no International Country to which we might give our allegiance. We must give it to the existing nations which are all particularistic. Otherwise we turn out in practical life to be disloyal, however conscientiously we may be true to our dreams. We cannot speak a universal language. We may speak one tongue or many. We cannot be everywhere. We must be in one place or in many places. Universalization cannot be promoted by abolition of nations (they cannot be abolished by fiat, nor can an international humanity be created by fiat) but by the multiplication of the number of nations toward which we feel sympathetic, leading to an emphasis upon the international elements in each nation.

There is, of course, the well recognized danger in such a multiplication of allegiance. It sometimes permits a *double and sinister political* allegiance to mask under the cover of a *cultural interest.* Sometimes, too, the humane interest may lead to a political allegiance conflicting with patriotism. When this leads to the ascendancy of right as against selfish national prejudice, then it cannot be considered as anything but beneficial. When it leads to the loyalty to a foreign government as against right, it is reprehensible. But the chances for such an unrighteous foreign allegiance are small under the influence of our own environment, provided that our scheme of education is such as is assumed here, where every child must attend the public schools. When such a disloyal foreign allegiance does occur, it must be treated as a separate problem. We do not maintain that people should not heed their conscience, because that may lead to the conscientious objector, who is, as we think, unreasonable in his plea of conscience and, in effect, though not in motive, disloyal. We do not suppress individuality because its expression sometimes leads to selfishness. Nor should we suppress the double cultural allegiance which is essentially humanizing because under present conditions where war is possible (in itself a most irrational condition in civilized society) it may at times create difficulties.

Multiple cultural allegiance is in itself a force tending to remove the likelihood of war. The notorious fact that international science, art and religion were of little avail in stemming the tide of war and the surprising ease with which savants, social workers and ministers found it possible to lose sight of universal interests, even to turn chauvinists, should warn us against expecting too much from merely ideal bonds. One's closest friends are still for the most part in one's own country; and control of military and police forces, of education, of the means of forming public opinion and of a multitude of other conditions gives the national government a stranglehold upon the lives of its citizens. Nevertheless, the ever-present danger of conflict between nation and nation can be overcome only by a multiplication of international ties until they become numerous and strong enough to bear the strain of national separatism. A League of Nations can become effective only in so far as it is an expression of a community of international interests and is based securely upon a multiplicity of interdependences. The further development of communication, the growth of economic interdependence, the multiplication of many forms of international societies and above all revision of education so that it may make apparent, not obscure, the existence of these many interdependences must precede any lasting peace. Important among these interrelationships is the consciousness of kinship rising out of the multiple cultural allegiance. It is significant that the presence of foreign ethnic groups gave us great concern during the war. Only the conviction that the Central Powers had violated the peace of the world could break the force of this international bond. On the other hand, our best evidence that double allegiances are not fatal comes from the experience of the war. The presence of hyphenated Americans did not prevent us from winning the war. Perhaps it even aided us for it forced us to become clear as to our purposes. How could the many conflicting loyalties of our variegated population be met? Only by a stand that was above national prejudice could we be united for the tremendous undertaking. The multiple loyalty enhances the quality of patriotism and raises it to the level of an international interest.

Loyalty to a minority ethnic group, in addition to enriching the general culture, promotes the spiritualization of the individual's aims and purposes. It tends to make his outlook more universal, his perspective international, his approval to lie on the plane of intelligent conscious justification. He remains near to those intimacies of close family relationship which seem basic to a real human touch and understanding; but he must still maintain an open mind towards divergences. His sympathies remain deep while they are broadened. Understanding the keen and intense woes and joys that are possible when one lives in close proximity to those with whom one feels an emotional and almost sensuous consciousness of kind, the sympathies are broadened and extended to a reach of international scope, where the unities are broadly humane, and the kinship is on the plane of the intelligent.

These are general values which arise out of a multiple allegiance. In addition, each particular group will contribute in accordance with its own gifts and culture. No association of men capable of social coherence and self-consciousness and tending to maintain its identity midst conditions which naturally would disintegrate them can be conceived of as being altogether without a culture. How much each group can contribute will depend upon the excellence of its cultural accomplishments. The whole range of contribution may extend from cooking recipes, quaint melodies and legends, through customs, conventions, folkways, to language, literature, ethics, social oranization and religion. To describe these even briefly for the Jewish group alone would require volumes and the work of many masters. In the following pages it is the intention not to attempt to evaluate Judaism or describe the Jewish heritage, but to present several ideas which will give some hint of the depth and meaning of Jewish life.

V

The Hebrew Language and Literature

Greek literature, Professor Woodbridge has pointed out, bears a unique relationship to Western philosophic notions. Greek thought is reflection upon experience spontaneous and original. Western philosophy is in great part a translation of the terms used to describe this experience. Between the original words and the translation a whole system of thought is often interpolated. Thus the unsophisticated ἡ ἀρχή (the beginning) of Greek literature, becomes the Latin 'principium' and the English 'principles' with the implication that there are underlying principles at the beginning of things. The significance of this difference lies not alone in the fact that Greek literature must be read in the original to prevent a perversion of thought. Even more important, the original writings, since they describe experience significantly, must remain permanent sources of reflection and of intellectual life, while Western modes of philosophy, being translation, must become out of date as the current system of thought gives way.

The Hebrew writings collected in the Bible bear a similar relationship to Western ethical and religious conceptions that Greek literature bears to the intellectual life. The Hebrew writings were literature before they became dogma. To read them in the original is sufficient to divest them of the conventional theology. The poet giving expression to the prayer of his people in defeat cries, "Come and help us." The translation has it, "Come and save us." The one thought will remain a natural appeal as long as men are capable of conceiving themselves in distress; the second idea suggests a sense of unreality that causes the secularist to smile. The Prophets' fierce cry for justice, intense with social realism, loses its passionate force midst the theologic phraseology. There are also errors due to mistranslation[1] in support of certain traditions as well as those that have crept in unconsciously as a result of the overshadowing conception. A knowledge of Hebrew furnishes the key to a natural understanding of Biblical literature and opens the gate to free interpretation. Hebrew, moreover, has

---

[1] As in the translation, 'virgin,' where the text means simply 'young woman' and though there is a distinct word to signify virginity. See Skinner on Isaiah VII, Cambridge Series.

the additional advantage that it is a living language and the connotations of its concepts can be learned more directly and truly.   Undoubtedly, the meanings have undergone changes through the
centuries of Jewish history.   But the development has been gradual
and continuous and changes of significance can be traced with no
great difficulty, while in the case of the classic tongues an. abrupt
translation must be made in thought.   If a considerable portion of
our population could acquire a literary knowledge of Greek and Greek
literature, it would undoubtedly lead to an enrichment of our cultural
and aesthetic life.   It can be of no less significance to further a knowledge of Hebrew and its literature.   The loyalty to the Jewish group
affords an unusual opportunity of obtaining an insight into one of
the richest sources of the world's spiritual experience which has been
particularly influential in the literature and in the mode of life of
the English speaking peoples.

The Jewish mind seems to have been keenly aware of the intimate
relationship between its language and its thought life.   Side by side
with the Jewish struggle for perpetuation has gone an insistence upon
the retention of Hebrew.   With the national reawakening has come
a renascence of Hebrew literature and a revival of Hebrew as a spoken
tongue.   But it is of significance to note that even in Yiddish, the
colloquial tongue of Eastern European Jewry, which is based on a
German of the fourteenth century, the ideas indicating important
ethical and religious concepts are never translated but always retained
in the original Hebrew.   One does not speak of *Religion, Glaube, Wohl-
thätigkeit* in Yiddish but of תורה, אמונה, צדקה, words which have different
roots and connotations.   To understand Yiddish it is necessary to know
hundreds of Hebrew concepts.   For one who does not know Hebrew,
Yiddish is an excellent medium for the interpretation of Jewish life.
Those who despise Yiddish as a jargon have really failed to grasp
the significance of this mixture of languages.   It was a successful
compromise with the environment.   For the masses who could not
speak Hebrew the current tongue was, so to speak, converted to
Judaism.

The social significance of retaining Jewish concepts in the Hebrew
can become clear through the description of the word רחמנות

(r a h a m o n u t, usually translated 'compassion'). In discussing the social instincts, Thorndike lays stress upon what he calls the instinct of 'motherly behavior,' which he portrays in terms of stimulus and response as, "a living thing displaying hungry, frightened or pained behavior, by wailing, clinging, holding out its arms and the like, provokes attention and discomfort, and may provoke acts of relief." (*Educational Psychology*, Vol. I, p. 102). Of this instinct, the noted psychologist says elsewhere, "Modern philanthropy and the acceptance of the brotherhood of man as a living creed rests at bottom on this original tendency." Thorndike notes the inadequacy of the term, 'motherly behavior,' to describe the instinct; it gives a false connotation for the instinct is present in various degrees in all human beings. In fact English has no good equivalent. The word 'pity' brings a sense of separation between subject and object; 'kindliness' and 'sympathy' lack the connotation of distress and the latter may be wholly intellectual or aesthetic; 'compassion' which comes closest is too classic and cold. It occurred to the writer that the Hebrew word רחמנות conveyed in a remarkably true sense both the meaning and emotional quality, so well indeed that it carries the intent of the definition even better than does the description given above. It contains both the notion of distress and kinship in suffering. *Mirabile dictu*, the root of the word רחם (r e h e m - womb) indicates the maternal and kinship relation which Thorndike's term aims to convey. The word also means to be tender and loving (r u h a m ah—Hosea, Chap. I) Furthermore, it has a central position in Jewish thought. God is אל רחום (elrahum—God compassionate) and Israel רחמים בני רחמנים (r a h a m o n i m b' n e r a h a m o n i m—the compassionate, children of the compassionate). But most important of all is the relation of the word to Jewish psychology. The mere utterance of the word is sufficient to evoke a psychological, almost a physiological response. In speaking before a Jewish audience, it is a word to conjure with. As the American orator would use the word 'liberty' as a means of arousing emotion, the Jewish orator would make his appeal on the basis of רחמנות. There is undoubtedly more than a chance connection between these various facts; the Jewish emphasis on the social attitude and the ethical tradition, the central position of the family and the conception of the Messianic age as a brotherhood, the conception of Israel and Israel's God as רחמנים together with the fact that for the instinct which lies at the basis of the social attitude the Hebrew has a remarkably good term. The word has become an institution and a motivating force in the life of the people. Translate it and you have dissipated energy. How much history would need to be lived again to make 'freedom' a word to rouse men with. Revolutions and civil wars would need to be fought and countless martyrdoms experienced. So רחמנות was created through centuries of travail.

To read Hebrew means to understand the symbols of what the Jewish People has conceived to be its most significant experiences. It means, of course, more than to read words of a different force and connotation. To read another language means to read other matter as well as other meanings. Each people retains in its body of classic literature those writings which are especially appealing and in which it excels. All Hebrew literature is so permeated with religious and ethical thought that any modern writer of Hebrew, whether in agreement with or in revolt against the traditional conceptions, cannot help but make his writings reminiscent of the ideas which have been for ages in the foreground of the nation's mind. The Jews unconsciously realizing this have laid great stress upon the teaching of Hebrew even in the definitely religious schools, while little time or none is given to instruction in formal principles. This is keen insight into what is undoubtedly a fact: that thought is transmitted more surely through the indirect method of teaching literature than through the direct method of the catechism. Living in a foreign land, where social background and atmosphere are lacking and institutions to a great extent are torn from their context, it is through the language and literature that we can most easily grasp the ideal life of a people. Individual speech reflects the person. Even more truly does the national language and literature reflect the soul of the nation; for only that which is harmonious with the people's ideal tends to survive. Institutions also must be considered expressions of the social idea. But they are more under the necessity of compromise and the idea is more easily lost in the performance. Words are more free and, therefore, reveal more truly the aspiration; they are less bound by the necessity of circumstances and by the responsibility of reckoning with actual life. In our own conception of a cultural loyalty, with the foreign political allegiance ruled out, the language and the literature must be the vital bond. In this connection it must be borne in mind that for the Jews the Bible is not the whole of the spiritual and literary heritage—rabbinic, mediaeval and modern Hebrew literature which has come with the national reawakening, continues the tradition to modern times. Though the later works have affected Western life but little, they are in themselves vast storehouses of thought and of great influence on Jewish life itself.

To the Jew, furthermore, Hebrew is an international language which symbolizes Jewish unity and through which he can communicate with Jews all over the world. It links him not only with the Jewish past but with the Jewish present. Hebrew, a national possession, thus tends to break the barriers of time and to cross the boundaries of countries. It has in itself a means for transcending the purely national consciousness in the direction of the international and universal.

VI

JEWISH HISTORY

Jewish history traces its course from the very dawn of civilization. In it is reflected the human race's struggle for life and its ideal vision. The record is crowded with prophets, heroes and martyrs; with strife, defeat and triumph; with events, philosophies and wisdom. To know it is to have a liberal education; for not only is it itself full with the content and significance of life but into its current stream the histories of many nations. Jewish history may be seen as the result of the interaction of the people of Israel with various civilizations of the ancient and modern world. Chaldea, Egypt, Assyria, Babylon, Greece, Rome, Spain, Russia, America; the Feudal system, the Church, the modern economic national organization and the struggle of democracy are bound up with the fortunes and the purposes of the Jewish People. The teaching of Jewish history easily becomes a pedagogical device for teaching the history of Western civilization.

With so much of the histories of nations in its own body Jewish history, nevertheless, presents a unique phenomenon—a striking individuality. This small nation never really strong in numbers or physical resources, subjected to the disintegrating force of exile, has been able to maintain its cohesion long after powerful empires had crumbled, because it became convinced that its life represented an ideal. לא נתקים ישראל אלא בשביל התורה Israel was not preserved except for the sake of the Torah—so says the teleologist who transmutes causes into purposes. It would be more true to say that Israel was not preserved except *through* the Torah. Consecration to an idea formed the bond of union when the territorial boundaries had been broken.

There arises out of the survival of the Jewish people a profound conclusion, vital for moral progress: the exaltation of the power of the Idea as against the power of environmental circumstances. The prophet had forseen that strength lay ultimately not in Power nor in military strength, but in Spirit. All subsequent Jewish history bears witness to this conviction. The Jewish People has survived in spite of untoward environmental conditions because it became self-conscious of the meaning of its life. The consciousness of the unity in an ideal cutting across generations, countries and circumstances has made it possible to maintain the national existence. The will to live and faith in the purpose of his life has found justification in the Jewish Survival.[1]

---

[1]Perhaps such a statement of the spiritual cause for Jewish perpetuation may strike the sophisticated student of history as a little sentimental. But the simplicity of the fact stands out against the learned theories of great historians. Wellhausen ends his masterly essay on the history of Israel and Judah saying, "The persistency of the race may, of course, prove a harder thing to overcome than Spinoza has supposed; but, nevertheless, he will be found to have spoken truly in declaring that the so-called emancipation of the Jews must inevitably lead to the extinction of Judaism wherever the process is extended beyond the political to the social sphere. For the accomplishment of this, centuries may be required." Wellhausen is in all likelihood wrong; keenly aware of the threatening danger, the Jewish people is already readjusting itself to meet the changed environmental conditions through the rebuilding of Zion and new forms of adjustment to Western democracies. The cause of the error is in the method of judging Jewish history. Wellhausen sees it altogether as the result of environmental forces. Jewish history cannot be written without due consideration of the Jewish will to live. Jewish history must be seen not only as a resultant of environmental forces, but as a resultant of the interaction of the Jewish personality with the environmental forces.

Opposed to this belief in the power of conscious will has arisen the idea that men are creatures of accident and environment, which finds aphoristic expression in the phrase, "*Der Mensch ist was er isst.*" Experience with life has indeed shown us that hope and the will are not absolutely free.   Mind is not independent of matter; hope and faith and will are not exercised in a vacuum.   But Jewish history doggedly maintains the belief in the ultimate supremacy of the inner forces, and its own experience gives a justification to what might otherwise seem a groundless faith.   In this sense the Jewish people is, indeed, a "witness unto the Lord."   Will is the master of circumstances, hope the guide of experience, and conscious purpose the conqueror of life.

In the possible truth of this faith in man's aspirations lies the possibility of salvation for the world.   It is through aspirations and ideas that mankind, midst racial, geographic and governmental diversities, can ultimately hope to become unified.   The rational, not the accidental, must become the basis of community.   In the advance of the world toward international organization hope must rest upon the confidence that common ideas will ultimately find their necessary institutional and environmental embodiments.   Jewish history is a testimonial to the strength of will and purpose against accident and circumstance.[1]   In the face of every great ideal project for the betterment of human life, when the chorus of diplomatists, business men and priests of the established order cries, "Impractical," it continues with prophetic insight to give the answer—"If you will it, this is no fairy tale."[2]

This belief in the idea is synthesized with the recognition of the place that environmental circumstance has in life in the movement of Zionism.   Never have the Jews as a people separated their hope for an ideal life from this world to the same extent as the Christian peoples have done.   Even in moments of despair when tears and prayers were the only possible means, the ideal itself was associated with the land of Israel.   Throughout the Exile they still continued

---

[1] Of course, Jewish history is also a testimony to the barrenness of wish and hope without proper consideration of political and physical means.
[2] Herzl's famous phrase in reference to the Restoration of Zion.   See Norman Angell, in *Menorah Journal*, January, 1917.

to study the מצוות תלויות בארץ (i.e., Commandments depending upon Israel's tenure of Palestine) against the time when Israel would be restored to Zion. Even when hunger and oppression conjured up other-worldly visions, the Messianic hope did not become altogether dissociated from its terrestrial basis. Zionism insisting on a socially autonomous background guaranteed by the world's political and legal organization brings about a complete *rapprochement* between the two inseparable factors of moral progress, a humane ideal and adequate political conditions.

VII

THE JEWISH PEOPLE—AN INTERNATION

Just as Zionism may be seen as a synthesis of ideal aspiration and material considerations, so, too, it may be regarded as aiming for a harmony between nationalism and internationalism. In the Zionist ideal the majority of the Jews must remain outside of Palestine, and the Jewish nation is conceived of as an international community with a centre in Palestine. In the various lands of the diaspora adjustment to the political and social conditions of the land will be necessary. Palestine with its politically and socially autonomous life will act as a uniting bond between the various communities. On the other hand, through these various communities the influences of the whole world are to be brought to bear upon the development of the Palestinian centre. Unity is conceived in cultural, not political terms; and the implications of nationhood become international. In such a type of organization the desire for full expression of national culture becomes compatible with the conception of an economic internationalism. Truly seen, it becomes ultimately dependent upon internationalization of the economic basis of cultural life. When we think of the Jewish loyalty, we must bear in mind that the allegiance is not to a land exclusively, but to an International Community of men whose interests include and are inextricably woven with the interests of many peoples and with the universal spread of liberal thought. One who is loyal to the Jewish People rightly conceived must become loyal to all the families on the earth among whom the Jews are scattered.

To this natural consequence of the form of its organization must be added the trend of its own thought. The Jewish ideal has long ceased to identify national greatness with territorial and political expansion. This is at the root of the confusion in understanding whether the Jews are a nation or a religious group. In form of organization they resemble a social community most like a nation. In aspiration they resemble the church, for their ideal is in the realm of the spiritual. The modern concept of nationality approaches most nearly a description of the Jewish group. It hopes to express its individuality not in the exclusive possession of larger tracts of land or in the control of economic assets, but through its contributions in the realm of art, philosophy, religion. Its supremacy is hoped for in terms of service, not in terms of acquisition. The Jewish People desires freedom to live in accordance with Torah, believing profoundly that the acceptance of the sovereignty of Instruction and Law is full of significance for the rest of the world.

Ultimately, as they think, it is the rule of Torah that can bring peace to the world.

> For from Zion shall go forth the Torah,
> And the word of the Lord from Jerusalem.
> And they shall beat their swords into plowshares,
> And their spears into pruning hooks.

It is a loyalty to an international community with an aspiration of service to the world that the Jewish allegiance requires. The consecration to the task of creating this new type of nationality or cultural internationality is a bold attempt in the face of the historic emphasis upon economic nationalism. It implies not only a devotion to the special task of the Restoration of Zion, but also a wholehearted support to those political tendencies which look forward toward the organization of the world on an international basis. For to the Jew every war is a civil war, and every national loss a loss to his own people. It is a sickly humanitarianism, a romantic idealism in the end negative and destructive, which sees severance from the Jewish people as emancipation from exclusiveness. A realistic sound-hearted and clear-headed insight would understand that to break with the Jewish group means to destroy international ties and an international vision.

To be born a Jew is an accident and signifies in itself nothing; but it may signify much, if the ideal implications of the fact are pursued and understood—if History is synthesized with Nature. It is an opportunity, just as to be born is an opportunity, to enter into an ideal life. To him who has the mind to grasp and the heart to be loyal it presents an added possibility of living the Life of Reason.

Those who oppose a dual cultural allegiance are consistent if they hold that a highly charged nationalistic spirit is the necessity of the age and if they exalt patriotism in the exclusive sense to the position of the highest virtue. But they cannot oppose it on the grounds that it is narrowing. Its tendency is to broaden the vision, make more conscious the loyalty, and raise the national aspiration to service of international ideals.

Once we look upon American nationality in terms of human service rather than selfish acquisition and agree that America's development of an international conscience is a good thing, then we cannot assume a *laissez-faire* attitude toward the question of the perpetuation of cultural divergences within the United States. The line of argument previous to this chapter at most defended the right of the sub-groups to maintain their cultural individuality. It did not propose that the State of its own initiative should further retention of ethnic loyalties. If, however, the analysis of this chapter carries conviction, it would be necessary to go a step further and say that it is the duty of the State to lend its aid and encouragement to the ethnic groups in their desire to maintain their spiritual heritage. What is the benefit if one tribalism is exchanged for another tribalism—if the exclusive Jew becomes the intolerant American? But if the necessity of adjustment can lead to an international and moral outlook, then, indeed, can we say that we have advanced a whole stage in the development toward humanism which is the essence of Democracy.

PART II

THE RELATION OF ETHNIC AND RELIGIOUS SCHOOLS TO THE STATE

CHAPTER V

THE RELATION OF ETHNIC AND RELIGIOUS SCHOOLS TO THE STATE

I

SECT AND ETHNOS

The educational process alone is the instrumentality properly responsible in a democracy for maintaining the national identity of minority communities. Neither local segregation nor governmental separatism would allow the undisturbed interchange of social forces which democracy demands. On the other hand communal organization with the school as the centre would make it possible to continue the ethnic loyalty and to preserve the cultural and spiritual personality of the group without of necessity interfering with the free play of currents demanded by the unity of American life.

The democratic ends which we are seeking would be defeated, however, if after agreeing to such a formal conclusion we should introduce a system of schools not in accord with democratic notions. Unless a principle manifests itself in concrete institutions, it really does not exist and formal adherence to it becomes meaningless. It will be necessary to know what is meant by the term 'school' in the plan of adjustment outlined. The remaining two chapters will accordingly be devoted to an analysis of the type of ethnic educational institution conceived to be proper for the school system of the minority group. The first and most important problem that will engage our attention is the question of the relation of the educational system of the ethnic group to the school system of the state.

Here we find evidence of the close connection between ethnic and religious groups to which we have already had reference in our second chapter. In truth, it is artificial to treat the problems of religious and of ethnic education separately. The distinction between the two types of groups is far from being absolute and the process of abstraction which differentiates the one from the other serves to over-emphasize the differences and to obscure the similarities. As is indicated by the frequent insistence on the use of the national tongue, the parochial school has developed in many cases because it served to perpetuate primarily national distinctions.[1] In fact, it is rather the truth that the main strength of parochial schools lay, at least in earlier times, in the circumstance that through them the foreign groups could preserve their nationality so closely bound up with their religion. On the other hand, when nationality is conceived in its cultural rather than political sense, the problem comes very close to what is considered generally a religious problem.

Especially in dealing with the relationship of the Jewish community to the State would it be futile to separate the ethnic from the religious problem. Neither the term 'ethnic group' nor the term 'religious group' taken alone is either exact or adequate in describing the nature of the Jewish group, nor would the two used together serve to cover the case. The terms obtained by translating these words into Hebrew could not be naturally used in Hebrew to describe the Jewish group. "*Am Yisroel*," the People of Israel, and "*Kenesseth Yisroel*," the Community of Israel, are the Hebrew phrases. While in the one case there is more of a national ring and in the other more of a religious connotation, the terms are not so sharply marked off and defined. To treat our people as simply ethnic or religious would veer the discussion into those conventional artificialities and false emphases which should be avoided and amount to a partial if not total begging of the question. Furthermore, by dealing with the two types of groups together, we may make explicit what is most important for our discussion. We are dealing with minority *communities* bound by common tradition. The fundamental matter to be borne in mind is that communities of men are involved. By treating the problem as one of 'religious education' a connotation of Bible Study and Catechism is conjured up, and the halo of literary and spiritual study is cast about what is in reality a question of the perpetuation of an association of men. On the other hand, the discussion of the 'national group' immediately rouses an apprehension of the intrusion of a foreign government, when only the question of an association of

[1]George V. Wenner, "Lutheran Parochial School," *Religious Education*, April, 1916.

men for cultural and idealistic purposes is involved. The matter which really concerns us is not the correctness of a dogma or the validity of a double political allegiance, but the perpetuation of a community existing for the pursuit of what they believe to be idealistic and cultural ends.

In both church and ethnic society the community is bound together primarily because of common traditions, customs and beliefs.   The unity is what would be termed a spiritual one.   Physical forces may have played upon the group in the past to make it a group and to create the common cultural heritage;   and some measure of physical contiguity is necessary to-day to make the community in psychic bonds possible.   But it is an ideational product, the result of having lived together, summed up in the term 'religion' in the one case, and in the term 'culture' in the other, which has now become the most important factor in maintaining the identity of the community. Left to the play of the present merely environmental forces it would disintegrate.   The unity of the group, whether it be ethnic or religious, is dependent upon its ability to remember its socially acquired characteristics, upon the memory of its history and culture, upon the process of education.

The ideas, customs and ceremonies to-day known as religious are really the cultural expressions of definite communities of men now crystallized into dogma, codes, and ritual.   What we call religion was, in the period when it was created, very much what we should call national culture to-day: the striving of a particular social group to transcend the limits of its own body of experience, and pursue ends humane, universal and eternal.   Thus Judaism, Hellenism and Taoism are as much national cultures as they are religion. It is rather a difference of *Zeitgeist* which makes the social aspiration of former ages express itself in the mystic terms of God and Salvation, and that of modern nations in the worship of Progress and Happiness. The differences are less real than external, more of logic and sociology than of psychological instinct and of human aspiration.   Catholicism cannot be rightly understood except in terms of the spiritual expression of Southern Europe, just as Protestantism is an aspect of the

North European national strivings.   When these social expressions
become transplanted into an environment which does not provide
the proper social *milieu*, they become formalized and tend to assume
the character of a body of principles or doctrines very often unrelated
to life.   Then we are sure that they are 'religion'.   But in reality, if
a religion is to remain vital, it must have its own social background.
So, too, a people transplanted must give up its government incidental
to its primary and intrinsic character as a community of social beings,
and it then tends to identify its life with certain principles for which it
stands.   But as in the case of the religious heritage, the principles
must remain meaningless without a social background.   What is
significant is that in both cases a spiritual product of a former social
life now becomes the *raison d'être* of continuing the society.

The discussion, then, relates to such groups as the ethnic and
religious, which as their distinguishing characteristics possess ideational (religious or cultural) heritages developed under other than the
present geographical and natural conditions.   As a matter of fact
the whole question has, in the past, generally been thought of in
religious terms even when an ethnic problem was involved.   So that
criticism of any existing mode of adjustment would be mainly a
criticism of the religious school.

It can hardly be said that we have reached a satisfactory solution
in the present adjustment.   Although the country as a whole has
accepted the state schools, the Catholics have never consented to
the present arrangement and protest against being forced to support
schools to which they do not send their children.   On the other
hand, many look askance at the very existence of parochial schools
and urge their total suppression by the State, as has been done in
France.   In addition, several new conditions warrant a fresh discussion of the question.   To the problem of religious minorities has
been added our own problem of ethnic minorities, made crucial by
the large immigration since 1881 of nationalities somewhat further
removed from the Anglo-Saxon American stocks than were the races
brought by earliest tides of immigration, and emphasized also by the
concurrent development of the idea of cultural nationality.   Especially is this important since such a large proportion of the recent

immigrants are Jews to whom religious and national identity are quite indistinguishable, for their nationality is religious and their religion national.   The Jewish group is undoubtedly an important factor in bringing to the fore the question of religious and ethnic education.[1]

In the second place, an awakened interest in religious matters seems to be astir.   A rationalistic and scientific impatience with the fantastic methods of religion, prayer, ceremonialism and dogmatism has obscured somewhat the ends which religion sought to attain, ends which had to do with enlarging the human vision, with the setting up of ideals of service, with great humane purposes.   A new psychology of religion is giving back to religion some place in the economy of human life, though this place and its proportion may be greatly changed.   Furthermore, the emphasis that has in recent years been placed upon the social nature of religion is leading to the realization that the present mechanical methods in religious schools are wholly inadequate for the development of a religious consciousness.

The recent excitement, especially on the part of Protestants[2] and Jewish reform ministers,[3] hailing the Gary scheme as a solution for the problem of correlation of religious and public education, is indicative of the tacit dissatisfaction with the present situation.   The interest of Protestant bodies in the development of week-day religious instruction is evidence of the growing disapproval of the formality of the Sunday school.   Among the Jews a wide experiment in religious education is being carried on.   The scheme ranges from methods of extension education through celebration of festivals, club work and literature, to the intensive work of the parochial schools.   Though the Jews on the whole do not favor parochial schools (over 99 per cent send their children to the public schools) the parochial school movement has recently received some impetus in the general increase of interest in religious education and in dissatisfaction with the

---

[1] It is interesting to note that of all immigrant groups the Jews have been the leaders in active Americanization work and even anticipated the public schools in reckoning with the problem (as in the Educational Alliance).   The term 'Melting Pot' is the creation of a Jewish writer, and the 'Federation of Nationalities' theory has been developed by a Jewish thinker.

[2] *Religious Education*, February, 1916.

[3] *System of Religious Education in Secular Schools*, Year Book of the Central Conference of American Rabbis, 1916.

present situation.   The variety of schools includes also those which
are purely secular in character or nearly so and which present the
antithesis to the denationalized 'purely religious' Sunday school.
Most interesting in this connection is the recent action of the 'Arbeiter
Ring' in introducing Yiddish and Hebrew into their schools.   This
strong, radical organization, consisting of over 100,000 Jewish workingmen, with their own organ, *Die Arbeiter-Stimme*, until now has
conducted Sunday schools for the spread of socialist ideas, and consistently opposed giving their children any Jewish instruction, religious or national.   In addition, the discussion in many circles of the
possibility of having Yiddish and Hebrew introduced into the public
school as culture languages is indicative of the unsatisfied need felt
for the retention of foreign ethnic cultures.   This newly awakened
interest, giving rise to variety of ideas and types of solution, makes
especially imperative a careful consideration of the fundamental
principles involved.

There are three modes of organization possible: (1) The parochial school, which displaces the public school.   (2) The inclusion of
particularistic teaching in the curriculum of the public school.
(3) A system of schools conducted by the group and complementary
to public school instruction.   Which of these three general schemes
satisfies in the greatest degree the needs of the ethnic group and at
the same time is harmonious with the criteria of democracy which we
have in mind?

II

THE PAROCHIAL SCHOOL

The first question, that of the Parochial School, has received the
most complete development among the Catholics, and for this reason
our discussion will deal especially with the position maintained in this
denomination.[1]   The Catholics have (1) consistently maintained that

---

[1]The following three books will be found valuable as indicating the attitude toward
religious education by the three denominations, Catholic, Protestant, and Jew: C. S.
C. Burns, *The Condition of Catholic Education in the United States* (also other works
by the same author);   A. S. Athearn, *Religious Education and American Democracy;*
A. M. Dushkin, *Jewish Education in New York City.*

the state schools do not serve their needs and that only the parochial school is adequate and (2) generally held that parents who send their children to parochial schools should be exempted from taxation for the support of public schools.   Their arguments may be summed up as follows:

The *Rights* Argument.[1]   To the parents belongs the 'right' by nature and by divine authority to choose freely under what system the child shall be educated.   The state, interfering with this right, either by suppressing parochial schools or by putting an additional burden upon those parents who send their children to the parochial schools, or by the unjust competition of providing free schools, is transgressing its own function, which is to regulate competition, not itself to compete; to protect the rights of individuals, not to interfere with them; and to step in when the parent fails to do his duty, not to abrogate the parental duties.   The education given by the state inculcates ideas inconsistent with the beliefs of the parent and thus makes a breach between the child and the parent.   Especially when a parent believes that the inculcation of his doctrine is necessary for securing the eternal life of the child does it appear heinous to compel the child to attend state schools; for the state will in such a case be robbing the child of his eternal life, a tyranny worse than arbitrarily convicting him to death.

The *Pedagogical* Argument.[2]   (a) Religion is as large as the whole of life.   It does not consist merely of the memorization of creed or the mechanical performance of ceremonies.   It must pervade all action and all thought.   Therefore, the whole education of the child must be permeated by its influence, the methods of teaching must exemplify the religious outlook.   The religious principles must be

[1]Pierre Binaut, *Les droits et les devoirs de l'état en matière d'enseignment.*   Monsignor P. R. McDevitt, "The State and Education," *Bulletin of the Catholic Education Association*, February, 1916.   John F. Fenelon, in *The State Catholic Education Association Bulletin*, November, 1916.   Rev. T. Bouquillon, *Education, to Whom does it Belong?* 1892.   Rev. R. I. Holland, *The Parent First*, 1892.   Rev. S. G. Conway, *The State Last*, 1892.

[2]Pierre Binaut, *Les droits et les devoirs de l' état en matiere d'enseignment.*   C. S. C. Burns, *The Conditions of Catholic Education in the United States*, 1917 (and other works by the same author).   Shields, T. E., "Relation Between Catholic School Systems and the State," *Catholic Education Bulletin*, November, 1916.

made manifest in every detail of the life of the school if they are to become active and significant.

(b)   The public schools cannot maintain a neutral attitude.   Even refraining from religious instruction is an attitude.   The relative emphasis on subjects and the interpretation of them develop an attitude in the pupil's mind, a point of view quite comparable with a religious point of view.   The teacher, too, having a mind, cannot be neutral and, even when he avoids favoring any one of the conflicting sects openly, his work and influence are bound to be unconsciously colored by his religious attitude.   The monopoly of education held by the state thus leads to indoctrination of the state's point of view.

(c)   The public school cannot teach religion.   The parochial school can teach citizenship.   Therefore, since education can be complete only if it is a unitary process, the parochial school should be favored.

The argument advanced concerning the conflicting rights of parent and state would be more convincing in the light of *laissez-faire* politics.   In this system of thought the state comes in to restrain one individual, who appears as a complete entity with definite and fixed rights, when he interferes with the equally definite and fixed rights of another individual;   or to judge between them when two individuals disagree;   or to fulfill the duties of the individual when he neglects to perform them.   In such a theory, with its weighing of right against right, the presupposition must be that rights are stable and unchangeable;   else how could they be measured?   In the particular application to the right to educate, in accordance with the argument, it is nature and authority that have standardized values.

All that one can mean, however, by maintaining that nature gives the right, is that because by original nature the parent tends in a variety of ways to take care of its offspring the parent should be the one to decide what the education of the child should be under the conditions of civilized society.   But origin alone cannot be considered as a sanction.   All civilized society exists because original nature does not satisfy the conditions of humane living;   original nature must be modified so as to permit the harmony of a rational life.   The antithesis 'natural-artificial' obscures the truth that the latter development also becomes natural.   The true antithesis would be *original* and *subsequent* nature.[1]

Sanction in a democratic conception comes from serviceableness. Authority and origin are sanctions only in so far as they give a hint of usefulness for the present situation.   One has a right to follow a certain course, when after consideration of as many as possible relevant elements it seems to be the right course to take.   The question of relevancy involves immediately our basic democratic principle. In the whole argument the contestants appear to be the parent and the state, while the individual mostly concerned, the child to be educated, is left altogether out of consideration.   Perhaps the profoundest element in democracy is the consideration that it urges must be given to the matter involved, especially if it be a person.[2] The object most closely affected must be the centre from which radiate all considerations and all reckonings.   Even when they reach far out from the immediate individual to more distant relationships, they must never lose this primarily important orientation.

But, as already implied, the whole conception of the relation of the individual to society involved in these arguments is itself faulty. The implication is that the individuals in society are fairly complete and separate entities; that they interfere with each other only on occasion; and that these interferences, when they do occur, are always overt, so that the state may take cognizance and step in.   The truth is that individuals living together in society are *never* such independent entities.   They are always interfering with each other, always helping or hindering, always influencing each other, actually and potentially. As long as men are in communication, they are already reacting one to another, interference being far more subtle than the *laissez-faire* theories would imply.   Even the *laissez-faire* principle that the state comes in when individuals interfere with one another, would make the state's function continuous and not spasmodic, were the true nature of the richness of relationship of individual to society fully realized.   Not each individual with his separate rights is the reality.

---

[1]Thorndike, *Educational Psychology*, Vol. I, page 293; Santayana, *Life of Reason*, Vol. I, page 276; Dewey, *Democracy and Education*, Chapter IV, page 331.
[2]See Chapter I.

Such an individual is an abstraction; but the very living process of interaction in which the 'individual' and 'society' are abstract terms is what actually exists.   The state, therefore, is a function of the interdependence of human beings in communication, not a means for maintaining independence in an exclusive and separatist sense.

The state's function to educate is a positive one.   It does not rise from the need to step in at times *in loco parentis*.   *Education exists to make explicit the significances of communication, to maintain interdependence, and to preserve its results in culture, in the arts and in the spiritual life.*[1]   It arises not because men are independent of each other—the words interdependence and communication are but pale shadows of the complexity and dynamic quality of the relation of men to men—but because they are completely interdependent.

Those living under one state affect each other, and a common educational system serves in the measure that it is efficient to further the benefits of the community it represents and to preserve and make more fruitful this interdependence.   Such an educational system must in a democratic community reckon with, represent and express the variety of forces in the community and must be conducted by the community as a whole, not by any part of it.   A failure on the part of the state to reckon with the groups it deals with or a failure on the part of one group to recognize the interdependence of all the groups in the state is alike undemocratic.   In so far as the common schools do not represent the broad interests of the country as a whole they may be objectionable; but they cannot be opposed on the ground that they do not represent the interests of one group.   For the very function of the educational system of the state rises from the fact that all within the state are in communication; they are members of one community.

The notion of right involved in the first argument harks back to a conception of politics untenable to-day and violates the fundamental

---

[1]The idea that education is a function of men in communication (both in the temporal and social sense), that it is a necessity of community (see how Mac Iver uses this word in his work "Community") seems to be fundamental and rich in possible implications.   Bouquillon, a Catholic writer, in a pamphlet entitled "Education, to Whom does it Belong?" foreshadowed this idea in the answer, "to every association."   A more direct treatment is to be found in Dewey, *Democracy and Education*, Chap. I and II.

principles of democratic thought. It rests upon authority for its sanction. It conceives of the problem from the point of view of the parent and the church and not from that of the child who is most intimately concerned. It fails to reckon in full measure with the responsibilities implied in the actual multiplicity of dependences upon which the nature and the good of the individual rest. This legalistic argument, which we have captioned the 'rights argument,' was the vogue in the parochial school controversies of the '90s, and is still used by some French writers of to-day. Among the present American defenders of the parochial school it has been superseded by the more utilitarian 'pedagogical argument.'

Pedagogical science will agree with the contention that the inculcation of formal principles is ineffective and that if these are to become active forces in living activities the reactions desired must be taught through actual situations. The atmosphere of the school and the example of the teacher in the daily life of the child are more potent than the precepts of a few hours a week. Especially in such a matter as religion which one could argue is a "completion, unification and organization of all life's experiences,"[1] must the influence pervade all action.

If the community in which the child lives were to consist only of Catholics such a contention would be correct in its practical conclusion as it is in its assumption of the pedagogical fact. But the point is just this, that the child who is to live in a community with non-Catholics ought to have his education in connection with a representative community; otherwise what guarantee is there that the reactions will function in the wider community? To teach faith, hope and charity towards Catholics in a Catholic environment does not insure practicing these virtues toward non-Catholics. Christian charity has often meant charity to Christians and intolerance of others. The argument that religion must be connected with life, then, in reality is an argument against the parochial school, for the life which the American must live is wider than the parochial school.

Further, it is possible to understand when religion is defined as a completion, unification and organization of one's experience why

---

[1] Coe, *The Psychology of Religion*, Chap. VI.

one's religion should pervade one's whole life. But that is quite a different thing from saying that one's church should pervade one's whole life. For the church is only one source of that religious experience which is described in the psychological definition of the term.[1] The church may embody in its history, creed and ceremonies the religious experiences of some group or some individual; but each man's religion, if he has any, is one individual experience and, if it is true and applicable to all his life, must be derived from all of his life, not alone from limited associations. Though the teachings of a great church with a long history be taken as valuable or even invaluable guides in life and though they have in a sense a relatively eternal and universal value, the democratic conception would never admit that truth has ever been completed or that it is anything but relative to the situation in which one is now placed. Not only must the religion be applied to a life which is most justly representative of the situation (and not to any parochial community), but the religion, too, which is to be applied to life, must itself be an expression and representation of the broader life. To assume the absoluteness, infallibility and completeness of the teachings of any church is itself contrary to the democratic notions that life's truths learned from life's experiences are subject to referendum and recall by life's experiences. The actual conditions, natural and social, under which the members of a modern democratic community, which is radically and religiously heterogeneous, live would make the pedagogical argument specious. The public schools are really more representative of the activities and ideals of the community in which the citizens must live than is the parochial school.

To the second charge of the pedagogical argument that the public schools cannot maintain an attitude of neutrality and that their teaching is disruptive of the church and parental authority, the public schools must plead guilty. They are certainly developing habits of reaction to situations. They are certainly building up the minds of the pupils. To deny this would be equal to saying that they were having no effect upon their pupils. But this is just what they should do. As long as the community con-

---

[1]Royce, *Sources of Religious Insight.*

tains a variety of forces, all of these must be permitted to play upon the child. Otherwise the child is subjected to a process which amounts to indoctrination; his horizon would be limited by a pre-arranged and delimited and delimiting education, that is, by an education parochial in outlook as it is in name. An opposite danger is pointed out in the disintegrating influence of conflicting teaching which leads to many a tragedy in the disruption of the family. But if this conflict is really representative of an actual and current conflict between the church and the state, is it not necessary for the child to go through it?

The harshness of the conflict, in a sense unavoidable, could never-theless be mitigated if the state schools, in democratic fashion, took into consideration the social life of their pupils and adjusted them-selves in some measure to it. On the other hand, the forces represent-ing the family community must also be modified. It is the stand-pat and therefore undemocratic attitude of both institutions which is the cause of the deplorable rending of social ties. Whatever scheme of education is finally favored must face frankly this important problem of maintaining the integrity of family life central to social stability and to the nation's welfare.

The foregoing discussion based on the Catholic position applies in the main also to the Jewish situation. But the organization and theory of the Jewish parochial school present important differences which affect the emphasis of the argument. In the first place the parochial school is the exceptional thing among the Jews, not the typical educational institution. As noted above, only a fraction of one per cent of the Jewish children attend parochial schools. From a practical point of view, therefore, the Jewish parochial school presents no crucial problem. Furthermore, the Jewish parochial schools are subject to lay control. They are communal, not clerical institutions, each managed by a separate board of trustees just as any hospital or recreational center might be. The teachers and principal generally are laymen, not rabbis; and the secular subjects are taught by teachers who have been trained in the public school system and have had experience in teaching in the public schools.

The Jewish schools differ from the Catholic schools in theory as well as in organization. The latter are apprehensive of a heretical doctrine and aim to safeguard their pupils from disrupting external influences. The Jewish defense rests on the following two contentions: (1) That the amount of time taken by the public school leaves no room for an adequate Jewish education. (2) That the teaching of the secular and the Jewish subjects under one roof by teachers who understand both Jewish and American life will avoid the conflict between "ultra oriental Judaism and ultra occidental Americanism" and the resulting tragedy of the disintegragion of homes.[1]

These differences of organization and underlying principles no doubt lessen the danger of divergence from the general ideas of the community. On the other hand, it should be realized that the differences between the Catholic and Jewish argument are not quite so wide as they may appear from the bald statement. Since the Jews have no centralized church and recognize no clerical authority, these schools could not be under other but lay control. The utilization of public school teachers for instruction in secular subjects is a makeshift made necessary by inability to procure any other type of teacher qualified to teach the secular branches. As a matter of fact a high school and a Talmudical academy are being developed at present with the aim of producing teachers who can teach both the secular and Hebrew subjects. The modern spirit, though not excommunicated, is rather tolerated than welcomed. Science, music, drawing, etc., are just permitted to enter and the pupils do not receive adequate instruction in these studies. Vocational subjects and the manual arts are neglected. An obscurantist spirit prevails. Until recently books in modern Hebrew were taboo and to read them was considered sacrilege. Even to-day the teachers are troubled and are at a loss to know what to do when a youngster puts the time-worn question concerning the validity of the Biblical or the scientific account of creation. Whatever is modern and scientific enters only perforce.

The main difficulty, however, lies in the fact that the Jewish parochial school, like the Catholic system, segregates the children along

[1] S. T. H. Hurwitz, "The Jewish Parochial School," *The Jewish Teacher*, December, 1917.

lines of creed.   The essential point of having the various elements of
the population, during the formative period of childhood, associate
with their neighbors with whom they are destined to live together as
American citizens remains unfulfilled.   No teaching of the common
branches in the classroom can take the place of actual personal
commingling as an educational force.   Bound as these children are to
come in contact with each other and to work together in later life,
their separation from each other in school days is poor preparation
for the coöperation and tolerance essential to a democracy.   Though
the perpetuation of significant elements of the culture of ethnic
groups is permissible under, and really a purpose of democracy,
segregation along any lines of either creed or race is thoroughly
undemocratic.

This main objection stands, also, against those who favor parochial
schools upon a cultural, not a religious basis.   The proponents of the
'Federation of Nationalities' theory, which was discussed in the preceding chapter, imply separate ethnic schools.   Among these are to
be reckoned also the Yiddish-Nationalists who favor the perpetuation of Jewish life through the means of Yiddish culture.   This
group conducts a number of complementary week-day schools at
present, but looks forward to a separate school system supplanting
the public schools.   No argument of clericalism or obscurantism can
be levelled against the Yiddish-Nationalists.   It must be admitted
that their standpoint is modern and that they base their contention
on modern sociological conceptions.   Though intense nationalists,
their idea of nationality is in accord with the most enlightened cultural notions regarding the nation as existing by the sanction of its
will to service in the development of literature, art and the ideal
life, not by the right of the will to power.

These protagonists of the separate ethnic schools point out that the
environment, the street, the press, politics, the vocation, the theatre,
literature and art will of necessity impress upon the individual living
here the culture of the land.   No one can avoid learning the language
and culture of the country even if he should endeavor to do so.   It
is the foreign ethnic culture having no natural or social background
which is in danger of being lost and which can be saved only through

the greatest effort.   With the hypothesis that the nature of the individual is determined mainly by his ancestral endowment, which is the basic underlying conception of these thinkers, it is only through the preservation of the ethnic culture that the individual can attain his full and free self-development and contribute his best to the nation as a whole.   Welcoming rather than apprehending segregation along ethnic lines, because they believe all culture and the higher life to be the fulfillment of ethnic strivings, they do not fear the possible disruptive influence of ethnic segregation, maintaining that the geographic, economic and political unities will enforce coöperation and mutual toleration.   Furthermore, the unique ethnic contribution enriching the life of the nation is of such great value that it will more than justify the organization along ethnic lines.

Sufficient has been said in the previous chapter to show that the general tendency of the evidence is against the assumption that race in the ethnic sense is the paramount force in the life of the individual. To create an institution which would tend to divide the country along the lines of assumed racial distinctions would be to perpetuate in an artificial manner differences which may have no natural basis in heredity.   Such a process would fall under the category of those artificial social arrangements which protect an artificial assumption rather than liberate inherent capacities.   In the end it would amount, as far as most individuals are concerned, to a process of indoctrination and to an undue exaltation of the place of the ethnic culture.   It is an essential American doctrine that citizenship, not lineage, makes one heir to the culture of America.

There is another very important, perhaps obvious though elusive element involved in the situation revolving about the question of allegiance.   The reference is not to the external matters of political and civic allegiance.   No one can seriously question the loyalty of those who have received a parochial education.   There is no evidence which goes to show that the graduates of parochial schools fall short of the duties and responsibilities involved in citizenship.   The attempt to cast doubt of loyalty in these matters succeeds only in obscuring the real issue.   It is a psychological aloofness rather than a political defection which is to be apprehended; a type of disloyalty, if that is not too strong a word, which will affect possible contribution rather than reveal itself in overt wrongdoing.

The school system of a nation exists ultimately for ideal purposes; to clarify its vision, to reveal its soul, to sanctify the sons of the people for the pursuit of the ideal things inherent in the life of the nation. If the school is conducted by the ethnic group and the child is taught by teachers representative of the group culture, while the American ideal is either picked up casually or interpreted by foreign teachers, it will be natural for the allegiance of the pupils, in the sense of a spiritual devotion, to be given rather to the ethnic group. For it is in the ethnic school that the pupil will find the clear consciousness of an ideal and the finest personalities. He may still fulfill all the legal obligations and sincerely pledge his allegiance to the flag of his country; but his moral wholehearted devotion will tend to be inspired toward the promotion of the ethnic culture. A separate school system for the ethnic group may involve a loss of positive spiritual allegiance to the society represented by the geographic community.

The parochial school neither in its Catholic, Jewish nor national form would seem to fulfill the demands of the democratic idea that the school system must be representative of the community at large; that to organize it along the lines of one sect or ethnos would tend to segregation and indoctrination. Should all children, then, be compelled to attend public schools, since these further the public good, and, as is done in France, all parochial education suppressed? Indeed, if those who send their children to parochial schools would avow their indifference to the public weal such a procedure might seem justifiable. But, in reality, the supporters of the parochial schools insist that it is the welfare of society which they have at heart. They, therefore, appear as a minority diverging from the opinion of the majority.

Here may be utilized the principle formulated in our first chapter with reference to the suppression of minority opinion and activities. The idea set forth there is that objective demonstration of the evil of an activity is necessary before it may forcibly be suppressed. Objectivity of proof of evil is the sanction of suppression. In the degree that in any case objectivity of proof is possible and care is taken to determine actual evil results, in that degree can it be said that democracy prevails in any situation.

Now it would be difficult to prove that the graduates of parochial schools are appreciably inferior to other pupils or that parochial schools are a menace to the social order. If it does happen that certain schools do not measure up to the objectively accepted standard in certain particulars, whether it be in instruction in English or in scientific subjects, the state may demand improvement in these subjects. But beyond that the state may not go. It dare not suppress institutions which do not obviously endanger the public welfare. If the opinion offered above, that parochial education is not proper in a democracy, has a rational basis, it must ultimately have its effect without resorting to force. There is nothing so disintegrating to an unjust established system as an opposing idea founded on change of social conditions. When the danger is crucial, it may not be practical or possible to wait for the slow-working influence of theoretical discussion. But when the menace is not immediate or obvious, nothing can be said against such a policy. No social or educational institution is so perfectly sealed that it can prevent the forces of the environment from ultimately disintegrating it, if it does not come to serve real human needs.

The strength of the parochial school in all likelihood indicates that it satisfies a justifiable demand not provided for by the public school system. No doubt much of its strength is artificial—upheld by the threat of clerical punishment or by the public opinion of the social group. But it is highly questionable whether it could maintain itself if it did not have something to contribute. For one thing, the parochial schools stand as a protest against the exclusion of all religious teaching from our scheme of education, which implies a monopoly of the right to educate on the part of the state. If a monopoly of education by the church is no solution, neither is a monopoly on the part of the state equitable. It may be shown that the state really cannot have a monopoly of education, for general social contact and literature are permeating educational influences. But the same can be said also in reference to the parochial school, the term monopoly being used relatively and particularly of the school system. It may be argued that the state in a democracy like ours is more likely to be democratic and that its schools are more representative of the common interests of the country as a whole, that its ideas of education are more responsive to the demands that the life of the environment makes upon us than a system bound by a historical and parochial tradition. If we must choose, it is said, let us choose the more democratic monopoly and the danger of indoctrination will be mitigated. But that a great danger does lurk in indoctrination by the state cannot be gainsaid. The state is still mainly an economic organization, though it no doubt has its cultural and spiritual aspect. Its strength, however, has come because it has given adequate emphasis to the physical and economic bases of life and has recognized the supreme superiority of machinery as against magic in the accomplishment of ends. This emphasis, however, has had its counterpart in a materialism which, fixing its attention upon economic and political factors, has exalted these into ends. Professor Dewey quotes someone as saying that as a result of modern economic and political organization one sinner can with a machine make more bricks in one hour than a saint could previously make in a whole day with his hands. But one might retort that that is just the trouble, and we wonder what the sinner is going to do with the bricks. The education of the parochial school may present obstacles to a perfect harmonization of the heterogeneous elements within the state. It may even be quite ineffective, filling the mind with other-worldly visions and with the fantastic methods of sacrifice and prayer dubious in their potency for actually reconstructing the world. But the indoctrination by the state may lead to attention upon economic and physical forces which taken together with an anti-social point of view may be disastrous.

Undoubtedly the presence of the parochial school is an indication of the unsatisfactory state of adjustment between public and other education. To solve our problem it will not be sufficient to suppress the parochial schools, which are the results of a maladjustment and not the root of the evil. It will be necessary to provide for the element in the demand which the parochial school comes to serve that has a rational support. That done, the better cause is bound to win in an environment where the interchange of social forces is as sure as it is in this country.

On the other hand, those who claim that the state ought to contribute to the support of parochial schools cannot receive justification in accordance with the foregoing analysis, that education is a function of the state community, not alone a parental duty. The taxation which supports the public schools is not a sort of charge (as a private firm might make) to the members of the state for services rendered to these particular members. It is a means of supporting an institution which safeguards that ideational community which is the necessity of and ultimately the most significant thing in the governmental unity. The wealth of individual citizens is possible only because the community provides the conditions and protects the rights necessary for its acquisition. Wealth is really communal in its nature and even when entrusted to the 'care' of individuals a part of it must go back to support the institutions which make wealth possible and give it significance. The parent is taxed not because he is a parent, but because he is a citizen, as is evidenced by the fact that all citizens whether they have children of school age or not are taxed in equal measure. The parent who sends his children to a parochial school has no more right to a rebate than has a bachelor. Citizenship and not parenthood is what involves the responsibility of maintaining schools. Minorities who differ from the public view can maintain their individuality only at a greater cost. Society penalizes divergences whose good is not recognized, whether these ultimately benefit the public welfare or not. Every minority, even when its objects are social, must fight its way to recognition and support. When an activity is directed mainly to preserve the interests of one group, even when these interests are thoroughly compatible with the interests of all other groups, and in the long run even contribute to the general social welfare, it is that group alone which must support the particular institution. Perhaps the best way to ameliorate this condition, unjust from an ideal point of view, though under present conditions perhaps the only feasible one, would be to take from the religious communities the financial burden of the charities, such as hospitals and recreation centers, which are in reality public, not parochial questions, and permit the funds usually expended on these tasks to flow to the causes which the minority community can alone rightly further, i.e., the preservation of the ideas and life of the religious group and the ethnic community.

III

RELIGIOUS EDUCATION IN THE STATE SCHOOLS[1]

The second suggestion, to introduce religious and ethnic instruction in the state schools, follows the plan which has been adopted in some of the European countries and in Australia.   On the theory that the State has taken over the parents' function to educate, it is held that the state schools must do all that the parents would have done had the education of their children remained under their control. In accordance with our own analysis, however, which makes the state's function rise out of the necessity of maintaining and furthering the society which the state government represents, it becomes clear that particularistic teachings have no place in the curriculum of the state's schools.   The function of the state's system is to be interested in whatever is common to all citizens by reason of their living together. A movement in line with democracy would eliminate whatever vestiges of religious teaching are still retained in the public schools, like the reading of the Bible and the celebration of religious holidays. The division of our pupils within the school into groups for the study of particular doctrines or ethnic heritages presents enormous practical difficulties from the administrative point of view.   In order to have proper grading, religious or ethnic schools in any neighborhood have to draw their pupils from many public schools, for the total school population is divided into a variety of sects.   And second, not all parents are desirous of giving their children religious instruction.   But more important from the point of view of the treatment of the subject in this chapter is that such a separation of pupils within the school savors of the spirit of segregation so antithetical to democracy.

---

[1] A. Riley and others, *The Religious Question in Public Education;* M. E. Sadler, *Moral Instruction and Training in Schools,* 2 vol.; G. Spiller, *Moral Education in Eighteen Countries.*

Particularistic teaching which aims to preserve the society of some one group of the population is a function of the society which is to be preserved. It is not a function of the state.

The objections from the point of view of the religious and ethnic schools are even more forcible. Wherever religious teaching in public schools has been in vogue, it has assumed a formal nature. It is bound to be so, for religion and ethnic culture are not abstract ideas that can be put into phrases and memorized, as seems to be the notion prevailing among many. All that the Catholics say concerning the need of atmosphere and of the example of personalities, of opportunity for application in every possible phase of school life, is here very much to the point. Only when a religion has lost its vitality and no longer has a message to bring will memorization of phrases be regarded as religious teaching. When an ethnic culture is involved, the task is even more complex; another language, literature and history must be taught. The effort and enthusiasm needed for such a work is beyond what state schools could give. The perpetuation of the life of a community is a task not to be attained through incidental attention. Religious and ethnic teaching is never mere intellectual erudition. There is involved a loyalty directed to the preservation of a social group. Special schools for music and art are established, because a permeating atmosphere is necessary. A social attitude within the school must be developed to inspire a devotion to the pursuit of these arts. Even more is it necessary to have separate schools for the religious and ethnic communities, because there is here involved allegiance to a society.

Whenever elements in the heritage of a religious group or of an ethnic community have become objects of universal as well as particular interest, nothing can be said against the introduction of such subjects into the public schools. If any portions of ancient Hebrew history and literature are regarded as important in the development of Western civilization, there seems to be no valid reason why these subjects should not take their place with the classic languages and Roman and Greek history. If in any given locality Yiddish or modern Hebrew is deemed important, there is no more reason for excluding these than there is for eliminating any other modern language. This can be maintained only with the proviso that the subject be taught in a disinterested manner, not as a 'religious' subject with a distinctive halo spread about it. The plan introduced in North Dakota and Colorado, of giving credit for Bible study outside of the classroom, can meet with no objection, for the idea is to treat the Bible as literature.[1] But such schemes should not be looked upon as praiseworthy steps in the development of religious education. So, too, there seems to be no reasonable argument against reading good translations of ancient Hebrew writings and of the classics of the New Testament in school assemblies alongside of selections from Plato, Shakespeare, Walt Whitman, or any other great writer. The exclusive reading of the Bible, as such, in the authorized and, therefore, not disinterested version is reprehensible. Those who argue that the Bible should be read because it is great literature are not consistent when they demand reading it exclusively.

The problem of religious education cannot be solved through such movements as the Australian plan, the North Dakota idea, and the introduction of Bible reading in public schools. Both Catholics and Jews who really desire to maintain a specific form of culture and ideal—and those among the Protestants to whom Protestantism still implies some elements of a distinctly Christian tradition, and does not merely mean a halo thrown around the contemporaneous national spirit,—do not find such literary studies adequate for maintaining the continuity of the community whose ideals they wish to preserve. What these communities must do if they are to justify their existence is to enrich the personalities of the communicants and through them the life of the nation. The formal teaching of religious subjects in the public schools is as little adequate to solve our problem as a high school study of Latin or Greek is potent to recreate the Roman or Greek societies with their specific types of personality. If the ethnic and religious communities remain satisfied with such instruction they will soon be as dead as are the classic peoples.

---

[1] C. A. Wood, *School and College Credit for Outside Bible Study.* W. F. Crafts, *Bible in School Plans of Many Lands.*

IV

COMPLEMENTARY ETHNIC AND RELIGIOUS SCHOOLS

The plan that seems to harmonize best with the principles laid down is a dual system providing that ethnic and religious education be given in special schools.[1] In such a scheme each system of schools would assure the integrity of the community which supports it; the public schools would further the society of the state; the religious and ethnic schools, the society of minority communities. Neither group is conceived of as having a monopoly on the right to conduct a school system. Our first principle is that each community undertake the responsibility of the maintenance of its own culture.

These schools must be correlated with each other. They must reckon with each other and adjust themselves to each other. Otherwise one school might interfere with the work of the other to such a degree as to make the right to conduct a school empty. This principle of correlation fundamentally affects arrangements of schedule. More fundamental, in order to prevent a breach in the pupil's life, not only external matters like time schedules must be adjusted with mutual regard, but the curriculum and general spirit in each school must be developed with cognizance of the situation in the other schools. Whatever schemes are developed must fulfill at least these two basic principles, separation of control and support on the one hand and correlation and adjustment on the other.

The validity of such an arrangement between the public schools and other educational agencies has recently received recognition in the Gary plan. One of the many arguments for the Gary plan was that the free time between school sessions could be utilized by churches for religious education. Unfortunately, in this case, while there was accord in principle, the actual schedule proposed proved unsatisfactory to some groups and really would have interfered with schemes of supplementary education already existing or in process of development to a far greater extent than it would have promoted new work. A number of Protestant ministers and

---

[1]See A. M. Dushkin, *Jewish Education in New York City*. A. S. Athearn, *Religious Education and American Democracy;* B. S. Winchester, *Religious Education and Democracy;* G. V. Wenner, *Religious Education and the Public Schools*.

Reform Jewish rabbis, who had hitherto contented themselves with remaining unsatisfied with the Sunday School, approved the plan, for, naturally, it did not disturb any of the work that they were carrying on and offered at least a plan, even if impracticable, to satisfy their aspiration for better work.   To the Catholics the issue was less important, for nothing less than the parochial school is considered a solution.   The Jews were affected most because they are already conducting quite an extensive educational activity supplementary to the public school system after school hours.   Since the Gary schedule kept some of the children in school until 5 and 5:30 p. m., it would have meant the complete disorganization of these activities. The arrangement of free hours in the Gary schedule would not have permitted reorganization on an efficient basis.   The plans being developed by Protestant groups for week-day religious instruction would also have been seriously hampered.   The technical difficulties of this scheme of correlation cannot concern us here.   What is necessary to point out, however, is that the idea of correlation becomes meaningless, unless we see how it affects definite plans.   The Gary scheme, heartily endorsing the *principle* of correlation and mutual adjustment, actually would have greatly handicapped the development of supplementary week-day instruction had it been adopted in New York.[1]

The Sunday School offers another example of a separate system of education by minority groups.   This is the agency for religious instruction best known in America and the normal one for the Protestant groups.   Since the work is conducted on a day when there are no public school sessions, the problem of the adjustment of schedules is eliminated.   Instead of this one problem, however, there are many others.   So far as the Jews are concerned, it is altogether inadequate as a solution, and its introduction as a means of Jewish education has on the whole perhaps done more harm than good.   Although the Protestants practically have no other schools for religious education, there is complete dissatisfaction with its accomplishments.   For the Catholics, with even more stringent demands for religious instruction,

---

[1]Dushkin, *Jewish Education in New York City*, p, 217,   Berkson in *The Jewish Teacher*, May, 1917.

the Sunday School is out of the question as a solution. There are a number of fundamental objections. The time given is insufficient; religious teaching becomes disconnected from everyday life; since it takes but two hours a week, teachers cannot be expected to devote themselves professionally to the work and to follow a course of study to prepare themselves adequately. From the point of view of preserving the society of the ethnic group the Sunday School is as impotent as the plans for the introduction of religious education into the public schools.

The problem is to create a school system complementary to the public schools, correlated with them and yet adequate for perpetuating the life of the community which it represents. Both in time schedules and in content and spirit of the studies the two parallel systems must adjust with mutual consideration. In neighborhoods where certain ethnic or religious minorities predominate the teaching staff in the public schools must have adequate preparation so that they may understand the social background of their pupils. Elements of the history of the culture and of the arts of the minority group should be introduced in the course of study. Especially in the case of immigrant groups there is a great deal that the public schools can do to get closer to the life of the pupils. This phase of the problem of adjustment has already engaged the attention of American teachers and educators and is undoubtedly fraught with great possibilities. On the other hand the supplementary schools of the ethnic minorities must do their part in the adjustment to the schools of the state.

The Jews have been carrying on such supplementary educational activities as are proposed here. The Talmud Torahs, to which reference has already been made, conduct sessions on week-day afternoons and Sunday (occasionally also on Saturday). Their function is to transmit the Jewish spiritual heritage. In the beginning the attempt was to transplant to this country the school of the Eastern European ghetto and to crowd in as many hours and traditional subjects as possible. Gradually the need of adjusting to the new conditions has impressed itself and the Talmud Torah is taking on the aspect of a community centre with a broad educational and recreational program. The Central Jewish Institute represents at this writing the furthest development in the attempt to work out a plan in which the two elements, preservation of the ethnic culture and adjustment to America, will be duly considered.[1] The plan of work followed in this institution was formulated and initiated by the writer and may, therefore, be regarded in the main as his conception of a concrete application of the general principles presented. Instead of elaborating a theoretical plan of supplementary ethnic education and discussing problems likely to arise, it will serve our purpose best to describe the activities of this institution. A chapter, therefore, has been added dealing with the work of the Central Jewish Institute.

More detail than is necessary for understanding the general plan has been submitted. A careful reader although he might agree broadly with the foregoing theoretical analysis might yet wonder what it would mean in any given situation. The description of the activities as well as of the plan of the Central Jewish Institute should give an adequate idea of what is considered to be the proper educational agency in our democracy for preserving the culture of the ethnic community and should serve as a sound basis for judging the validity of the proposed theory of adjustment.

---

[1] For a general account of Jewish educational efforts, see A. M. Dushkin, *Jewish Education in New York City*.

THE CENTRAL JEWISH INSTITUTE

CHAPTER VI

THE CENTRAL JEWISH INSTITUTE[1]

I

Its Significance

The description of the work of the Central Jewish Institute should prove especially instructive in our study of the problem of adjustment not alone because it gives ample consideration to the two factors of our problem—carrying on the ethnic tradition and adapting to the conditions of America—but more so because it was conceived in a clear consciousness of this double task which faces Jewish life in America. Throughout the whole plan is manifest the realization that the institution is to work under American conditions. Nevertheless, the Hebrew subtitle תלמוד תורה (Talmud Torah) aligns it definitely with the educational agency whose specific purpose is the perpetuation of Jewish life. Its comprehensive plan of work is the culmination of two lines of endeavor in Jewish communal activities.

The adaptive tendency is best illustrated in those recreational and educational agencies which have been established through the initiative of the Jews who came here in the earlier wave of immigration between 1850-1870. These immigrants, coming mainly from Germany, have been eminently successful in attaining success and position in American life. Very early they turned their attention to

---

[1]Much more detail has been included in this chapter than is necessary for illustrating the foregoing theoretical analysis; its size is undoubtedly disproportionate to its relation to the rest of the book. After consideration, however, I have decided to leave it in the original form, hoping that the description of plan and methods will help to draw a concrete picture and that it may be suggestive to others who are interested in the development of the Jewish Community Center.

The Central Jewish Institute has been selected because it comes nearest to a consistent application of the ideas elaborated in this book. Undoubtedly, there are other Talmud Torahs and Y. M. H. A.'s where some elements of the work are carried on and in some instances more thoroughly or with greater success. Some of the Talmud Torahs have a more intensive curriculum; some of the Y. M. H. A.'s give a greater place to recreational activities. But no other institution could have served as an illustration of what is essential in the plan, *the adjustment* of forces, the *balance* of work, the *organic relationship* between the activities, the *conscious realization* of the problem.

the organization of Jewish charitable institutions and they have made for themselves a most praiseworthy record by the generosity of their gifts, the orderliness of their methods and the administrative efficiency of their leadership.   To-day, though a minority in the community, the so-called "German-Jews" still bear the financial burden and retain the ruling power in Jewish philanthropic affairs. With the general extension of public interest beyond helping the poor, curing the sick and caring for the orphan, educational, recreational and 'social' activities have been added during the last thirty years. Into this new work the older philanthropic notions are carried over and the feeling still persists that the beneficiaries are maladjusted persons, abnormal or potentially abnormal.   Thus the Educational Alliance seeks to Americanize the immigrant who is conceived to be out of harmony with the general civic and social life.   The Y. M. H. A.'s[1] hope that their recreational activities will provide a prophylactic against possible vice.   The social activities have an implication of "doing good" for the people in the slums.   Always there is an attitude on the part of the directors that they are conducting an institution for others, not for themselves, to serve needs which they themselves or their children do not feel.   Even the "religious classes" are conducted for the purpose of giving ethical instruction which is supposed, in some mysterious way, to keep the children of the poor in the straight path of virtue.   Little thought is exercised upon questioning what should be the normal to which the individual must adjust his life.   Some current conception is accepted as the standard and the person rather is regarded as the misfit.   The endeavor is to adjust the individual to prevailing sociological conditions.   In a word, we might say that these institutions endeavor to square the Jew with his new geographical environment and to the conditions rising out of it.

The other factor, stressing the retention of the Jewish consciousness, has been contributed mainly through the more recent immigration dating from 1881, consisting largely of immigrants from Eastern Europe.   These newcomers are still in the throes of economic adjustment.   Nevertheless, many have already gained a foothold among the ranks of the comfortably situated and are beginning to play a part in

---

[1] The reference is to the Y. M. H. A.'s in New York City.

Jewish communal work.   Together with the more Americanized Jews of the earlier wave of immigration they are coöperating in the endeavor to care for the poor and sick and are from year to year assuming a larger share of this common Jewish responsibility.   Their distinctive contribution, however, lies in their interest in the development of the Talmud Torah or Communal Jewish School.   As distinguished from institutions which rose from the need of meeting the new conditions, the Talmud Torah draws its purpose from within Jewish life.   Its purpose is to transmit the Jewish heritage so that the Jewish community consciousness may be preserved and Jewish spiritual life perpetuated in the new land for the coming generations.   Its work is conceived in terms of education for the normal child, not as a method of saving individual souls.   The institutions mentioned above have their origin fundamentally in the *new geography;* the Talmud Torah, we may say, finds its *raison d'être* in *Jewish history*.   It is because the Jews have a past crystallized into a social, cultural and spiritual heritage, together with a will to carry it on, that the Talmud Torah becomes necessary.

In recent years both types of institutions have tended to broaden the scope of their work.   On the one hand, the Jewish schools have begun to realize that they must take social conditions into consideration if they are to be successful in their effort to preserve Jewish life in this country.   Unsanitary and dilapidated buildings, mechanical and drill methods exercised upon equally uninteresting material, unkempt and untrained teachers, repel the child born and bred in America, accustomed to a highly developed and systematized public school.   It is being realized, furthermore, that the education of girls traditionally neglected by the Jewish school can no longer be left out of account. The adolescent boy and girl, too, present a most harassing problem, for here the disintegration of Jewish life becomes patent.   Even the parent, it is seen, must be earnestly considered in the problem of bridging the gap between the old and the new generations.   In answer to these problems the movement among the Talmud Torahs in recent years has been to include social and recreational activities in their scope of work.   On the other hand, some of the social settlements, beginning to understand the anomaly of being Jewish institutions with no characteristically Jewish work, have commenced to lay more emphasis on what they call their "religious classes," and a steady increase in attention to the study of Hebrew can be noted. The tendency, therefore, in both institutions—though the approach of the one is from Jewish tradition and of the other from present social conditions—is toward an institution which will harmoniously fuse both ideas and complete the synthesis of Jewish history and American geography with all that these two facts imply.

The older institutions, however, are laboring under very difficult handicaps in their endeavor to meet the new demands made upon them. In the original plans the present needs were not taken into consideration and the attempts at improvement are impeded by the inadequate facilities. The buildings of the Talmud Torahs, seldom up to standard even for classroom work, are in most cases totally unfit for the variety of extra-curricular activities demanded by the new conception. On the other hand, the social settlements are often deficient in proper accommodation for specifically school work. Even more important than the almost prohibitory physical difficulties inherent in the buildings is the mental attitude of the boards governing the institutions. Conditions rather than a changed philosophy may be said to be at work in whatever modifications are taking place. In neither of these types of institutions has there been a policy carefully thought out with reference to the problem involved. Both have been imitative, though in different ways. In the one type the prevailing conceptions and methods have been adopted whole-heartedly, including often the bad, inadequate and irrelevant elements as well as the good. Conformity to current social opinions and institutions has marked the work. In the development of the Talmud Torah, on the other hand, traditional methods are the main guides. The yoke of the past weighs heavily upon every detail of method and curriculum in the Talmud Torah. Change, whether in method or in content, tends in itself to be regarded with suspicion.

The Central Jewish Institute, erected but recently, is the first institution planned at its very inception to meet the problem with full cognizance of the two forces shaping Jewish life. Its facilities for classroom and school work are unexcelled. On the other hand, both in aesthetic effect and in facilities for the variety of work necessary in a social centre it surpasses the older settlements. It addresses itself not to child alone, nor to any one age of the population, but regards every member of the family as its patron. In fact, it looks upon the family as a whole, rather than the individual, as the unit of its work, regarding the family as the keystone of the Jewish social structure. It is a Community House, endeavoring to serve the neighborhood in every way it can, but with the additional and specific purpose of perpetuating for the community, and through it for the nation as a whole, whatever is considered of significance in Jewish cultural and spiritual life.

What makes the Central Jewish Institute particularly interesting to us is its conscious attempt to contribute to the large, general problem of developing an educational agency that will be potent to preserve a vital Jewish life under conditions prevailing in the United States. In its beginning, however, the Institute was a response to a local need. It will be of aid in understanding what is of permanent and general importance and what is merely local, what has entered on principle and what adventitiously, if we briefly examine the local conditions from which the Institute came into being. Incidentally we may also gain added insight into the problem of Americanization.

II

NEIGHBORHOOD AND HISTORY

The Central Jewish Institute (125 East 85th Street) is located in Yorkville, as the central portion of Manhattan, east of Fifth Avenue, is known. As differentiated from the East Side, which lies to the south, and Harlem to the north, this neighborhood presents rather the appearance of an older and more settled population. Still predominating in foreign elements,—either of first or second generation— it differs from these other two sections in several ways. In the first place, the neighborhood is not inhabited exclusively by foreigners— quite a sprinkling of old inhabitants is noticeable—and a far greater number of the inhabitants are the American children of foreign born, or foreign born who came here in the '80's and 90's. In addition, the neighborhood contains an unusually large percentage of Germans and Irish, giving a racial distribution reminiscent of the 'old' immigration rather than of the 'new.' The Jewish population, heterogeneous within itself, is scattered amongst the rest of the population.

Religiously as well as racially an unusual heterogeneity will be found. A Catholic parochial school flanks the synagogue adjoining the Central Jewish Institute and several other Catholic institutions are in the nearby vicinity. As in every American community, the Protestant churches, nevertheless, predominate. From the point of view of economic classification, wide though graded divergences exist. Lexington Avenue forms a dividing line. West of it through Park, Madison and Fifth Avenues, the gradation rises from middle class to ultra rich. This division of Fifth Avenue represents one of the wealthiest sections of New York. East of Lexington Avenue the gradation descends from middle class to poor, from respectable retail storekeepers to those who need the assistance of charity.

The neighborhood as a whole thus shows a wide heterogeneity, racially, religiously and economically. On the other hand, the social problems of sanitation, charity and assimilation, though not absent, do not appear in the acute form characteristic of the congested neighborhoods of the more recent immigrants. Conspicuously there are no ghettoes, the various foreign elements being distributed throughout the neighborhood. The conditions are more nearly like what one would expect in a section where the immigration problem was not the all engrossing question. Perhaps for this reason the educational agency proper for such a neighborhood would be typical of the ethnic school in a normal American urban community.

The Jewish element in the population shows within itself a heterogeneity as widely distributed as that in the general community. The total Jewish population within easy walking distance from the Institute numbers thirty-five thousand. For convenience in description it may be classified into four divisions. In the first division are those of the highest economic class who live in the Fifth Avenue district. These, however, are a small proportion, and perhaps should not be counted as a part of the neighborhood, for Fifth Avenue is rather a national than a municipal or local thoroughfare. Still, certain individuals in this population have taken an interest in the Central Jewish Institute, albeit from a communal rather than local point of view. The second and third divisions center around two prominent synagogues, the Congregation Kehillath Jeshurun, adjoining the Central Jewish Institute, and the Congregation Orach Chayim, on Lexington Avenue near 95th Street.

The most influential element in the work of the Central Jewish Institute is the group associated with the Kehillath Jeshurun synagogue. This group consists mainly of Russian Jews who hail from Lithuania and represent the first wave of Russian Jewish immigration of the 80's and 90's. These are carefully to be distinguished from the new Russian immigration which has a strong element of radicalism and Yiddishism. In contradistinction to the latter these Jews are of the bourgeoisie, well-to-do and distinctly conservative. In religion they are orthodox, which implies adherence to Jewish ceremonies and customs and an allegiance to Jewish life. Although most of this group arrived in America poor men and have acquired their wealth here, they come from families which were respected in the social life of the Eastern European ghetto, where learning was the distinguishing class mark. In many cases the rise to social position through wealth is merely a recuperation of status previously enjoyed by dint of reputation for learning. To these, of course, have been added others whose claim to be included in this community rests not upon similarity of nativity or of social class in the old country, but upon their economic status here together with their adherence to 'orthodoxy.' This entire group represents the highest economic class among the Russian Jewry of New York City.[1]

The third division is a community very similar to the foregoing group but consisting of German-Jews and centering about another

---

[1]Although the richer portion of this group has now moved to the west side of Central Park.

It is most interesting to note that the group has a certain amount of neighborhood community spirit within itself; families know each other, marriage takes place among them, and gossip easily spreads. This is unusual among Jewish communities, because in most sections of the city the Jewish population is so mobile that no neighborhood feeling can exist. It is the synagogue primarily which has promoted the community of spirit.

synagogue, namely the Orach Chayim.   The economic status of the
German-Jewish group is similar to the second group (i.e., of Russian
Jews just described), although these tend to be professional men and
commission merchants rather than manufacturers.   They represent
also an older stratum of neighborhood population and have been in
the country a longer time, their immigration dating from the period
prior to 1880.   This group also has a community spirit among its
members, but has tended to merge with the Russian Jewish group.
In spite of the feeling akin to a social class consciousness which
exists between Russian and German Jews, the two groups have been
drawn together in this neighborhood by their proximity, their similar
economic conditions and their stand on orthodoxy.[1]

These three groups live west of Lexington Avenue, which is the
residential district.   The fourth group will be found on the avenues
and streets east of Lexington Avenue.   They are more recent arrivals
consisting of small shopkeepers and workingmen.   Economically,
they range from those who make a living to the very poor.   In nativity they are Hungarian, Austrian and Polish Jews of the new immigration, though not perhaps of the latest tide.   Like most Jews who
come from Eastern Europe, they observe the dietary laws and attend
synagogue with greater or lesser frequency.   They are orthodox, if
we use this term to describe the social background and the type of life
rather than a creed.   In the former two groups orthodoxy has begun
to be crystallized into a convention.   It has become an issue, for the
Jews in these classes have had to resist the tendency toward the
Reform synagogue, a likely concomitant of elevation in economic and
social status.   With the Jew of the fourth group 'orthodoxy' is still
the natural mode of life.   This group rather than the former two
represents the ordinary everyday Jew that one has in mind in thinking of the Russian Jew.[2]

---

[1]Both synagogues are orthodox, aim at a decorous service, and favor English sermons.
[2]An element conspicuously lacking in this neighborhood is the more modern Russian
Jew, who had broken with the ghetto before he arrived and who already had been
influenced by the new forces of Russian life.   The Socialist of the distinct and easily
recognized Russian Jew type, the intellectual Hebraist-Zionist, and the Yiddishist-
Radical are all missing.   The neighborhood tends rather to lean toward conservatism
and is for a neighborhood of a considerable Jewish population unusually lacking in
"social movements."

These descriptions apply to the adult generation. To understand
the problem of the Central Jewish Institute it is necessary to have
some idea of the tendencies amongst those growing into manhood and
womanhood. As a matter of fact it was the anxiety for the coming
generation that brought the Central Jewish Institute into being.

The adolescents of the group described last present a good example
of the "half-baked second generation." They have become thoroughly "Americanized." They are a jolly crowd, know the batting
averages to a 'T', and support the musical comedies regularly. They
are adepts in "kidding," and their repartee, which is abundant,
can always be traced to the latest vaudeville shows. Gum chewing
is their distinguishing characteristic and they are very "padriodig,"
as they pronounce it. The better of these gather in "literary clubs"
which never have a literary program. The sessions of the club are
generally devoted to the business of preparing for the next dance or
minstrel show.

They know little of Jewish life, tending to associate it merely with
the ceremonies and especially with the prohibitions observed in the
home, the significances of which are very seldom, if ever, understood.
Their "Jewish culture" is limited to the ability to read the Hebrew
prayers mechanically without understanding the meaning of the text.
They are generally indifferent to, if not ashamed of, Jewish life.
Sometimes, when put to it, they assert their pride in being Jews,
the psychical compensation for their real self-depreciation. Having
gained a public school education and speaking English (with a New
York, not a foreign accent), they tend to regard themselves superior to their parents and everything associated with them. This
cocksure and "smart guy" attitude is carried over into their
general character. They have lost whatever culture was inherent
in the customs and institutions of their parents' traditional life, and
have substituted for it not a universal culture, or even an American
one, but the ways and ideas immediately surrounding them,—rag-
time and jazz band, baseball averages and, at the height, musical
comedy, together with an individualistic attitude acquired from the
bitter competitive industrial scheme into which they have been
thrown. The type described, it will be recognized, is not particularly

a Jewish type, but a well known product of the larger American city where the street corner, the movies, the baseball scores and musical comedy are the true educational influences for the adolescents of the economically poorer groups.

While this description would apply to an easily recognizable portion of the second generation, there is also a goodly percentage where the home influence has not completely broken down.   This would be true most often where the family had some social status in the past and where it has been able to meet the struggle for existence with some success.   In these cases, especially when the children have gone on through high school and college, the crudities in general personality are minimized.   As far as Jewish knowledge and Jewish loyalty are concerned, however, the same general conditions exist.   There are, indeed, instances when an unusually favorable family influence has been able to withstand the disintegrating environment or when the college Zionist or Menorah society has kindled a spark of loyalty to Jewish tradition in the vision of the ideal of a renascent Jewish cultural life.   But these are the exceptions, not the rule.

Among the well-to-do similar conditions prevail, except that a greater number have gone to college, and more often crudeness has been avoided.   Business and the professions ultimately absorb these and the attachment to Jewish life, if it continues, becomes quite formal.   Most often Jewishness for these is a matter of strange ceremonial, observed either from superstition, as a mark of respect for parents, or as the convention of the social set.   There are here, too, notable individual examples of sympathy with and intelligent devotion to Jewish life.

The prevailing characteristic among all groups, however, is the disintegration of the ethnic and religious culture in the second genera- tion.   Too often the process is not counterbalanced by an acquisition of general culture.   With a superficial knowledge of the socially approved language and conventions the younger members of the family tend to regard themselves as superior to their parents, espe- cially in those cases where in the fierce economic struggle the young people contribute to the support of the family.   They do not realize that their parents, apparently not knowing, may still be wiser and more cultured than they. For the old generation represents a tradition which embodies a long social experience, while the children are bereft of all but a very superficial outlook. Frequently, when as among the 'better' classes an attempt has been made to acquire the manners of the land, the lack of deep roots becomes apparent, and the phenomenon of affectation associated with *nouveau-riche* is often marked. No adequate agency is at hand to bridge the gap between the generations, to interpret the old tradition in terms of the new.

The work that led to the creation of the Central Jewish Institute was initiated among the members of the Kehillath Jeshurun Congregation, the synagogue of the well-to-do Russian Jewish group. Loyal to Judaism and anxious that their children should remain loyal, they found themselves at a loss when they saw their children drift away. Professor M. M. Kaplan, then the Rabbi of the congregation and principal of its religious school, had been continuously emphasizing the importance of Jewish education in the task of fostering Jewish life and the necessity of reorganizing Jewish school work with consideration of the surrounding social life. It was due to his influence that discussion arose in 1908 that culminated in the establishment of the Central Jewish Institute. This underlying motive is significant in that it marks a new era in Jewish institutional life. The earlier communal efforts had been conceived in a philanthropic spirit, as means for the betterment of others, Here it was the interest of their own children that the founders had in mind.[1]

A second important departure from the then current notions is the conception of what was meant by a Jewish School. Not only was it

---

[1] So strong was this point made that some interpreted this to mean an institution for their own use exclusively. Subsequently the most influential of this group moved to the other side of Central Park, and a new and very interesting institution, "The Jewish Center," was established by them. The Jewish Centre modernizes the old idea of the Synagogue as a "Meeting House," "House of Study," and "House of Prayer." It is planned as a palatial ten-story structure with complete facilities for educational and social work. It provides for club rooms, gymnasium, dining hall, classrooms, auditorium, etc., but the *synagogue* is at the centre of the entire conception. The conception is unique, for the synagogue is built right into the structure, as its central architectural feature. It is not a general public institution, but a clubhouse, so to speak, for the families of the members. It is an interesting experiment in modern reconstruction of the synagogue as a social centre. While strictly orthodox, it completely surpasses any Reform Temple in modernity of conception.

planned for adequate classroom instruction; the idea of 'school' was broadened to include auditorium, reading room, social room and gymnasium, to provide for recreational, social and general educational activities. Naturally the idea, being new, provoked opposition. In this center of 'orthodoxy' the close propinquity of shower bath and religious school seemed sacrilegious to some of the older members of the congregation. The differences were so violent that the large plan, which involved an expenditure hitherto unheard of with reference to Talmud Torah, might have fallen through had it not been for the aggressive personality of one of the leading spirits. Samuel I. Hyman, to whom is due the honor of being the founder and first president of the Central Jewish Institute, was himself a character indicative of a new attitude. Though born in America, he was doggedly loyal to orthodox Judaism. With his strict Jewish adherence he combined an intense loyalty to America, and believed wholeheartedly in the possibility of harmonizing the two forces. Seeing in the local educational need the possibility of contributing to the solution of a general Jewish problem, he determined that the Institute should be built on model lines so that it might become the prototype of the educational institution potent to preserve Jewish life in America. It was due to his tireless efforts that the building was erected without compromises. The cornerstone was laid in May, 1915, and activities began in the fall of 1916. From its very inception the Institute coöperated with the Bureau of Jewish Education of New York City.[1] Under its auspices a survey of the neighborhood was made, before activities were initiated, with the purpose of determining possibilities and character of work. This procedure of studying the district before beginning work symbolizes the new attitude of the Institute, the substitution of a plan consciously elaborated for haphazard and traditional methods.

Throughout the plan of work is found the realization that the new situation demands new methods. Nevertheless, at many points conditions had to be reckoned with. From the foregoing account may be gathered some of the circumstances which must be taken into

---

[1]For the scope and functions of the Bureau of Jewish Education, see Dushkin, *Jewish Education in New York City.*

consideration in gauging to what degree the Central Jewish Institute meets the ideal of the ethnic Community Center. In the description of the building and its activities which follows, it will be instructive to point out other instances where the Institute fails to fulfill ideal requirements. However, our main purpose is to present the general principles underlying the work, to show what types of activities are carried on, their purpose and emphasis.

Before entering upon his duties as Executive Director in 1917, the writer submitted a "Policy and Plan of Work" which the Trustees agreed should become the basis of the work. This statement can still serve very well as a concise outline of the plan.[1] Its main ideas were summarized in several paragraphs at the first annual meeting held in February, 1918. It may be interesting to state them here before proceeding to the detailed description of the work of the institution.

"The underlying idea of The Central Jewish Institue is 'Talmud Torah,' as is indicated by its 'sub-title. The preservation of Jewish spiritual life is the idea which gives point and purpose to all the activities of the institution.

"With all its strong insistence on a Jewish purpose, it nevertheless recognizes the need of adjusting to the conditions of American life and thought. The harmonization of Jewish purpose with American life is the institution's *raison d' être*.

"Insisting on an intensive course in Jewish subjects for the Talmud Torah, it nevertheless maintains that those who cannot be induced to enroll in the intensive work must not be entirely neglected; they must be reached through a scheme of extension education.

"In addition to specifically Jewish work, the Jewish center must carry on activities which make for the physical and social well-being of the people who live in the neighborhood. Health and good citizenship are a part of, and not opposed to, Judaism.

"Just as the activity of the Institute should not be limited to one aspect in the life of the individual, so, too, it should not be limited to one age in the population. The older brother and sister and the parents must be reached. Indeed, no member of the family is more important than the other. For the task is to bridge the gap between the generations, to integrate the family. The family is the cornerstone upon which rests the integrity and continuity of Jewish life.

"In fine, the Central Jewish Institute hopes to make a contribution to the solution of the problem of creating the educational institution that will be potent to preserve a vital Jewish life in America."

[1] The statement appeared in *The Jewish Teacher*, December, 1917, under title "The Community School Center."
The plan of work was initiated by the writer, but is now being carried on under the capable direction of Mr. A. P. Schoolman.

III

The Building

The structure is itself a vital part of the plan.   The Central Jewish Institute is a thoroughly fire-proof four story building, standing on a lot 60 x 100 feet.   It contains, in addition to ten classrooms, two kindergarten rooms, two social rooms, a sitting and reading room, an auditorium, gymnasium, kitchenette, and two roof-gardens, one adjoining the kindergarten room, the other on the top of the building. Such a combination of facilities has hitherto not been associated with the Talmud Torah.   In recent years the need of facilities for general work has begun to be recognized.   Talmud Torahs have included an assembly hall for lectures and for synagogue purposes.   One Talmud Torah has even added a gymnasium.   But the Central Jewish Institute is the first Jewish educational institution in New York City that has combined all facilities for social work with thoroughly adequate accommodation for school work.

Both from a practical and aesthetic point of view it sets a new standard.   It has made admirable use of its space and at the same time is undoubtedly the most beautiful structure in New York City devoted to school purposes among the Jews.   It has been done in exceptionally good taste and with an eye to comfort as well as to the needs of hard usage.   Two principles of primary importance for any community school center have been well illustrated.   The first is that of the *convertible unit*.   A room utilized for one purpose at one time may be converted to serve with equal adequacy other purposes when necessary.   Thus the auditorium may serve as lecture platform with cinematograph and stereoptican facilities, as a stage for dramatics, and as a synagogue.   What is meant is not only that the auditorium can be made to serve these various purposes, but that through change of fixtures and decorations it is actually *converted* from one type of room to the other.   So, too, the gymnasium, ordinarily used for calisthenics, athletic games and dances, can be converted into a lunch room and banquet hall.   A kitchenette and collapsible tables are at hand to make such a transition of usage convenient as well as possible.   The classrooms have been provided with movable, instead of stationary seats, and with additional closets, so that they are equally available for the regular school work in the afternoons—and for the clubs and organizations that meet in the evenings. So throughout the building the addition of many carefully planned details enhances greatly both the convenience and possibility for a variety of use.

The second principle observed was that of *organic relationship*. In many of the older institutions where numerous facilities have been provided no plan or purpose or underlying motive is felt. There is a shapelessness and ungainliness about the building that has led to the characterization of 'barns.' In the Central Jewish Institute a definite tone prevails and the unity of the whole institution impresses itself upon the visitor. It has also been carefully saved from assuming the institutional and barrack-like character that the public schools as well as many social centers have. The trees and ferns in front of the building, the flowerbeds in the windows, the furnishings in the library and social hall, all help to give a more genial and intimate impression. An effort has been made to illustrate that a community house, though primarily a school, ought to be more like a home than like a public asylum.

There is one direction, perhaps, in which the institution should have gone further. The Ethnic Community House, in its architecture and interior decorations, should be representative of the type of civilization which it is conceived of as furthering. Jewish buildings should, wherever possible, although built in harmony with the surroundings, utilize whenever possible Jewish motifs and designs. One should be able, in passing a Jewish Community House, to know what it is, just as one can recognize a Gothic church or a cathedral. For the present, in view of the fact that there is no developed original Jewish architecture, nothing more than the utilization of certain decorative designs can be hoped for. Something along this line has been done in designing the stage curtain and the pulpit and readers' desk in connection with the synagogue. More will need to be done through appropriate pictures, hangings and decorations. The underlying principle should be borne in mind that the embodiment of Jewish ideas in architecture and decoration is a cultural contribution and an educational influence.

The observation of these concepts, *variety of usage, organic relationship to give a unity of character, a warm and intimate rather than institutionalized atmosphere, and the unique character of the ethnic group embodied so far as possible in architecture and decorations,* is prerequisite to a full realization of any plan of work that may be laid out for ethnic community centers.

IV

CONTROL AND ADMINISTRATION

The responsibility is vested in a virtually self-perpetuating Board of Directors, consisting of thirty-five members.[1] The large size of the board is due, as in similar cases,[2] to the fact that in the past the main function of boards of Jewish schools has been to raise the funds necessary for the maintenance of the institution. The members were generally chosen either because of their large contributions or their ability to solicit funds from others. The directors in the Central Jewish Institute actively interested in the work number less than ten, and as soon as the financial difficulties shall have been adjusted the tendency will be to reduce the number of members on this board more nearly to the active workers.

It is important to note that the board is a lay body, responsible to itself alone; it is not subject to any clerical or other organization. Though the Institute is the outgrowth of the congregational school of the adjoining synagogue, the board is an entirely separate body. It includes a number of rabbis, but these enter as individuals with the same duties and functions as the lay members. The directors are drawn mainly from the second and third classes of the population described above, and represent the two synagogues, Kehillath Jeshurun and Orach Chayim. The Institute is an 'orthodox' institution; but this word is used in its general psychological and social

---

[1] In accordance with the constitution the board should consist of twenty-five members to be elected annually by the members contributing to the support of the institution. As in most Talmud Torahs, this institution is governed by custom, not by constitution.

[2] See A. M. Dushkin, *Jewish Education in New York City*, page 197 ff. Dr. Dushkin recommends a board of nine representing the parents, neighborhood and community at large. This is undoubtedly theoretically correct from the purely administrative point of view, but, as Dr. Dushkin recognizes, difficult to introduce under present conditions where adequate income is not assured.

meaning, rather than in any creedal sense; i. e., to indicate respect for tradition and for Jewish ceremonial practice and to point out that in the present transitional stage in which all forces are naturally making for change and disintegration the Institute sees its own task as one of conservation. Perhaps most of all the term 'orthodox' here indicates that the central interest comes from within Jewish life and has not been forced upon it from the outside. Neither the organization of the board nor its policy are parochial in spirit.

The independent and private form of organization is counterbalanced in actual practice by several unofficial checks. The policy of Jewish schools, generally speaking, is wholly dependent upon the wish of its directors or trustees. A number of influences, semi-official and unofficial, have become active in the work of the Central Jewish Institute that tend to make its control in reality communal, though in form it is private. The Institute no longer depends entirely upon the philanthropic efforts of its trustees. Together with other large Talmud Torahs, social and charitable institutions, it receives a large part of its income from the Federation of Jewish Philanthropic Societies of New York City.[1] Although the Federation is prohibited by its own laws from interfering with the internal policy of any institution, it serves nevertheless as a check upon communal work through its power to refuse admission to institutions and to determine upon the budgets of constituent societies.[2] In presenting its needs to the Federation the Central Jewish Institute acts, together with the other Talmud Torahs affiliated with the Federation, through the Board of Jewish School Aid, a voluntary organization representative of the Jewish schools and interested in the development of Jewish education. There are thus two communal checks: in distributing the funds the Federation must reckon with the needs of all the communal institu-

---

[1] The Federation is a central organization which collects and distributes the funds for one hundred and five of the largest Jewish communal institutions. The institutions affiliated with it may accept no contributions for current expenses from members; their membership must contribute to the Federation which pools the resources of these nstitutions. (See *Jewish Communal Register*).

[2] The Jewish schools were admitted only after a difficult struggle. The directors of the Federation, who conceive of social work as philanthropy, did not at first recognize educational work as coming within their scope. The Jewish schools, however, pointed out that the presence of a central organization attracting all the larger contributions preempted the field for them and prevented their obtaining support.—*The Jewish Teacher*, May, 1917.

tions and the Jewish schools must keep pace with the rest; second, each school must accommodate itself to the needs of the other schools.

There is a more direct force arising out of the income derived from self-supporting sources, the largest part of which consists of the tuition fees paid by the children who attend the Talmud Torah, as the intensive class work is called. During the year 1917–1918 an active Parents' Association was formed which is making itself felt in the work of the Institute. The plan is to give the parents official representation on the board. Especially will this be possible when a greater proportion of the funds come from the neighborhood sources.[1]

An additional unofficial influence is exerted by the workers and teachers of the institution through the Executive Director. Responsibility for carrying out the policy of the board has been centralized in the executive head, and the committee form of administration in which the various departments were directly responsible to committees of the board has been wholly eliminated.[2] The success of the work of the Institute has in great measure been made possible by adopting the centralized as against the decentralized method of administration. This form of organization has permitted the Executive Director to exert a guiding influence in the development of the work. Through the workers and teachers a number of educational influences are indirectly brought to bear upon the Institute. Among these are to be reckoned the Bureau of Jewish Education, the Hebrew Principals' Association, and the Jewish Teachers' Association. In addition, contact with the general secular educational influences is maintained through the professional interests of the workers. Coöperation with various civic bodies establishes also relationships with the general community at large.

The government of the Central Jewish Institute is thus responsive to a wide variety of influences and can in no sense be regarded as subject to the opinions of a small number of private individuals. In *form of organization*, however, the Institute is defective, for it will be recalled that the various influences make themselves felt through unofficial channels. Much now depends upon the good will and

---

[1]Since the above was written this idea has materialized; the president of the Parents' Association has been elected a member of the Board of Trustees.
[2]See A. M. Dushkin, *Jewish Education in New York City*, Part II, Chap. IV.

wisdom of the present Board of Trustees, and the strength of the Executive Director. If the neighborhood and communal forces were made regular and official, as well as occasional and voluntary, the government of the Central Jewish Institute would become truly representative of a democratic conception.

V

The Plan and Content of the Work

1. The Talmud Torah

The central activity of the Institute embodying the purpose for which it was established is the Talmud Torah. It is the emphasis upon this phase of its work which differentiates the Central Jewish Institute from the recreational and social settlements which may appear very similar to superficial observation. It is not alone that more time is given to the Jewish activities and that they occupy a larger place among the total activities. What is more important to bear in mind is that the Talmud Torah is the *central* activity and gives meaning and character to the whole institution. It is this differentiated purpose of the promotion of Jewish life that gives to the Central Jewish Institute its peculiar significance. Properly speaking, the work of Americanization done by the Educational Alliance is a state function, as is also the recreational work of the Y. M. H. A.'s. Such activities should be public, not sectarian. Many of these institutions are of great temporary benefit, and they will be necessary until the state has equally adequate facilities for such work. But it is in the study of particularly Jewish things that Jewish institutions must ultimately find their *raison d'être*.[1]

THE CURRICULUM

The curriculum, presented on pages 196–97, is partly a response to the wishes of the parents and partly the conception of those in charge of the school. It represents a modification of the traditional course to the needs of the child living in America. The discussion will bring out in the most important instances what is due to principle and what to the necessity of compromising with prevailing conceptions.

[1]See Chap. III especially pp. 100–106.

Year	Prayer Book	Hrs. per Wk.	Hrs. per Yr.	Hebrew Language and Literature	Hrs. per Wk.	Hrs. per Yr.	Biblical Literature (in Hebrew)	Hrs. per Wk.	Hrs. per Yr.
First	Mechanics of Reading and Translation of Simple Prayers and Blessings.	2½	120	Graded Course in Hebrew. Conversation, Reading, and the Elements of Composition.	3	144			
Second	Sabbath Service. Reading and Selections for Translation and Explanation.	1½	72		4	192			
Third	Weekday Services. (As above)	¾	36		2½	120	Pentateuch (Children's Edition).	3	144
Fourth	Holiday Services. (As above)	¾	36	Supervision of Home Reading. Grammar and Composition.	1¾	84	Former Prophets, selections from Psalms and Proverbs.	3	144
Fifth	Ethics of the Fathers. (As above)	¾	36	As above.	2½	120	Latter Prophets. (selections).	2½	108
Sixth	Review of Various Services.	¾	36	As above.	1¾	84	Latter Prophets (selections).	2¼	108
Total Hours			336			744			504

CURRICULUM

AGE OF ENTRANCE: 8

History	Hrs. per Wk.	Hrs. per Yr.	Customs, Ceremonies, Contemporaneous Life.	Hrs. per Wk.	Hrs. per Yr.	Singing	Hrs. per Wk.	Hrs. per Yr.	Total Hrs. per Wk.	Total Hrs. per Yr.
40 Jewish Heroes. (From Abraham to Herzl).	¾	36	Jews of Many Lands, Customs and Ceremonies of the Home.	¾	36	Melodies for Services in the Home. Folk Songs.	½	24	7½	360
Biblical History to the Destruction of the First Temple.	¾	36	As above	¾	36	As above and Synagogue Responses.	½	24	7½	360
Destruction of the First Temple to Arabic Period.	¾	36				As above.	½	24	7½	360
Arabic Period to Modern Times.	¾	36	The Jewish Calendar; The Synagogue.	¾	36	As above.	½	24	7½	360
History of the Jews in America.	1½	72				As above.	½	24	7½	360
Review. The Story of the Jewish People.	1½	72	The American Jewish Community and Its Problems.	¾	36	As above.	½	24	7½	360
		288			144			144		2160

Hebrew. Of the 2160 hours in the entire six-year schedule 1548 hours are devoted to Hebrew subjects: 744 are devoted to the Hebrew language and secular literature, 504 hours to the Sacred Literature which is read and taught in Hebrew, and 300 hours to the Hebrew Prayer Book. To those who regard the Jewish school as a religious school and who think of religion in terms of ethical and theological teachings, this condition of affairs may be surprising, all the more so when a further study of the curriculum does not reveal any special place for direct religious or ethical instruction. This can appear strange only when the nature of the Jewish group and what Western thought terms its religion are not understood. As we have already noted above, Judaism is a term like Hellenism, in which it is implied that the social heritage is the product of a definite national group. What makes the whole matter confusing is that while Hellenism finds its expression mainly in artistic and intellectual fields, Israel finds its highest national expression in social ethics and ethical religion. Judaism is a religious civilization. It will be noted that most of the "literature" would be called "religious literature." Even the selections in the secular literature would deal very often with matters of religious interest like the Jewish holidays or with Jewish ethics or Jewish history. The proportion of time under the subject of Hebrew devoted to belles lettres is very small. On the other hand, a Jewish school is never a place merely for the study of creed and ceremonies. The emphasis upon the study of Hebrew is the central characteristic of all traditional Jewish schools.

The so-called "natural method" has been adopted in the teaching of Hebrew. Competent authorities agree that this method is pedagogically superior in the teaching of foreign languages and its excellence in this respect would have sufficiently warranted the elimination of the older methods of translation, vocabulary building and drills in grammar. The introduction of the new method in Jewish schools has undoubtedly been influenced also by the development of the hope for national regeneration and by the growth of modern Hebrew literature. The use of Hebrew in conversation tends to make the pupil feel that the language is living and that the people still lives. It makes the ancient literature live again and opens the gateway to the modern literature and to the new life developing in Palestine. A knowledge of Hebrew gives the individual direct access to the means of a true understanding of the literary sources of Jewish spiritual life which are also the sources of many of the religious and moral conceptions of Europe.[1] The study of Hebrew, furthermore, is of supreme significance for the present and future of Jewish life. With the passing of Yiddish as the Ghetto breaks up, Hebrew alone can remain the distinguishing Jewish language. While the language of the country of citizenship must become for Jews their ordinary medium for intercourse, the community of All Israel must have its common language. Hebrew must serve as means of interchange of thought between the various Jewish communities of the world and between them and Palestine. The complete forgetting of a distinctive tongue will undoubtedly mean complete obliteration of the Jewish group. No Jewish community is ever known to have survived long after it had given up its distinctive mode of expression. Language and the thought of life seem inextricably bound up. Professor Schechter's dictum, "When the last word of Hebrew shall have been heard in our Synagogues, then, too, there shall be the last of Judaism," finds a deep echo in the Jewish consciousness.[2]

The Prayer Book. In the study of the Prayer Book we come upon a subject more distinctly a part of the religious phase of Jewish life. The aim of the course is to enable the pupils to read the liturgy (which, of course, is in Hebrew), to know the order of the various services, and to understand the most important passages. Religious services in both the home and the synagogue are such an integral part of Jewish social life that the teaching of the Prayer Book is traditionally considered the first step in any system of Jewish education.

Paradoxical as it may seem, this emphasis upon the teaching of prayers has proved a serious obstacle to the development of an effective curriculum of Jewish instruction.[3] The father through daily repetition of the prayers for many years has attained great skill in saying them off very rapidly, not realizing that his accomplishment

---

[1] See Chap. IV.
[2] Solomon Schechter, *The Problem of Religious Education in Seminary Addresses.*
[3] See Dushkin, *Jewish Education in New York City,* p. 350.

has been gained through practice outside of the school as well as through attendance in the 'cheder' (which was in his Eastern European home an all-day affair). He expects the Hebrew school, with its comparatively few hours, to reach an exacting standard of rapidity in reading. In America, where parents do not expect too much from their children in the matter of Jewish education, the ability to read Hebrew mechanically is often completely identified with Jewish education. In response to this demand a considerable portion of the time is devoted to the Prayer Book, in the first and second years, although its content is for the most part beyond the understanding of the child. In a properly ordered curriculum, this subject should be postponed until the higher grades. The difficulty of the Prayers, at this age, necessitates the use of the translation method instead of the more interesting and more effective 'natural' method adopted in the course in Hebrew and Literature.

It must be remembered in this discussion that the Hebrew Prayer Book, furthermore, is as much a body of literature as it is a collection of liturgy. It includes excerpts from the Bible and from Psalms and the portions of direct prayer are few. It is a service of the People of Israel to its God rather than a relationship of the individual to the deity. Nationalistic Jews, disclaiming the religious tie, might still study it as a literary expression of the national soul. Thus the most 'religious' of the subjects of the curriculum has a literary and national aspect, just as the cultural and literary aspect has a religious bent. It is necessary constantly to bear in mind the unitary character of the curriculum, so as not to fall into the artificial 'religious' and 'nationalistic' emphasis.

History and Customs and Institutions. The subjects under history, customs, ceremonies and contemporary Jewish life are taught in English and represent studies descriptive of Jewish life. The function of these subjects is to summarize, to put in proper perspective, to clarify the significance of the events, products and customs of Jewish life.

Several points are worthy of note in connection with the method followed in the teaching of history. Jewish history, even in the biblical periods, is treated as history, not as a groundwork for 'moral lessons.' Whatever 'ethical' or 'religious' training is given results from the study of the content, not from any direct attempt to inculcate moral maxims or catechetical solutions to problems. For this reason as well as because the Jewish people is conceived of as still living, Jewish history is brought up to modern times, and equal emphasis is given to biblical and post-biblical periods. The course includes, for instance, a year's work in the history of the Jews in the United States. Too often the teaching of 'history' in the Sunday schools has left the pupils with the notion that the Jewish people is a strange extinct people who lived in the dim past, governed by supernatural laws of development. It is perhaps not surprising that their conclusion would be that such a people could really have no place in our modern natural world. The organization as well as material and spirit of the course differs from the usual mode of procedure. The history is taught in a series of cycles. This permits the child who attends only one or two years to attain the perspective which is essential in the teaching of history. It permits also review of historical periods from various points of view as the child develops in age.

The course in social life includes both strictly religious ceremonies, social customs and much that falls in between. Beginning with a description of "Jews in many lands," the course proceeds to study those customs which identify Jews. This course also includes in the last year a survey of Jewish communal life in the United States, with an attempt to present in a simple way the problems which confront it.

The Jewish Sabbath and Holidays. The Sabbath and Holidays, though not appearing as separate subjects in the curriculum, form, nevertheless, an important element. These institutions which embody the most significant ideas in Jewish life are really a subject of study in all the courses in the curriculum. In addition to treating these holidays in numerous places both incidentally and directly, the course of study is interrupted for a lesson or two whenever a holiday appears on the calendar and time is devoted to a study of the particular holiday, from its various phases, liturgic, ceremonial, historical, etc. Special children's services are conducted on the Sabbath and on the Festivals, though not on the High Holy Days. As described below, in addition extra-curricular activities, entertainments and plays are conducted for the neighborhood to mark the festivals.

AIMS OF THE CURRICULUM

The aims of the curriculum of the Talmud Torah may be summarized as follows:

1. To give a knowledge of the Hebrew language.
   a. To open up for direct appreciation the storehouse of classic (Bible, etc.) and modern Hebrew literature.
   b. To teach its peculiarly significant concepts which deal with social and religious ideals.
   c. To form a bond of union with the Jewish past and the Jewish present in other lands, especially with the new life in Palestine.
2. To transmit the significant cultural, religious, and social heritage of the Jewish people through a knowledge of its history, literature, customs, and religious practices.
3. To bind the child in loyalty to the Jewish People so that he may strive for a continuous development of its ideal—cultural, social, religious—aspirations.
4. To give some notion of the general problems facing the Jewish People in its desire to perpetuate itself as a free society and the particular problems involved in the task of adjustment to life in America.

In short, the work of the Talmud Torah consists in converting the physical Jew, who is so by birth, into a spiritual Jew, who remains so by reason of the ideal significance of Jewish life.

THE SCHEDULE

The most serious administrative problem of the Talmud Torah is to organize its work properly within the limited number of hours at its disposal. As the many references have already made clear, the Talmud Torah is a complementary weekday school, i.e., sessions are conducted afternoons and Sundays so as not to conflict with public school hours. This gives rise to two difficulties. The rich curriculum must be taught in a minimum number of hours, so as not to

encroach unduly upon the child's study and play time. In the second
place each teacher must have sufficient hours of instruction to enable
him to earn a livelihood. Only professionally trained teachers are
qualified to teach in the Talmud Torahs. The standard of scholarship is far beyond what would be expected of a teacher in the public
schools. Full time positions require from twenty to twenty-four
hours of service on the part of the teacher.[1] The necessity of crowd-
ing more than twenty hours into the afternoons of Monday, Tuesday,
Wednesday and Thursday[2] and on Sunday mornings has forced a
schedule upon the Talmud Torah which requires attendance for some
of the pupils at late hours; most of the Talmud Torahs are conducted
up to 8 P. M. and some even as late as 9 P. M.

The schedule adopted at the Central Jewish Institute endeavors to
eliminate this condition as well as to arrange the hours in number
and distribution so as not to interfere unduly with the free time of the
child. Each teacher has two classes and each class about eight hours
per week (inclusive of auditorium session).

The sessions are conducted from 4 to 6 P. M., on Mondays, Tues-
days, Wednesdays, Thursdays; on Saturdays from 2 to 5 P. M. and
Sundays, 9 A. M. to 12.30 A. M. The schedule would run as follows:

Monday 4–6	Tuesday 4–6	Wednesday 4–6	Thursday 4–6
Class A	Class B	Class A	Class B

Saturday	Sunday
Class A 2–3:30	Class A 9–10:30
Sabbath Services 3:30–4:30	School Assembly 10:30–11
Class B 4–6	Class B 11–12:30

The improvement in time distribution, it will be seen, is due to the
reduction of the number of sessions per teacher with a consequent
reduction of the total number of hours from 20 to 16, which must be
compressed into hours left free from public school, and to the introduction of Saturday as a school day. Although in the traditional
Talmud Torah, Saturday is not used as a school day, it is not in dis-
accord with Jewish thought to 'learn' on the Sabbath. The freedom
from public school lessons and the opportunity of conducting services

[1]The average number of hours of instruction per week per class in the Talmud Torahs
is about eight, although many classes receive as many as 10 hours and occasionally
even more.
[2]Friday afternoon is too close to the Jewish Sabbath which begins on Friday evening.

combine to make Saturday valuable as a day of study. The new
schedule, which permits the child to have three afternoons free from
school work and on the other days keeps the children only until six, is
excellent in comparison with the old schedules followed in the Talmud
Torahs. Nevertheless, it still presents two difficulties. The children
must attend school for two hours additional to the public school on
two days a week and the long school day is not wholly eliminated.[1]

In the second place, even this scheme is hardly feasible for the
average Talmud Torah. The reduction in the number of sessions
and total hours allotted to each teacher increases the per capita cost
of teaching over 50 per cent. For this reason the Central Jewish
Institute, too, may be forced much against its will to adopt a schedule which will keep the school open till 7 P. M.

The difficulties involved in the schedule cannot be ultimately
solved without a recognition on the part of the state schools that
sufficient time must be left from the school day for such private
agencies as are represented by the ethnic schools. The Gary scheme
has recognized the validity of the principle of correlation, but the
particular schedule suggested would have been even worse, so far as
Jewish schools are concerned, than the present scheme.[2] As conditions
are to-day the ethnic schools are placed under a handicap so difficult
as to be almost prohibitory and some have been led to propose separate schools for the ethnic and religious groups which will give a
fairer distribution of time between secular and other subjects. In
fact, the whole argument of Jewish parochial schools is based on this
question of distribution of time. It is seen here how failure on the
part of the state to reckon with what may be considered the justifiable
demands of a group may force the group into an equally unjustifiable
position.

The French system where the children are excused on Thursdays for
religious instruction offers an example of correlation between public
and other education. Under the prevailing conditions in New York
City, if the Jewish children who wish to attend Hebrew schools were
excused two afternoons during the week, a schedule could be worked

---

[1]The younger children have only one hour sessions on the public school days, but
come four times, Monday, Tuesday, Wednesday, Thursday instead of two.
[2]See Chap. V, pp. 171-2.

out which would offer a satisfactory solution. Such a suggestion seems Utopian at present. The various ethnic and religious bodies are not sufficiently conscious of the importance of education for the retention of the group identity; nor are those who do realize this fact at one in the acceptance of a weekday school as a solution. With such lack of organization of the ethnic and religious viewpoint no forceful demand can be made upon the schools of the state. Furthermore, the prevailing spirit among public school leaders would perhaps not favor such a plan. While the minority ethnic groups are expected on every occasion to adjust themselves in line with reasonable demands of the state, it is questionable whether the state is yet amenable to the virtue of *noblesse oblige* in such matters. The essential theoretical point in reference to the schedule is that the argument long carried on between Church and State rights in education must receive its solution in a denial of exclusive monopoly for either the one or the other and in the acceptance of a conception of sovereignty limited by the need of mutual consideration.

To what degree each should modify its present plan is no endless academic question. The debatable ground is very narrow. Few, if any, of those granting the principle of a double system would encroach very much on the present allotment of time to the state schools. The great majority of Jews would be satisfied with an educational scheme that devoted eight hours a week to Jewish studies. Utilizing Saturday and Sunday, this would mean that the highest demand of by far the largest percentage of Jews would be satisfied with a schedule that would excuse the child from public school about four or five hours a week. Undoubtedly this would not interfere with the good or rights of the state; and, were the public educational mind ready for such a conception, there would be no real obstacle to the attainment of such a solution. The real difficulty is the profound, if unconscious, belief in the exclusive sovereignty of the state.

2. JEWISH EXTENSION EDUCATION

The intensive curriculum of the Talmud Torah is a development from the traditional course of Jewish study, as the name Talmud Torah already implies. The necessity of present circumstances and modern conditions have entered to modify both content and method;

but in the main the basic elements, the central position of book learning and classroom method, are still the distinguishing characteristics. Although the variety of conditions has led to the development of several types of curricula, these basic elements are always repeated.

In recent years it has become recognized that this single type of intensive Jewish instruction for all is not adequate for the conditions confronting Jewish life in America. In the old centers of Jewish life the traditional custom of giving boys an intensive Jewish literary training had a strong hold upon the masses and practically all boys were sent to a 'cheder'. Those who could, assimilated the difficult course of study. Those who could not, were, nevertheless, not deprived of Jewish influence. The Jewish school in the Ghetto, though much more intensive than the Talmud Torah in America (it was an all day school), was but one element in the Jewish education of the child. The home and the whole social environment, language and social intercourse were Jewish and there was no active divergent culture to lessen the influence they exerted. Even the girls who seldom went to school received through the home and through participation in Jewish life an education adequate to their Jewish responsibilities. The transition to conditions of life in America has completely changed the situation through the elimination of these spontaneous indirect educational influences. In a large and heterogeneous Jewish population the pressure formerly exercised by social opinion in the well-organized Jewish communities in Eastern European countries is no longer felt. The emphasis which the struggling immigrant must place upon the economic aspect of his life, the disintegrating influence of new and diverging ideas, the presence of the public school usurping most of the child's time, together with the extra burden of an additional tuition fee in the face of apparently free public schools, are all factors which deter many from sending their children to intensive Jewish schools. Only twenty-five per cent of the Jewish children of school age attend Hebrew schools at any one time. The problem thus arises to develop some system of extension education with small per capita cost, which would not take too much of the child's time but which would give some modicum of Jewish education to those who for one reason or another cannot or do not wish to attend the intensive work of the Talmud Torah.

For adolescents there is no traditional scheme to take the place of the educational influence of the general social environment. For the young people intensive classroom work is no solution at all except for the very few. Even in public education the comparatively small number that attend the high schools are motivated in great part by an ultimate vocational aim. It is not to be expected that a great number of young people will after a day's work or after high school hours, with the difficult program of 'home work,' devote themselves to Jewish studies which have no 'practical' application. The absence of any Jewish educational scheme for adolescents suitable to conditions in America presents a crucial problem in the task of the perpetuation of Jewish life in this country. In this critical period of questioning and doubt, when many new desires, interests and loyalties are awakened, the Jewish loyalty involving some spiritual vision and kept at times only through personal sacrifices, becomes very difficult to retain. Without providing some educational scheme it becomes absurd to expect the Jewish youth not to drift away, with the consequent disintegration of Jewish life.

The parents also no longer have the same opportunities for continuing their Jewish life through participation. For them, too, is needed some agency to acquaint them with the new problems arising out of the changed conditions of life. In short, the new situation, that of attempting to live a Jewish life outside of the confines of the ghetto, has taken from Jewish life the spontaneous and natural influences of a permeating Jewish social life and has given rise to the necessity of creating some scheme of direct education for the masses.

It is evident that no classroom work can combat with these problems. There have developed in recent years a number of plans of Jewish extension education, especially in reference to the problem of the children. The most comprehensive of these is the extension work planned for children and young people by the Bureau of Jewish Education known as the Circle of Jewish Children and the League of the Jewish Youth. The plan of extension education carried on in the Central Jewish Institute in the work with children and young people follows these general schemes. In the work with the parents current ideas of Parents' Associations have offered the suggestions.

A full description of the extension work is beyond the scope of our purpose. The following brief analysis will give an idea of the lines of work. Schedules of regular activities, calendars of seasonal events and several illustrative programs are presented from which a more complete picture may be drawn.

The Circle of Jewish Children. The work of the Circle of Jewish Children is carried on through mass activities centering about the celebration of the Jewish Festivals and through supervised club work correlated with the festival celebrations. The plan differs from similar schemes of mass and club activities in two important ways. In the first place, an attempt is made to reach the same child through a number of celebrations and record is kept on a cumulative record card of the activities in which each member has participated. In the second place, the activities compose a regular curriculum of studies carefully planned to make the greatest use of the limited time.

The organization of members is controlled through the children attending the Talmud Torah. Leaders are selected from among the brightest and most active pupils. Each leader then finds ten playmates in the neighborhood and arranges them into a group. These become members of the Circle by signifying their desire to join and receiving a button and certificate. By selecting the leaders with reference to the block upon which they live, it is possible through this scheme of organization to cover an entire neighborhood. The leaders themselves form a club or council where they receive instruction and training in the proper performance of their duties.

The leader thus serves as the agent between the school and the unaffiliated child. Whenever a holiday celebration takes place, each leader receives ten tickets for distribution among the members of his or her group. Likewise the holiday story pamphlets, childrens' newspaper, ceremonial toys and whatever material of instruction the Circle provides are distributed through the leaders. In the same way, if a member wishes to join a club or a class in the Hebrew school, the leader directs to the proper channel. The leader thus forms an inexpensive and effective means of bringing the extension activities of the Institute within the reach of the many children of the neighborhood who do not attend Hebrew schools.

THE CIRCLE OF JEWISH CHILDREN

Office open daily—4 to 6 P. M.—Room A
Sunday—10 A. M.—12 M.

Senior Clubs are open to boys and girls between the ages of 11 and 13.
Junior Clubs are open to boys and girls between the ages of 7 and 10.

SCHEDULE OF ACTIVITIES

FESTIVAL CLUBS

CHOIR
Senior Girls	Thursday	5 P. M.	Auditorium
Senior Boys	Thursday	6 P. M.	Auditorium

DANCING
Senior Girls	Tuesday	5 P. M.	Gymnasium

DRAMATIC
Senior Boys	Sunday	3 P. M.	Room D

DANCING
Junior	Monday	4 P. M.	Gymnasium

DRAMATIC
Senior Boys	Sunday	1 P. M.	Room C
Senior Girls	Sunday	2 P. M.	Room A

BEZALLEL CLUB
Senior Boys	Sunday	1 P. M.	Room B

MACCABEAN SQUAD
Senior Girls	Monday	6 P. M.	Gymnasium
Senior Boys	Thursday	6 P. M.	Gymnasium

ORCHESTRA
Senior	Sunday	4 P. M.	Room B

RED MOGEN DOVID
Senior Girls	Wednesday	4 P. M.	Room B

OUTDOOR
Senior Boys	Tuesday	3.30 P. M.	Park

SCRAP BOOK
Junior Boys and Girls	Tuesday	4.30 P. M.	Room B

SEWING
Senior Girls	Thursday	4 P. M.	Room B

REPORTERS' CLUB
Junior Boys and Girls	Monday	7 P. M.	Room C

STORY HOURS
Boys and Girls	Monday	5–6 P. M.	Room C
	Thursday	4–5 P. M.	Room C

LEADERS' CONFERENCES
	Monday	4–5 P. M.	Room A
	Thursday	5–6 P. M.	Room A

READING AND STUDY   Open Daily   Room C

GAMES   Open Daily   Room D

The "Circle Bulletin" appears Sunday 9 A. M.

(SAMPLE SCHEDULE OF REGULAR ACTIVITIES FROM PROGRAM OF 1919)

The League of the Jewish Youth.   The plan of work for the young people resembles in general outline the work of the Circle of Jewish Children.   However, the League of the Jewish Youth is conceived of as coördinate in extent with the Jewish community of the city and each branch is regarded as one district.   In the Circle the local district is the unit of active work although here, too, there is coördination between various branches and inter-branch activities.   The organization of the older group is replete with symbolic significance and with historical reminiscences.   Each district is a Galil (גליל); each Galil is divided into Tribes (שבטים); each Tribe into Households (משפחות), etc., and various forms of initiation ceremonies exist for the Junior, Intermediate and Senior members.   Naturally much more initiative is permitted the young people and to a greater extent they conduct their own activities.   In addition to holiday celebrations, literature, training groups for 'organizers' and forum for discussion of Jewish and civic questions, the young people are given opportunity to participate in communal efforts, both Jewish and civic.   Thus the League has been utilized in drives for Federation members, Kehillah, Relief, Restoration Funds, Liberty Loan and Red Cross.   While dealing mainly with large numbers, the organization is so planned that through a series of concentric groups of varying sizes, organizers' councils, local councils, city council, inner council, etc., the elders, as the directors and supervisors are called, can come in close personal contact with the leading spirits among the young people to guide them and select for more intensive work those capable of leadership.

The Parents' Association.   No plan of education is complete which does not include the parent.   Especially is this true in Jewish life, where the family is the keystone of the whole communal structure.   The problem of bridging the gap between the generations cannot be solved without the parent.   Not only is it necessary to arouse interest in the problem of Jewish education.   Of equal importance is the problem of bringing the parents nearer to their children through teaching them the language of the new land and interesting them in the general problems of the civic community.   To deal with this aspect of the work a Parents' Association has been formed which

LEAGUE OF THE JEWISH YOUTH

Office open daily (except Friday) from 8 to 10 P. M.—Room C.

Senior activities are open to members between the ages of 18 and 21,
Intermediate activities are open to members between the ages of 15 and 17.
Junior activities are open to members between the ages of 13 and 15.

SCHEDULE OF ACTIVITIES

FESTIVAL CLUBS

CHOIR			
Senior	Thursday	8.30 to 10 P. M.	Room B
Intermediate	Thursday	7.30 to 8.30 P. M.	Room B
DRAMATIC			
Senior	Sunday	8 to 10 P. M.	Room D
Intermediate	Sunday	8 to 10 P. M.	Room A
Junior	Sunday	4 to 6 P. M.	Room D
ORCHESTRA	Sunday	8 to 10 P. M.	Room B

INTERPRETATIVE DANCING	Wednesday	7.30 to 9 P. M.	Gymnasium
POSTER CLUB	Wednesday	8 to 10 P. M.	Room B
ENTERTAINMENT AND DANCE	Alternate Sun.	2.30 P. M.	Gymnasium

ORGANIZERS' TRAINING GROUPS

Junior Girls	Alternate Wed.	7 to 8.30 P. M.	Room E
Junior Boys	Tuesday	7 to 8.30 P. M.	Room E
Intermediate Boys	Tuesday	8 to 9.30 P. M.	Room E
Intermediate Girls	Wednesday	8 to 9:30 P. M.	Room F
Senior	Alternate Wed.	7 to 8.30 P. M.	Room E

LOCAL CABINET MEETING	Saturday	8 to 10 P. M.	Room E
CITY CABINET MEETING	2d Saturday	8 to 10 P M.	Room E
EDITORIAL BOARD—HED HA-GALIL	1st & 3d Sat.	8 to 10 P. M.	Room E
ELDERS' TRAINING GROUP	1st and 3d Sun.	8 to 10 P. M.	Social Rooms
JEWISH FORUM	Friday Evening		Social Rooms

"Hed Ha-Galil"—Bulletin of the L. J. Y. A. appears on the 15th of each month.

(SAMPLE SCHEDULE OF REGULAR ACTIVITIES FROM PROGRAM OF 1918) begins with the natural interest that the parents have in the work of their children and leads out into Jewish communal and general civic activities of concern to the parents themselves. Monthly meetings are held for the discussion of the problems of the school and the questions of wider Jewish and civic interest. On bi-weekly occasions, Sunday afternoons, the parents of the children of a selected class observe model lessons and discuss the work of their own children with teachers and principal. These meetings have their social aspect and the parents act as hosts. On these as well as on other social occasions the mothers contribute cakes of their own baking, mix the punch, etc. A cooking class is led by one of the parents who has a good knowledge of Jewish cooking and understands something of the elements of dietetics and correct form of table service. A study circle in Jewish subjects is carried on weekly. Furthermore, through the Association the parents are brought in contact with the general activities such as classes for English to foreigners, public lectures, Red Cross work, etc. Pains are taken to make the parents feel at home in the building. A room has been appropriately furnished as the meeting place for the parents and a "social evening" is conducted once a week, the parents taking turns in acting as hosts. All of the activities are conducted by the Parents' Association, the institution assisting with the plans and subsidizing certain of the activities. These activities generally involve only comparatively small numbers. The large numbers of parents are reached through activities centering about the Holy Days and Festivals. The parents conduct their own services on the High Holy Days in the auditorium of the Institute. In addition every Festival is celebrated through some appropriate entertainment as in the case of the children's and youths' organizations.

Each age, then, has its separate organization, its festival celebrations and its special reading and meeting room. All the work, however, is connected by the organic purpose of the Institute, and there are occasions when the different ages are brought together. The Institute regards the family, not the individual, as the pupil. The attempt always is to reach the several members of the same family rather than to scatter energy amongst single individuals. One of the main principles upon which the Central Jewish Institute bases its work is the belief that only by dealing with the family as a whole can the integrity of Jewish life be preserved.

Jewish Holiday Celebrations. The Festival celebrations may be regarded as the nucleus of the extension curriculum. The work of many of the clubs in the Circle and in the League consists of preparing for them and much of the work of the Parents' Association centers about the Jewish holidays.

The holiday celebration is conceived of as a unit, but separate entertainments are conducted for children, the young people, and parents. In the entertainment of the Circle of Jewish Children, two performances are generally given, one for the older children and one for the younger. In these entertainments, the children who attend the School and the members of the Circle are brought together. Every number on the program is designed to bring out some significant aspect of the holiday. The ceremonial, historical and ethical significances are each treated either directly or indirectly. The play, tableau, illustrated lecture, and song are utilized. Usually the entire assembly is taught a holiday song, and pamphlets telling the story of the holidays are distributed. While most of the program is rendered in English, some Yiddish and Hebrew is introduced, especially in songs and in recitations.

The holiday program of the League is similar in scope. The chairman is generally the president of the branch of the League of the Jewish Youth. Addresses both by one of the young people and by an 'elder' of the community are a feature.

The Parents' Evening is made up of selections from the program of the League and the Circle. In addition, a parent and a member from the community at large deliver addresses on some timely topic or Jewish community problem. One of these addresses is always in Yiddish. An officer of the Parents' Association acts as chairman, and the parents themselves act as ushers.

In the entertainments for the young people and the parents programs are generally printed which, in addition to giving the arrangement of the program, also bear some educational message. The history or significance of the holiday is brought out and correlated with some event of civic or current Jewish interest.

CIRCLE OF JEWISH CHILDREN ENTERTAINMENTS

SUNDAY, DECEMBER 1, AT 10 A. M., *for* JUNIORS
MONDAY, DECEMBER 2, AT 4 P. M., *for* SENIORS

———

PROGRAM

1. AMERICA ....*Audience*
2. CHAIRMAN'S REMARKS......................*Miss Leah Konowitz, Chairman*
3. LIGHTING OF THE CANDLES......................*A member of the T. T. Choir*
   Haneros Halalu.....................................*Talmud Torah Choir*
   Mo'oz Tzur
4. RECITATION: Judas Maccabeus.........*A member of the Junior Dramatic Club*
5. CHANUKAH DANCE...*Dancing Class*
6. RECITATION: Ten little boys...........................*Jr. Dramatic Club*
7. MASS SINGING.......................................*Choir and Audience*
   Circle Song
   Auf'n Pripitchik
8. A CHANUKAH STORY...............................*Mr. Mordecai M. Soltes*
9. THE MOTHER OF MARTYRS (A one act play)................*Sr. Dramatic Club*
10. HATIKVAH ....*Audience*

(FROM CHANUKAH PROGRAM 1918)

———

PARENTS' ENTERTAINMENT

SATURDAY, May 18th, 1918, at 8.30 P. M.

———

PROGRAM

1. THE STAR-SPANGLED BANNER....................................*Audience*
2. INTRODUCTORY REMARKS..................*Dr. Simon Tannenbaum, Chairman*
3. "DOS LIED VON BROT".................*Choir, The Circle of Jewish Children*
4. RECITATION: El Hatsipor—*Bialik* ....*Milton Jacobs*
5. SHEVUOTH DANCE....................................*Junior Dancing Club*
6. ADDRESS: The League of the Jewish Youth.............*Emanuel Hirshberger*
7. "PAGEANT OF OLD ISRAEL"................*Choir, The Circle of Jewish Children*
8. RECITATION: "Zamd und Shtern" ....*Adolph Tannenbaum*
9. PLAY: "Ruth"...............*Dramatic Club, The League of the Jewish Youth*
10. HATIKVAH........ ....*Audience*

(FROM SHEVUOTH PROGRAM 1918)

THE LEAGUE OF THE JEWISH YOUTH
YORKVILLE GALIL

PROGRAM

1. THE NATIONAL ANTHEMS OF THE ALLIES........................*C. J. I. Choir*
America, Rule Brittania, The Marseillaise, Hatikvah.
2. RECITATION: "Peace" (Isaiah, Ch. II, vs. 2–5).................*Rose Goldman*
3. SHOLOM ALEICHEM...*C. J. I. Choir*
4. CHAIRMAN'S REMARKS.........*George Hyman, President Yorkville Galil L. J. Y.*
5. LIGHTING OF THE CHANUKAH LIGHTS....................*Simon Yudelowsky*
Haneros Halalu
Mo'oz Tzur...*C. J. I. Choir*
6. TABLEAUX
   a. Mattathias
      RECITATION ....*Rose Goldman*
      "ALL WHO ARE FAITHFUL FOLLOW ME"
      Cast of Characters, etc.

   b. Battle of Beth Horon
      RECITATION ....*Emanuel Hirshberger*
      "LET OUR WATCHWORD BE THE HELP OF GOD"
      Cast of Characters, etc.

7. VOCAL SOLO.......................................*Miss Jennie Friedman*
"Oi Ihr Kleineke Lichtelach"
Words by Morris Rosenfeld; Music by Miss Sadie Cheifetz
8. THE DANCE OF THE CANDLES....................*Downtown Galil, L. J. Y. A.*
9. CHANUKAH, OY CHANUKAH..............................*C. J. I. Choir*
10. HANNAH (A one act play)......................*Dramatic Club, C. J. I.*
Place: Throne Room in Palace of Antiochus, King of Syria.
Time: In the Days of the Maccabees.
Cast of Characters, etc.
11. MASS SINGING...................................*C. J. I. Choir, Audience*
"HEAR THE VOICE OF ISRAEL'S ELDERS"
12. ADDRESS...*Mr. Isaac B. Berkson*
13. HATIKVAH ....*Audience*

(FROM CHANUKAH FESTIVAL 1918)

American Holiday Celebrations. Just as the work in the Talmud Torah is correlated with reference to Jewish life in America, so, too, the festival celebrations are correlated with American ideas and with current events. In addition to these references to American life in distinctly Jewish festivals, an attempt has been made to celebrate the American holidays as the Jewish holidays are celebrated, i.e., with the purpose of bringing out their spiritual significance.

The first of these was the celebration of "Lincoln Evening" in 1918, the program of which is presented here. American folk songs were utilized in the same way that the Jewish folk songs are used in the Jewish Festivals. The address of the chairman dealt with the growing Americanism, as illustrated in quotations from significant American documents. The concluding number was an address on Lincoln based on Professor Schechter's masterly essay, interpreting the character of Lincoln with added richness through the Jewish apperceptive mass. As an American holiday celebration the program presented undoubtedly valuable elements, in its dignity and seriousness of the conception of Americanism.

This type of program illustrates a principle not sufficiently grasped by the current notions in Americanization programs. The American holidays can assume untold meaning to the immigrant when approached from his own apperceptive mass and through the ideals with which he is acquainted in his own culture. Such celebrations as these give the immigrant a real kinship with the ideals underlying American life. In a similar manner, Washington's birthday, Thanksgiving, and Columbus Day have been celebrated with appropriate programs.

3. SOCIAL, CIVIC AND GENERAL ACTIVITIES

In addition to the specific purpose of conducting definitely Jewish educational activities the Central Jewish Institute also serves as a general social centre, welcoming every activity which promotes the physical, social and civic well-being of the community. The types of work carried on under this head of general activities are varied and resemble the recreational and educational activities usually carried

What is Americanism and what does it demand of us?

Can it demand that we deny who we are? Is it possible that it should ask us to become estranged from our fathers and mothers? Shall it ask us to forget the People from whom we are sprung?

No! For Americanism is something positive, not negative; it demands a loyalty, not a disloyalty.

America demands that we give to it what is finest and most profound in our People's life. What these things are we have sought to inscribe on the emblem of our League. "Torah, Avodah, Gemiluth Hasodim," symbolize for us all of those spiritual ideals and that spirit of service which we have struggled to develop throughout the forty centuries of our history,

But in no less degree does America demand that we also take from it what is finest and most profound in its own life. And we are gathered here tonight for just this purpose—to gain a little deeper insight into the great things for which America stands.

This, then, is the confession of faith of our League of the Jewish Youth.

Not by negation and neglect of our Jewish souls, but by contributing what is finest in us to America and by taking the finest in America unto ourselves can we become loyal to America.

PROGRAM

1. STAR SPANGLED BANNER......................................*Audience*

2. OUR CONCEPTION OF AMERICANISM
    The League of the Jewish Youth, recited by.................*Rose Goldman*

3. INTRODUCTION OF THE CHAIRMAN....*Daniel Cogan, Pres. Inter-Club Council*

4. INTRODUCTORY ADDRESS............................*Abraham A. Silberberg*
    Chairman, Social Activities Committee

5. VIOLIN SOLO CONCERTO No. 2.................................*Leonard*
    PHILIP GELLER

6. RECITATION: "The Jesters Recantation"...................*Mr. Philip Adler*

7. VOCAL SOLO { Swanee River
    Old Black Joe............................*Miss Rose Rabbach*
    Comin' Thru the Rye

8. ADDRESS: "A Jewish Conception of Lincoln"............*Rabbi Jacob Kohn*

9. HATIKVAH ....*Audience*
    MISS SADIE CHEIFETZ AT THE PIANO

10. DANCING

(FROM LINCOLN PROGRAM 1918)

This little hut was the cradle of one of the great sons of men, a man of singular, delightful, vital genius, who presently emerged upon the *great stage of the nation's history, gaunt, shy, ungainly, but dominant and majestic; a natural ruler of men, himself inevitably the central figure of the great plot.*

No man can explain this, but every man can see how it demonstrates the vigor of democracy, where every door is open, in every hamlet and country side, in city and wilderness alike, for the ruler to emerge when he will and claim his leadership in the free life. Such are the authentic proofs of the validity of democracy.

Lincoln, like the rest of us, was put through the discipline of the world—a very rough and exacting discipline for every man who would know what he is about in the midst of the world's affairs; but his spirit got only its schooling there. It did not derive its character from the experiences which brought it to its full revelation. The test of every American must always be, not where he is, but what he is. That also, is the essence of democracy, and is the moral of which this place is most gravely expressive. —PRESIDENT WOODROW WILSON's address at Hodgenville, Ky., accepting birthplace of Abraham Lincoln as a gift to the Nation.

1787

We, the People of the United States, in order to form a more perfect union, establish justice, insure domestic tranquility, provide for the common defense, promote the general welfare, and secure the blessings of liberty for ourselves and our posterity, do ordain and establish this constitution for the United States of America.

PREAMBLE OF THE CONSTITUTION OF THE UNITED STATES.

1823

The occasion has been judged proper for asserting, as a principle in which the rights and interests of the United States are involved, that the American continents by the free and independent condition which they have assumed and maintain, are henceforth, not to be considered as subjects for future colonization by any European powers.

We owe it, therefore, to candor and to the amicable relations existing between the United States and those Powers, to declare, that we should consider any attempt on their part to extend their system of government to any portion of this hemisphere, as dangerous to our peace and safety.

JAMES MONROE: *Message to Congress, December 2, 1823.*

1858

"A house divided against itself cannot stand." I believe this government cannot endure permanently half slave and half free. I do not expect the Union to be dissolved. I do not expect the house to fall—but I do expect it will cease to be divided. It will become all one thing, or all the other.

ABRAHAM LINCOLN: *From speech delivered at Springfield, Ill., June 16, 1858.*

1917

We are glad, now that we see the facts with no veil of fake pretense about them, to fight thus for the ultimate peace of the world and for the liberation of its peoples, the German people included: for the rights of nations, great and small, and the privilege of men everywhere, to choose their way of life and obedience. The world must be made safe for democracy. Its peace must be planted upon the tested foundations of political liberty. We have no selfish ends to serve. We desire no conquest, no dominion. We seek no indemnities for ourselves, no material compensation for the sacrifices we shall freely make. We are but one of champions of the rights of mankind. We shall be satisfied when these rights have been made secure as the faith and the freedom of nations can make them.

WOODROW WILSON: *Address delivered at a Joint Session of the Two Houses of Congress, April 21, 1917.*

(FROM LINCOLN PROGRAM, 1918)

on by social settlements. Their general character and scope are well known and need perhaps no more than to be mentioned.

Club Work. As in most social settlements, social and literary clubs for young people are conducted. These have their meetings, dances, debates, entertainments, athletic affairs, etc. A G. O. (general organization) exists in which the various clubs have representatives and in which are discussed and arranged matters of interest to all the clubs. The Institute puts whatever facilities it has at the disposal of the clubs and directs them in their work by suggesting programs and activities; but it in no way interferes with the autonomous organization. These clubs coöperate with the League of the Jewish Youth and are a binding link between the Jewish extension work described above and the general activities.

Jewish Societies. The building is used as a meeting place also by a number of Jewish organizations, not necessarily of the neighborhood, which are interested in various phases of Jewish communal life or in Jewish movements. These include clubs and societies interested in Jewish questions from the viewpoint of study, such as Zionist societies and also adult organizations for various philanthropic and communal purposes.

Civic Education. The Institute coöperates with civic agencies in bringing to the neighborhood educational activities of various nature. Under this head the Board of Education conducts public lectures and a class in English to foreigners. Lectures in citizenship, in problems of sanitation, sex-hygiene and the like are given from time to time under the auspices of various societies. A civic forum is conducted on Sunday afternoons. In all of the civic educational activities the non-Jews of the neighborhood are invited and attend.

Occasional Events. Besides housing these regular activities, the building is used for a great many occasional events of many sorts, such as concerts, recitals, dances, banquets, conventions, and celebrations representing a host of social and educational activities.

Summarizing, we may say that the work of the Central Jewish Institute can be thought of as being included within three concentric circles. The inner one, which forms the nucleus, deals with intensive Jewish education and is based upon the work of the Talmud Torahs. The outer one deals with the general civic, social and educational activities and follows closely the work of recreational and social settlements. The connecting circle, including the extension activities, is a phase which has no embodiment in a separate institution but rises out of the necessity of relating the other two phases; it is a consequence of looking upon the task as a problem of adjustment.

The importance of the function of the series of activities included in extension work, the Circle of Jewish Children, the League of the Jewish Youth and the Parents' Association, is as yet little understood. It is the linking force between the specific Jewish purpose and the general social activities. From the Jewish point of view it is the means of interesting those whose Jewish interests are lukewarm or for whom intensive class work is not adapted. It is the agency through which those who have little contact with Jewish life are brought together with those who have more intimate knowledge. The children of the Circle are brought into contact with the children of the Talmud Torah and the regular members of the League, with the more active leaders and organizers. On the other hand, those who come to the Institute primarily through their Jewish interests are brought into contact with wider community interests and civic affairs. The extension work thus forms a clearing house for the interchange and adjustment of the various forces. It is in the further development of the extension activities where the idea of adjustment is emphasized that we can expect to find the Jewish Community Center making its characteristic contribution.

Few of the many elements that have gone to make up the work of the Institute are new. But the similarity to other institutions in certain phases should not be permitted to obscure what is essential to the plan. The many activities are not a combination merely; the work has been unified by the main purpose. The attitude is distinctly not that of many social settlements and centers which

disclaim any purpose of their own, but are willing to provide whatso-
ever activities the neighborhood requests. The Institute is glad to
offer its facilities; but in addition it has its own central idea which
forms the criterion by which to decide upon what activities its money
and energies should be expended. The basic thought of the institution, to preserve Jewish life in harmony with American conditions,
controls the general scope of work and affects the manner of treating
subjects and activities. Nor is the Institute to be looked upon as a
compromise between Talmud Torah and social center. The word
'compromise' suggests a middle course not wholly satisfactory to
either side. The aim of the Jewish Community Center must be
synthetic, its Talmud Torah should maintain the highest standard
possible without relinquishing the other elements demanded by the
new conditions. Without this central emphasis upon the distinct
aim of preserving Jewish life the Central Jewish Institute could not
serve as an illustration of the type of educational agency through
which the 'Community' theory can become effective.

The 'Community' theory of adjustment, then, means concretely
that Jewish life in this country must depend mainly upon the existence of a sufficiently large number of Jewish centers built in the main
along the lines of the modernized Talmud Torah suggested in the plan
of the Central Jewish Institute. Jewish life, of course, will contain
many more elements. A certain amount of local contiguity will be
basic to any community spirit. The Jewish family, the synagogue
and philanthropic institutions must remain a part of any system of
Jewish life developed in this country. Theories will differ as to what
is regarded in them as most effective in preserving and fostering a
significant Jewish life. Those who regard Judaism as a religion
merely would logically make the synagogue or temple the central
agency. The nationalists and those who emphasize the racial
distinctiveness of the Jew would naturally tend to favor schemes
which allot definite territories and provide for some measure of political autonomy. The 'Community' theory, emphasizing the cultural
and spiritual heritage of the group, makes the school central, and in
the conditions confronting us in American life it would be necessary to
add that the school must complement, not supplant the public school.

Our discussion began with a theoretical argument based upon the demands of a democratic mode of thought. *What place has the Jewish group in our democracy? May it retain its identity or must it fuse entirely with the total group? Second, if it may retain its identity, under what limitations and through what agencies may it do so?* We may now face about and ask these questions in a more concrete form. *Shall ethnic communities be permitted to carry on such activities as are implied in the lines of work conducted at the Central Jewish Institute? Are such activities in accord with the aims of democratic America?* Perhaps few will give negative answers to these questions. *On the other hand, will such activities be adequate to prevent the ethnic group from disintegrating? Will they be adequate to conserve for the individual member of the ethnic group and through him for the community at large the valuable elements in the group heritage?*

The answer of the writer is implied in the recommendation. But, undoubtedly, the facts are not at hand which may permit us to make a scientific prediction. The Jews have had the longest experience in preserving a group heritage, though separated from their land. Yet the same conditions, psychological as well as material, have never confronted them. It is proposed that they live with their neighbors, not in ghettoes; democracy is spoken of; there is a sound desire to make a harmonious adjustment; the concept of cultural nationality has been developed; the homeland will be rebuilt; new events stress the importance of an international outlook—the combination of new circumstances and new ideas must make him pause who would wish to prophecy.

However, one thing seems clear: only the method proposed—in its main aspects—can serve in the conditions confronting us in America as a satisfactory solution for the development of a sound and normal Jewish life. Otherwise Jewish life in America must disintegrate; or become irrelevant, as in the petrified ceremonialism of American orthodoxy or the disembodied phrases of American Reform; or become narrowed and inward, as in the parochial outlook of the Mizrachi or the racial nationalism of the Poale Zion. Of irrelevancies, suppressions, and abnormalities Jewish life has had enough in the last two thousand years of ghetto. If it is impossible to develop in America a sound Jewish life which reckons with the environment, it would be best to allow the forces of assimilation to run their course. We would arrive, then, at the position of משוללי הגלות (those who negate the diaspora) who look to Palestine alone for the continuance of Jewish life. All energies would need to be turned to the upbuilding of a sound, healthy and significant Jewish life in Palestine. Under such conditions Jewish life might indeed be preserved; but it would be deprived of its international organization fraught with so much significance and might even tend to be narrowed again to the limitations of a nationalistic cult. In this disintegration of Jewish life in the diaspora not only the Jews, but America too, in common with other countries, would undoubtedly sustain a cultural and spiritual loss.

A solution of our problem harmonious with basic principles becomes imperative, not alone because we love our people and cherish its traditions, not alone because we recognize our duty to America and appreciate its great cultural possibilities, but in a profoundly moral sense also because we are beginning to grasp the significance that a proper adjustment of the foreign ethnic groups in our midst may have for the relations of one nation to another, in raising the basis of national life from a materialistic to a spiritual plane, in transmuting its very essence from the gross metal of economic imperialism to the pure gold of cultural self-determination. And in this development of a new conception of nationality, with its implications for the New World order, there is a part to play, not only for the Jewish group, be it understood, but for every ethnic community in America which has transcended the limitations of national fetichism and has caught the vision of a universal humane ideal.

SELECTED REFERENCES

AHAD HA'AM.   *Al P'rashat D'rahim.*
ADDAMS, JANE.   *Democracy and Social Ethics.*
——.   *Newer Ideals of Peace.*
ALEXANDER, HARTLEY B.   *Liberty and Democracy.*
ANTIN, MARY   *The Promised Land.*
ATHEARN, A. S.   *Religious Education and American Democracy.*
BERKSON, I. B.   "The Community School Center," *The Jewish Teacher,* Dec. 1917.
BINAUT, PIERRE   *Les droits et les devoirs de l'etat en matiere d'enseignment.*
BOAS, FRANZ.   *Changes in Bodily Form of Descendants of Immigrants.*
——.   *The Mind of Primitive Man.*
BOUQUILLON, REV. T.   *Education, to Whom Does it Belong?*
BRIDGES, HORACE J.   *On Becoming an American.*
BURNS, C. S. C.   *The Condition of Catholic Education in the United States.*
CARPENTER, EDWARD.   *Towards Democracy.*
CONWAY, REV. S. G.   *The State Last.*
CRAFTS, W. F.   *Bible in School Plans in Many Lands.*
CROLY, HERBERT.   *Progressive Democracy.*
CUBBERLEY, ELLWOOD P.   *Changing Conceptions in Education.*
DEWEY, JOHN   *The Influence of Darwin on Philosophy,* and other essays.
——.   *Democracy and Education.*
——.   "Nationalizing Education" *Proceedings of N. E. A.,* 1916.
DRACHSLER, JULIUS.   *Democracy and Assimilation.*
——.   *Intermarriage in New York City.*
DUSHKIN, A. M.   *Jewish Education in New York City.*
FENELON, JOHN F.   "The State," *Catholic Education Association Bulletin,* Nov. 1917.
FITE, WARNER.   *Individualism.*
FRIEDLANDER, ISRAEL.   *Past and Present, a Collection of Jewish Essays.*
ZHITLOWSKI, CHAYYIM.   *Gesammelte Schriften.*
GIDDINGS, FRANKLIN H.   *Democracy and Empire.*
GOTTHEIL, RICHARD.   *Zionism.*
GRANT, MADISON.   *The Passing of the Great Race.*
HERZL, THEODORE.   *The Jewish State.*
HESS, MOSES.   *Rome and Jerusalem.*
HOBHOUSE, L. T.   *Liberalism. Social Evolution and Political Theory.*
HOLLAND, REV. R. I.   *The Parent First.*
HILL, DAVID JAYNE.   *Americanism, What is It?*

Hurwitz, S. T. H.   "The Jewish Parochial School," *The Jewish Teacher*, Dec, 1917.
Jewish Encyclopedia.   Article, "United States,"
James, William.   *Pragmatism.*
Kallen, Horace M.   *Constitutional Foundations of the New Zion.*
———.   "Democracy versus the Melting Pot," *The Nation*, May, 1915.
Kellor, Francis.   *Straight America.*
Lowie, Robert H.   *Culture and Ethnology.*
MacIver, R. M.   *Community.*
MacVannel, John A.   *Outlines of the Philosophy of Education.*
Munsterberg, Hugo.   *Eternal Values.*
McDevitt, Monsignor P. R.   "The State and Education," *Bulletin of the Catholic Education Association*, February, 1916.
Pinsker, Leo.   *Auto-Emancipation.*
Ravage, Walter E.   *An American in the Making.*
Religious Education.   Articles in February, 1916, number.
Riley, A.   *The Religious Question in Public Education.*
Ross, Edward A.   *The Old World in the New.*
Royce, Josiah.   *The Sources of Religious Insight.*
Ruppin, Arthur.   *The Jews of To-day.*
Sadler, M. E.   *Moral Instruction and Training in Schools.*
Sampter, Jessie E.   *A Guide to the Study of Zionism.*
Santayana, George.   *The Life of Reason.*
Schechter, Solomon.   *Aspects of Rabbinic Theology.*
Spiller, Gustav.   *Moral Education in Eighteen Countries.*
———.   *The Interracial Congress.*
———.   "Science and Race Prejudice," *Sociological Review*, October, 1912.
Shields, T. E.   "Relation between Catholic School Systems and the State," *Catholic Education Bulletin*, November 16.
Thorndike, Edward L.   *Educational Psychology.*
Triggs, Oscar L.   *Browning and Whitman, a Study in Democracy.*
Wellhausen, J.   *The History of Judah and Israel.*
Wenner, George V.   Religious Education and Public School.   "Lutheran Paro-
———.   chial School," *Religious Education*, April, 1916.
Weyl, Walter.   *The New Democracy.*
Whitman, Walt.   *Democratic Vistas.*
Wiernick, Peter.   *The Jews in America.*
Winchester, B. S.   *Religious Education and Democracy.*
Wood, C. A.   *School and College Credit for Outside Bible Class.*
Woodruff, Charles E.   *The Expansion of Races.*
Zangwill, Israel.   *The Melting Pot.*
Zimmern, Alfred.   *Nationality and Government.*
———   *The War and Democracy.*